DATE DUE FOR RETURN

HITLER SPEAKS

HITLER SPEAKS

*A Series of Political Conversations
with Adolf Hitler
on his
Real Aims*

By

HERMANN RAUSCHNING

LONDON
THORNTON BUTTERWORTH LTD.

First Published .. .. December, 1939
Second Impression .. ,, 1939

CONTENTS

FOREWORD

THESE conversations with Hitler took place in the last year before his seizure of power and the first two years (1933 and '34) of the National Socialist regime. The writer jotted them down under the immediate influence of what he had heard. Much may be regarded as practically a verbatim report. Here, in the circle of his intimates, Hitler speaks openly about his innermost ideas—ideas which have been kept secret from the masses.

Only in exclusive circles is it known what Hitler really intends and what National Socialism is. Only among close friends has Hitler given free expression to his political and social aims. It is in such exclusive circles that I myself have heard them from his own lips.

To have published these conversations only six months ago, would have earned me at that time a reputation for malicious invention and defamation. Even hints which left the essentials unspoken aroused surprise and suspicion. As the author of *Germany's Revolution of Destruction*, I was repeatedly criticised because my statements contradicted the clear statement of National Socialist aims in *Mein Kampf*, for example, with regard to an alliance between National Socialism and Soviet Russia. As long as National Socialism was seen as nothing more than a German nationalist movement aiming at the removal of some of the worst features of the Versailles Peace Treaty, no one took seriously my frank revelation of the real aims of Hitler. Not until to-day is the world prepared to accept the truth : that Hitler and his movement are the apocalyptic riders of world annihilation.

PART I—1932

Contemporary Events

Jan. 7.　　Chancellor (Dr. Brüning) discussed presidential election with Hitler and proposed extension of von Hindenburg's term.

Jan. 11.　Hitler rejected the proposed extension without an election.

Mar. 13.　Von Hindenburg obtained large majority with Hitler second on the poll.

April 13.　President ordered forcible dissolution of Hitler's army.

April 24.　In the Prussian State elections Hitlerites headed the poll, but not sufficiently to place them in power without allies.

May 25.　Fight in Prussian Diet between Hitlerites and Communists.

May 30.　Dr. Brüning and his Cabinet resigned.

May 31.　Von Papen nominated as Chancellor.

June 3.　President dissolved Reichstag.

June 9.　Hitler fined £50 for contempt of court and unseemly behaviour as witness in a Munich court.

June 15.　President raised ban on Hitler's private army.

July 17.　Hitler opened his electoral campaign.

July 31.　Hitler gained an increased representation in elections for Reichstag, but failed to secure majority.

Aug. 1.   Raids by Nazi troops.

Aug. 13.   President rejected Hitler's claim to be Chancellor.

Aug. 22.   Riots in Beuthen, Silesia, after death-sentence on five Hitlerites for murder of a Communist.

Sept. 2.   Death sentence on five Hitlerites commuted to imprisonment for life.

Nov. 6.   General Election in Germany.

Nov. 17.   Resignation of von Papen Cabinet.

Nov. 21.   President invited Hitler to explore possibilities of forming Cabinet under certain conditions.

Nov. 22.   Hitler declined to meet President's desires.

Dec. 2.   General von Schleicher became Chancellor and Baron von Neurath Foreign Minister.

CHAPTER I

THE NEXT WAR

"THE next war will be quite different from the last world war. Infantry attacks and mass formations are obsolete. Interlocked frontal struggles lasting for years on petrified fronts will not return. I guarantee that. They were a degenerate form of war."

Hitler gazed fixedly across from the little glass veranda of his mountain eyrie to the precipitous wall opposite.

"We shall regain the superiority of free operations."

"Is it true, Herr Hitler, that Germany has prepared secret inventions which will break down every resistance, inventions against which even the French Maginot Line will be defenceless?" The Danzig *Gauleiter* (district leader) Albert Forster indicated by a sign to me that he had now led Hitler into his favourite subject.

"All armies have secret inventions. I am sceptical as to their value," Hitler returned.

"But the penetrative power of our new S-munitions. Isn't it true that electrical warfare yields entirely new possibilities of attack?" Forster persisted. "And the new poison gases and bacterial warfare? Will bacteria be used as a weapon in the next war?"

"A nation denied its rights may use any weapon, even bacterial warfare." Hitler's voice rose. "I have no scruples, and I will use whatever weapon I require. The new poison gases are horrible. But there is no difference between a slow death in barbed-wire entanglements and the agonised death of a gassed man or one poisoned by bacteria. In the future, whole nations will stand against each other, not merely hostile armies. We shall undermine the physical

13

health of our enemies as we shall break down their moral resistance. I can well imagine that there is a future for bacterial warfare. We have not quite perfected it yet, but experiments are being made. I hear that they are very promising. But the use of this weapon is limited. Its significance lies in wearing down the enemy *before* the war. Our real wars will in fact all be fought before military operations begin. I can quite imagine that we might control Britain in this way. Or America."

" Do you believe, my Führer, that America will again interfere in European affairs ? " asked the third of the company, the young leader of the then Danzig S.A.

" Certainly we shall prevent it from trying again," was the reply. " There are new weapons which are effective in such cases. America is permanently on the brink of revolution. It will be a simple matter for me to produce unrest and revolts in the United States, so that these gentry will have their hands full with their own affairs. We have no use for them in Europe."

" You said that we should poison the enemy with bacteria even before the war starts. How can that be done in peace-time ? " Forster asked.

" Through agents, harmless commercial travellers. That is the surest method—at the moment the only effective one," Hitler replied. " The results would not be immediate. It would take several weeks, if not longer, for an epidemic to appear. Perhaps we shall introduce bacteria at the height of the war, at the moment when the powers of resistance of the enemy are beginning to fail."

Our conversation then dealt with some details of a future gas and bacterial war. We sat in the rather narrow veranda of Wachenfeld House in the Obersalzberg. Hitler's magnificent Alsatian sheep-dog lay at his feet. The mountains on the opposite side of the valley glowed above a pleasant meadow. It was a magical August morning of that austere, autumnal clarity which is so refreshing in the Bavarian highlands. Hitler hummed *motifs* from Wagnerian operas. He seemed to me preoccupied and moody. From having been communicative, he fell suddenly into a dry silence. The political moment was full of danger. National Socialism was approaching one of its crises. The Party was in a well-nigh desperate position. But Hitler's every word rang with the firm conviction that he would soon be in power, and able to lead the German people to a new destiny. We spoke of the result of the war, and the tragical turn of all German victories.

" We shall not capitulate—no, never," Hitler exclaimed. " We may be destroyed, but if we are, we shall drag a world with us—a world in flames."

He hummed a characteristic *motif* from the *Götterdämmerung*. Our young friend of the S.A. broke the silence by saying that it was the superior armament of our enemies that had brought about the unhappy conclusion of the last war.

" It is not arms that decide, but the men behind them—always," Hitler rebuked him.

" But surely new inventions and superior weapons do decide the fate of nations and social classes? Is not that what you meant, my Führer, when you said the next war would be quite different from the last one? The new weapons, the technical inventions will change the whole course of the war. They make strategy completely superfluous. To-day Germany is supreme in weapons and technical inventions."

" No, strategy does not change, at least not through technical inventions. That is quite wrong." Hitler's manner became lively. " Has anything changed since the battle of Cannae? Did the invention of gunpowder in the Middle Ages change the laws of strategy? I am sceptical as to the value of technical inventions. No technical novelty has ever permanently revolutionised warfare. Each technical advance is followed by another which cancels out its effects. Certainly the technique of warfare advances, and it will create many more novelties until the maximum of destruction is reached. But all this can only produce a temporary superiority."

Hess, at that time Hitler's private secretary, who had retired at the opening of the conversation, here intervened.

" The gentlemen do not seem to understand," he explained, " how Germany, in view of the limited value of technical inventions for warfare, will be able to escape getting bogged again for years in a war of position."

" Who says I'm going to start a war like those fools in 1914 ? " cried Hitler. " Are not all our efforts bent towards preventing this ? Most people have no imagination." Here his face twisted into an expression of contempt. " They can imagine the future only in terms of their own petty experience. They are blind to the new, the surprising things. Even the generals are sterile. They are imprisoned in the coils of their technical knowledge. The creative genius stands always outside the circle of the experts.

" I," he went on, " have the gift of reducing all problems to their simplest foundations. War has been erected into a secret science and surrounded with momentous solemnity. But war is the most natural, the most every-day matter. War is eternal, war is universal. There is no beginning and there is no peace. War is life. Any struggle is war. War is the origin of all things. Let us go back to primitive life, the life of the savages. What is war but cunning, deception, delusion, attack and surprise ? People have killed only when they could not achieve their aim in other ways. Merchants, robbers, warriors—at one time, all these were one. There is a broadened strategy, a war with intellectual weapons. What is the object of war, Forster ? To make the enemy capitulate. If he does, I have the prospect of wiping him out. Why should I demoralise him by military means if I can do so better and more cheaply in other ways ? "

Hitler went on to develop the outlines of his war as he has since widely tested it. At that time it seemed a novel and not very convincing doctrine. It was evident, however, that he had given much thought to these matters. He looked upon himself as a great strategist of a new kind, a future war-lord in a sense and to a degree hitherto unknown.

" When I wage war, Forster," he declared, " in the midst of peace, troops will suddenly appear, let us say, in Paris. They will wear French uniforms. They will march through the streets in broad daylight. No one will stop them. Everything has been thought out, prepared to the last detail. They will march to the headquarters of the General Staff. They will occupy the ministries, the Chamber of Deputies. Within a few minutes, France, Poland, Austria, Czechoslovakia, will be robbed of their leading men. An army without a general staff ! All political leaders out of the way ! The confusion will be beyond belief. But I shall long have had relations with the men who will form a new government—a government to suit me.

" We shall find such men, we shall find them in every country. We shall not need to bribe them. They will come of their own accord. Ambition and delusion, party squabbles and self-seeking arrogance will drive them. Peace will be negotiated before the war has begun. I promise you, gentlemen, that the impossible is always successful. The most unlikely thing is the surest. We shall have enough volunteers, men like our S.A., trustworthy and ready for any sacrifice. We shall send them across the border in peace-time. Gradually. No one shall see in them

2

anything but peaceful travellers. To-day you don't believe
me, gentlemen. But I will accomplish it, move by move.
Perhaps we shall land at their flying-fields. We shall be
capable of transporting, not only men, but arms, by air.
No Maginot Line will stop us. Our strategy, Forster, is to
destroy the enemy from within, to conquer him through
himself."

" Do you know," whispered the awestruck Forster, " a
few weeks ago he laid a new plan before the East Prussian
generals, a plan of defence against Polish aggression. They
accepted the plan. Hitler is a genius, he is an expert in
every field ! "

Linsmayer, our S.A. leader, now asked to be allowed to
photograph Hitler in a group with the rest of us. We went
outside and took up our position beneath a steep cliff.
Hess took the picture with Hitler in the centre. We then
walked a few steps down the road, which at that time was
still narrow, and led from the back of the house into the
woods. I looked across to the inn on the opposite side,
Zum Türken. Summer visitors were standing outside
training their field-glasses on us. Hess pointed to the
green slope rising to a rounded summit that offered a good
landing-field for 'planes, thus avoiding the inconvenient
car-drive down to the valley. Hess had just been a successful competitor in a flying competition. Forster spoke to
him about it.

" You must give that sort of thing up in future," Hitler
told him. " There are better things in store for you. I
need you, Hess."

Hitler resumed the conversation.

" In the air we shall of course be supreme. The air
offers many possibilities. We shall surpass all competitors.
We have only one serious rival in this field : the English.
The Slavs will never learn to fight in the air. It is a manly
weapon, a Germanic art of battle. I shall build the largest

air fleet in the world. We shall have the most daring pilots. Of course we shall have a great army as well."

"Will you introduce universal conscription again?" Linsmayer asked.

"Not only that, but a universal conscription of labour to which Hindenburg's auxiliary conscription will seem a petty half-measure. We need armies, not only highly qualified special formations, but mass armies as well. But we shall not use them as in 1914. The place of artillery preparation for frontal attack by the infantry in trench warfare will in future be taken by revolutionary propaganda, to break down the enemy psychologically before the armies begin to function at all. The enemy people must be demoralised and ready to capitulate, driven into moral passivity, before military action can even be thought of."

He went on with growing enthusiasm : "How to achieve the moral break-down of the enemy before the war has started—that is the problem that interests me. Whoever has experienced war at the front will want to refrain from all avoidable bloodshed. Anything that helps preserve the precious German blood is good. We shall not shrink from the plotting of revolutions. Remember Sir Roger Casement and the Irish in the last war. We shall have friends who will help us in all the enemy countries. We shall know how to obtain such friends. Mental confusion, contradiction of feeling, indecisiveness, panic : these are our weapons. Of course you know," here Hitler turned to me, "the history of revolutions. It is always the same : the ruling classes capitulate. Why? Defeatism ; they have no longer the will to conquer. The lessons of revolution, these are the secret of the new strategy. I have learnt from the Bolsheviks. I do not hesitate to say so. One always learns most from one's enemies. Do you know the doctrine of the *coup d'état?* Study it. Then you will know our task."

We listened, none of us guessing how close we were to the realisation of these ideas. I thought of the experiments of the highest commanders of the German Army during the last war with the Bolshevik leaders. What had seemed mere improvisations to disable the enemy were here reduced to a system, a universal law.

" I shall never start a war without the certainty that a demoralised enemy will succumb to the first stroke of a single gigantic attack." Hitler's eyes took on a fixed stare, and he began to shout. " When the enemy is demoralised from within, when he stands on the brink of revolution, when social unrest threatens—that is the right moment. A single blow must destroy him. Aerial attacks, stupendous in their mass effect, surprise, terror, sabotage, assassination from within, the murder of leading men, overwhelming attacks on all weak points in the enemy's defence, sudden attacks, all in the same second, without regard for reserves or losses : that is the war of the future. A gigantic, all-destroying blow. I do not consider consequences ; I think only of this one thing."

He paused as if to give us time to take in this terrific programme and some at least of its fearful implications. His next words were spoken with impressive calmness :

" I do not play at war. I shall not allow myself to be ordered about by ' commanders-in-chief.' *I* shall make war. *I* shall determine the correct moment for attack. There is only one most favourable moment. I shall await it—with iron determination. I shall not miss it. I shall bend all my energies towards bringing it about. That is my mission. If I succeed in that, then I have the right to send youth to its death. I shall have saved as many lives then as could be saved. Gentlemen, let us not play at being heroes, but let us destroy the enemy. Generals, in spite of the lessons of the war, want to behave like chivalrous knights. They think war should be waged like the tourneys of the Middle Ages. I have no use for knights. I need revolutions. I have made the doctrines of revolution the basis of my policy."

Hitler paused again. His next words came like a peroration :

" I shall shrink from nothing. No so-called international law, no agreements will prevent me from making use of any advantage that offers. The next war will be unbelievably bloody and grim. But the most inhuman war, one which makes no distinction between military and civilian combatants, will at the same time be the kindest, because it will be the shortest. And together with the fullest use of our arms, we shall grind down our enemy with a war of nerves. We shall provoke a revolution in France as certainly as we shall *not* have one in Germany. Take my word for it. The French will hail me as their deliverer. The little man of the middle class will acclaim us as the bearers of a just social order and eternal peace. None of these people any longer want war and greatness. But *I* want war. To me all means will be right. My motto is not : ' Don't, whatever you do, annoy the enemy ! ' My motto is : ' Destroy him by all and any means.' *I* am the one who will wage the war ! "

CHAPTER II

A MORNING AND EVENING ON THE OBERSALZBERG

WE had come down from Danzig—Forster, Linsmayer and I. Our train ran into Berchtesgaden shortly before midnight, and Hitler had sent his car to fetch us. It was a good twenty minutes' drive up a steep road to the Obersalzberg, but Hitler wanted to receive us there in spite of the lateness of the hour. It was a breakneck journey.

Hitler came forward to receive us. He had visitors, ladies. The house was a small, agreeably modest one. A lounge extending through the whole width of the house was furnished in the style of a Bavarian peasant cottage. A plain bench surrounded the great fireplace. From a shrouded bird-cage came the frightened chirping of song-birds awakened by the bustle. Hess greeted us, and we were introduced to the other guests. Hitler offered us some cherry brandy, though he himself is a teetotaller. It was quite cold up there—the air of the mountains was harsh after a hot train journey.

That August of 1932 was not the first time I met Hitler. I had looked into his famous eyes before this. But now for the first time I saw him in his private home, which combined good middle-class taste with highland scenery and refined peasant style, as was customary in our pre-war middle class. Dimity curtains, and what is known as rustic furniture, everything small and dainty. Not really the right background for the future liberator of Germany.

What impression does Hitler himself make on one ? This is a question I have been asked many times, and I must admit that as far as I personally am concerned, it was with mixed feelings that I made his acquaintance. The great popular orator in these surroundings was reduced to the insignificance of the *petit bourgeois*. There was a general atmosphere of geniality, but there was something impersonal in the furnishings. I myself was rather taken aback at the midnight company of decidedly over-blown ladies. Did he really crave the credulous devotion of women to retain his belief in himself? Hitler is not physically attractive. Everyone knows that to-day. But at that time stories were circulated in the party and among sympathisers about his deep blue eyes. They are neither deep nor blue. His look is staring or dead, and lacks the brilliance and sparkle of genuine animation. The timbre of his harsh, uncommon voice is repellent to the North German. The tone is full, but forced, as though his nose were blocked. Since then this voice, guttural and threatening, has become familiar to the whole world. It embodies the torment of these years.

There is something peculiar about the magic of a personality. I have found in myself and others that one succumbs to such magic only if one wishes to succumb to it. I have noticed that Hitler made the strongest impression on such people as were either highly suggestible or somewhat effeminate or accustomed by their education and social background to formalism and hero-worship. Hitler's physical appearance certainly does not heighten the impression made by his personality. A receding forehead, with the lank hair falling over it ; a short, unimposing stature, with limbs somehow ill-fitting and awkward ; an expressionless mouth beneath the little brush of a moustache —such are the traits of the outer man. His only charm lies perhaps in his hands, which are strikingly well-shaped and expressive. What a difference to the strikingly youthful, intelligent countenance shown in Napoleon's death-mask !

Hitler greeted us cheerfully. It was shortly after the perpetration of a certain bestial murder in Upper Silesia.

The National Socialists had dragged a political opponent
out of his bed in the middle of the night and trampled
him to death.   Von Papen, then the Reich Chancellor, the
man who was later to implement Hitler's summoning to
power, had issued sharp decrees against these political
criminals.   The murderers of Potempa were condemned to
death.   Hitler, in a sensational telegram, had publicly
announced his solidarity with the murderers.   He
justified their deed and called them his comrades.   This
cost him many sympathies at that time, and his star began
to fade.

Our conversation dealt with the latest events.   Hitler
was indignant at the opposition shown him by the nationalist
middle class.   He stigmatised them as the real enemies of
Germany.

"I shall have the *Stahlhelm* dissolved," he declared
with the firmness of a man who is sure of his case.   (The
Stahlhelm was a union of national soldiers of the front, the
real defence corps of the German Nationalists.)   Then he
castigated what he considered the dishonest and criminal
policy of Papen.   He attacked the death sentence of the
court, calling it a mockery of justice.   The violence of his
tone showed how much he felt he had exposed himself by
his telegram.

" Such savage judgments," he said, " are never forgotten
by a people.   In such critical times as these, a nation will
suffer and forget anything done openly in the political
struggle.   If I were to allow the S.A. a free hand, or if
twenty or thirty thousand Germans were to lose their
lives in street fighting, the nation would be able to forget
it.   The nation would console itself.   Such things are like
the incidents of the open battlefield.   But a miscarriage of
justice, a cold and considered judgment, a death sentence
that outrages the unfailing moral sense of the people, the
branding as common murderers and the execution of men

who have acted from purely patriotic motives—that is something that the nation will not forget or forgive."

I must confess that at the time I was influenced by this passionate pleading, though, like most people, I saw in the abominable Potempa murder only a foul stain on the brown shirt, which was at that time still regarded as an honourable uniform. How many brutal murders and tortures have been done since then by S.A. and S.S. alike, not in the heat of national passion, but in the lust of cruelty or with sober calculation ! I do not know whether Hitler ever recalled, in all his many death sentences on alleged traitors to their country, his own comment on Papen's judgment in the open court. Probably not. Hitler, like most of his hysterical *Gauleiter*, like the Danziger Forster, for instance, can change his opinions completely without even knowing that he is doing so.

" Papen will have to answer for this one day," Hitler said. " I guarantee that. And the *Stahlhelm* will get its accounts settled. I will have it dissolved for its treacherous attacks on my S.A. It has lowered itself to the level of the Red Front."

It was late, and the ladies intervened. Hitler had allowed himself to be carried away in spite of the late hour. A sleepless night was before him. We exchanged only a few further unimportant remarks. Hitler denounced the monotony of travel by air as compared with the ever-changing and delightful glimpses of the landscape, and of country and city life, obtained from a motor car. He advised us to return home by car. He himself, after his first amazement at the view from above, had long since ceased to enjoy air travel.

Hess indicated that we were to retire, consoling us with the prospect of the following morning. He would indicate to us when we might bring up our own problems. Hitler accompanied us to the door. It was long past midnight, but

fresh and clear.   Already the grey of dawn was beginning
to show.   Linsmayer and I walked the short distance across
to the *Türken*.   Forster was stopping at another house.

" We Must Be Ruthless "

I slept badly, partly, perhaps, owing to the unaccustomed
air of the mountains, which affects us plain-dwellers, but
also because I couldn't get out of my mind what I had heard.
I shared a room with Linsmayer.   This young S.A. leader
was one of the many charming, honest and genuinely
patriotic young men who joined the movement from the
purest and noblest motives.   It is particularly necessary to
recall this to-day for the benefit of those who paint everything in black and white, and do not understand that
countless Germans allowed themselves to be carried away
on a strident current, firmly believing in the necessity of
their sacrifice.   Young fellows like Linsmayer felt genuinely
that they were making the sacrifice of their youth in a
great cause.

It was already late when we received a message that
Hitler was up and wished to speak to us.   Our conversation
opened on the theme of the previous evening.

" We must be ruthless," said Hitler.   " We must regain
our clear conscience as to ruthlessness.   Only thus shall we
purge our people of their softness and sentimental
philistinism, ' *Gemütlichkeit* ', and their degenerate delight in
beer-swilling.   We have no more time for fine sentiments.
We must compel our people to greatness if they are to
fulfil their historic mission."

" I know," he resumed after a pause, " that I must be
a harsh master.   I must demand harshness from myself.
My task is more difficult than Bismarck's or any other
German's.   I must first create the nation before even
beginning to tackle the national tasks before us."

Everyone who knew Hitler during the early years of struggle knows that he has by nature an easily moved and unmistakably sentimental temperament, with a tendency towards emotionalism and romanticism. His convulsions of weeping in all emotional crises are by no means merely a matter of nerves. The maudlin, sobbing tone in which, for example, he appealed to the Berlin S.A. when the Stinnes conflict threatened to split the party was genuine. For this very reason, there lies behind Hitler's emphasis on brutality and ruthlessness the desolation of a forced and artificial inhumanity, not the amorality of the genuine brute, which has after all something of the power of a natural force. Nevertheless, in the harshness and un-exampled cynicism of Hitler there is something more than the repressed effect of a hypersensitiveness which has handicapped its bearer. It is the urge to reprisal and vengeance, a truly Russian-nihilistic feeling.

Hitler's thoughts at this time were wrestling with the temptation to break his own resolve to reach power by legitimate means only. He was being tempted to place himself in possession of the supreme power by a bloody revolution, a " march on Berlin." Hitler was continually being implored by his closest confederates to drop his restraint and take up the revolutionary struggle. He himself was torn between his own revolutionary temperament, which impelled him to passionate action, and his political astuteness, which warned him to take the safe road of political combinations and postpone his " revenge " till later.

There is not the slightest doubt that an open outbreak of the National Socialist revolution was imminent at the time of the autumn elections of 1932. It would have meant the end of the party. The rising would have been ruthlessly suppressed by the *Reichswehr*. Over and over again in conversation this sentence cropped up : " Clear the streets

for the brown battalions ! " For himself and his friends,
Hitler painted the chances of a surprise occupation of the
key points of political and economic power, and he lingered
with special interest over the chances of a bloody destruction
of Marxist resistance in the streets. Events of the summer
revealed the extent to which plans for a *coup* were already
elaborated. They were not the sporadic enterprises of
local party leaders, but came from Hitler himself. They
suited his temperament, the needs of his imagination and
his conception of historical greatness as not to be achieved
without the spilling of blood.

We can see here the same conflict of feeling as that which
recently caused the Führer of the Third Reich to vacillate
between his desire to be " the greatest general of all times "
and the devious road of " combinations," the art of
manœuvring himself into power, of gaining his world
empire by cunning. Incidentally, Hitler's followers
reproached him with the charge that he had missed the
most favourable moment to strike. And in truth the
economic crisis began in 1932 to ease a little. The influx
into the party fell off. Hitler's opponents began to draw
together, and seemed well in the running. Driven to the
wall, outflanked in all his chances of action, Hitler saw his
plans to capture power melting away. The *Reich* presidential election was a heavy defeat for his party. After
Papen's accession to power, he saw the hated rival, with
the ease and nonchalance of the young cavalry officer,
clearing many of the political hurdles that Hitler had
reserved as his own objectives, such as, for instance, the
direction of the Prussian police and the removal of the
basis of Marxist influence in Prussia. Urged to action by
his fiery impatience and passion, he had nevertheless to
play the part of an idle summer visitor to the Bavarian
mountains, while time passed and Papen anticipated his
plans.

The Plan in the Drawer

Hitler's questions as to the position in Danzig led us directly to the economic problems. I mentioned Hitler's insistence that the party must compose a programme for the creation of employment. The highly amateur fashion in which ambitious experts in all varieties of labour problems had collated their plans, so as to form some sort of joint programme for ending unemployment, had awakened great doubts as to whether the party was to be taken seriously. Such doubts were not removed by the party's two economic and technical experts, the civil engineers Feder and Lawaczek, whose curious theories, propounded in "intellectual gatherings," invited the ridicule of economists and caused acute embarrassment to all intelligent party members. I therefore asked Hitler, whose relations with Feder were not at the time known to me, about the possibility of financing the economic programme. I could not see, I remarked, that Feder's theory was anything but financing by means of an inflation.

"How do you mean?" said Hitler, eyeing me with displeasure. "I am not worrying about financing our programme. You may safely leave that to me. As long as speculators are kept out, there are no difficulties."

"But," I ventured to interpose, "it will not be possible to keep prices stable if the creation of employment is financed thus. Feder's money theory will also have an inflationary effect."

"You get inflation if you want inflation," Hitler retorted angrily. "Inflation is lack of discipline—lack of discipline in the buyers, and lack of discipline in the sellers. I will see to it that prices remain stable. That is what my S.A. is for. Woe to the men who raise prices! We need no legal instruments for that. It will be done by the party alone. You shall see—if our S.A. once clean up a shop, such things will not happen a second time."

Forster nodded contentedly. This type of economic
discipline appealed to him.

" Besides," Hitler continued, " I do not worry about
the theories of Feder and Lawaczek. I have a gift for
tracing back all theories to their roots in reality. I have
nothing to do with pipe-dreams. You need not take this
man Feder and his associates literally, even though officially
the party does so. Let them talk as they please. When I
am in power, I shall see to it that they do no mischief. If
these men cause confusion, Forster, you will no longer
allow them to speak. These people cannot think simply.
Everything has got to be complicated. I have the gift of
simplification, and then everything works itself out.
Difficulties exist only in the imagination ! "

Hitler's repudiation of Feder was at that time new
to me. It was interesting as an indication of Hitler's
supremacy over his entourage. There is no doubt that
he did possess this gift of simplification, even in a creative
sense, up to a point. He has the gift, like many self-taught
men, of breaking through the wall of prejudices and conventional theories of the experts, and in so doing, he has
frequently discovered amazing truths.

Hitler continued to fulminate :

" I shall not be deceived by these captains of industry
either ! Captains indeed ! I should like to know what
ships they navigate ! They are stupid fools who cannot
see beyond the wares they peddle ! The better one gets to
know them, the less one respects them."

Hitler made a disdainful gesture with his hand. Forster
began to wax enthusiastic over the plans for employment
that had been collected by a so-called " technical engineering division " in his district against the time when they
should seize power. I observed Hitler's impatience and
suggested that this was merely a rough draft ; elaboration
was still lacking. It seemed to me that a guiding

principle would have to classify the various projects
for financing.

" It all depends on the initial spark," Hitler returned.
" How I shall bring that about is of no interest. The
economic life of the country must be set in motion, and
we must close the circle so that our economic strength is
not drained out of the country. I can accomplish just as
much by rearmament as by housing or colonisation. I
can also put more money in the hands of the unemployed,
so that they may cover their needs. In this way I create
purchasing power and additional trade. But these are
simple, uncomplicated processes which we shall master
by sheer determination not to shrink from unavoidable
difficulties. None of this is a secret science, as the professors
pretend, but a matter of sound sense and will-power."

Hitler did not appear to attach much importance to the
employment plans. Evidently they were to him more a
mental distraction in this period of complete inactivity, a
means of occupying his mind with town planning, colonisation, agricultural improvement and technical progress.
The whole " plan in the drawer " was, like so much else,
merely a means to an end. It was a scintillating soap-
bubble, not serious labour. The party leader himself
set no store by these efforts. He allowed them to be made
public for propaganda purposes, for pedagogical reasons,
but was entirely indifferent as to the results. In other
words, looked at in the light of day, there was nothing
in the famous drawer. The sum of the expert equipment
with which Hitler seized power consisted in his unlimited
belief in himself, his faith that he could deal with things,
in accordance with the primitive, but effective maxim :
orders will be carried out. Haphazard, perhaps, but it
worked for a time, and later he would see.

Nevertheless, Hitler's attitude showed both an open-
mindedness and a peasant cunning that one is tempted

to describe as sublime. The empty drawer, even later, was most effective in Hitler's view. The difficulties that arose were due to the hostility of the reactionaries who would have liked to sabotage his purposes. Hitler did not recognise any difficulties as inherent in a problem. He saw only human incompetence and human ill-will.

Incidentally he was fortunate in his empty drawer. Herr Schacht filled the yawning void with his ingenious projects. It is pretty certain that without this " magician," Hitler's self-assurance would soon have suffered a number of heavy blows. A pity ! It thus became possible for Hitler, shortly before Schacht's dismissal, to refuse the latter's demands for a sterner control of expenses. Hitler was always able to point to his own past financial successes. Whenever, in the " struggle for power," he had demanded money from Schwarz, the party treasurer, Schwarz had regularly replied :

" Herr Hitler, there are no funds."

Then Hitler had pounded his fist on the table and shouted :

" To-morrow morning, Schwarz, I must have a thousand marks ! "

And lo ! and behold, next morning the thousand marks were there.

" Where he got them doesn't interest me ! " Hitler would say.

The question of finance, indeed, has never troubled him much. For a time, perhaps, that was an added strength. At any rate, all the *Gauleiter* imitated him in it.

" There is money, unlimited money," Forster, our Danzig leader, replied to my doubts as to the financing of his ambitious building plans. At the time of our visit to Hitler he was chiefly interested in the problem of technical inventions.

" Herr Hitler," he resumed the conversation, after

the Führer had been for some time lost in a brown study,
" what is your opinion of new, revolutionary inventions ?
Can we count on any such ? Is it not a fact that only such
inventions compel industrialists to make really big invest-
ments, and that it is in this way that industry flourishes
again, and a permanent prosperity is created ? I mean "—
apparently the implications were not entirely clear to
Forster—" a further technical improvement of the whole of
existence, as after the invention of the steam engine—an
improvement of the electrical industry, and then of machines
and chemicals ? "

I pointed out that Lawaczek himself believed that the
day of the great, revolutionising inventions was past. This
was the very reason why he had formulated his uncon-
vincing theory as to the cheap storage of electrical power
by means of the electrolytic production of hydrogen and
his systematic development of graded falls as a means of
producing cheap electric current.

" Engineers are fools," Hitler cut in rudely. " They
have an occasional idea that might be useful, but it becomes
madness if it is generalised. Let Lawaczek build his
turbines, and not try to invent industrial booms. Don't
get mixed up with him. I know his hobby-horse. This
is all nonsense, gentlemen. History does *not* repeat itself.
What was valid in the nineteenth century is no longer so in
the twentieth. Inventions no longer appear of their own
accord as a piece of unprecedented good fortune. To-day
we control them. We can foretell when and where inventions are to be expected. But the crucial point is this :
we do *not* develop them. We allow the possibilities to
moulder. It is all a question of the will. One can no
longer allow things to work themselves out. The wealthy
countries that have everything no longer need inventions.
What should they do with them ? They are merely an
embarrassment. They want to get rich in the old way.

3

They want to sleep, these rich countries—Britain, France,
America."

He paused ; and then went on excitedly, gesticulating
with his hands and pounding the table, his voice rising in
crescendo :

" In one respect Lawaczek is right : what was once accident
must become planned. We must do away with accident.
We can ! This is the meaning of the ' great works ' that
states undertake to-day—not the speculators and the
bank Jews, in whose interests it is that nothing should go
forward. For this reason we must liberate Germany from
all such connections. We must stand on our own feet.

" But Germany, as it is to-day, is not a biological unit.
It will be Germany only when it is Europe as well. Without
power over Europe we must perish. Germany is Europe.
I give you my guarantee that there will be no more unemployment in Europe. An unequalled renaissance will
come. We shall awaken the world from its sleep. We
shall undertake tasks of which the world does not dream
to-day. And we shall perform them successfully. But
we must have Europe and its colonies. Germany is only a
beginning. No European country to-day is a complete
whole. But Europe is for us. Whoever conquers it will
press his seal on the coming age. We are the chosen.
If we fail, we shall die out, as all Europe's nations will
degenerate. The stake is life, or death. Lawaczek,
Feder—they're old women ! I have no use for their
bourgeois wisdom ! "

Hitler broke off. It was the first time I had heard
anything of his real aims.

DANZIG, FREE CITY AND SANCTUARY

But our immediate business was Danzig. From these
great plans we had to return to the ugly reality. The

National Socialist Party in Danzig was at that time in a
difficult position. Unlike its position in the Reich, the
party was not in the opposition but, as the strongest
party since 1930, supported a minority government in
which German nationalists were the leading influence.
Since the latter were more or less openly working against
the National Socialists, Forster desired a new election ; this
was being resisted by the Danzig Senate. He therefore
wished now to withdraw his support from the government
in order to undermine it. The question was : did Hitler
approve of the overthrow of the government, and was the
opposition of the National Socialists in Danzig in his
interests politically ? It might have seemed an irrelevant
question, but it gained significance in the light of the
general position of the entire party at that time.

The first question Hitler put to us was this :

" Has Danzig got an extradition agreement with
Germany ? "

I did not at once understand, and replied that we had
at any rate an agreement arranging for mutual legal aid.
Hitler elucidated his meaning :

" If the German Reich demands it, is Danzig compelled
to hand over political personalities of German citizenship
residing in Danzig ? "

I still failed to see what Hitler was driving at, but I
gave him a negative reply. It was not the custom to hand
over political personalities if they had committed no
criminal act.

" It might," Hitler explained, " be necessary for me to
transfer my party headquarters outside German territory.
Conditions may become more difficult for our party very
soon. It might, therefore, be my intention to carry on
the leadership temporarily from abroad. In Germany
itself we might be subjected to such great pressure as to
prevent our free functioning. I must be prepared for any

eventuality, and possibly even leave Germany overnight. Danzig would be a supremely suitable spot, in the immediate vicinity of the German frontier. I might make my decision about an election in Danzig dependent on whether Danzig could offer me the guarantees I require."

I replied that certainly the present government of Danzig would not be likely to offer sufficient guarantees for the security of the party's political work if this should be prohibited in the Reich, even though we probably need not fear any actual extradition for political reasons.

He turned to Forster :

" Forster, we must consider whether it would not be wiser to make friends with the present government of Danzig, rather than precipitate an election which may not make it possible for us to challenge the new government alone."

Forster did not reply at once.

" What is the earliest date at which you could have an election ? " Hitler asked.

" The late autumn," Forster replied.

Hitler shrugged his shoulders.

" That's too late."

We had an extended discussion of the possibilities of an election and the chances of persuading the present government to permit the setting up of Hitler's headquarters in Danzig. I could not overlook the probability that if the party and the S.A. were to be prohibited in Germany, Danzig would follow suit, as this would offer the present minority government the most favourable opportunity of getting rid of its guardian. For the rest, Hitler's estimate of the position was a complete surprise to me. I did not hear until later that the German government had in fact considered the possibility of a general dissolution of the National Socialist party, and had shelved it temporarily only under pressure from the Reichswehr. The work of an underground party interested Hitler—fascinated him, in fact, since he expected to receive fresh stimulation from an illegal status. He could then carry on the struggle more ruthlessly, more treacherously, as it were. Hitler gave us to understand that his will was " ungovernable," that he was determined to succeed all the more, that such proscription would only end very soon in the triumph of the party. But he must have a free hand. He must not be under police supervision.

We came to no conclusion. Danzig, the free city, as a sanctuary for the once more persecuted, once more illegal National Socialist party, remained an unsettled project, and remained so largely because the Papen government preferred not to outlaw the party. In view, however, of Danzig's subsequent position as the storm-centre of a world crisis, it is not without irony that Hitler was at one time strongly in favour of Danzig as an independent state, and that he intended to exploit this independence for his own safety.

We began next to discuss the dangerous position in East Prussia, and the rumours of a Polish attack on it. Hitler spoke of the worsening of relations with Poland with undisguised satisfaction. This, incidentally, was quite in line with his attitude soon afterwards towards Pomerania, where the local party pronounced that it was not interested in the possibility of an attack by Poland on East Prussia, Danzig or Pomerania. In any case the party would await developments. Not for the first or the last time Hitler proved that his party interests far outweighed the common national interests.

We then began to discuss the coming war, and the secret armament and defence measures of the Reich. Even at that time, Hitler thought the chances of an isolated war against Poland very favourable. He had a very poor opinion of the Polish soldier, whom he classed with the Rumanian and Italian, as the worst in Europe. But he denied that he would initiate his coming to power with a

war, even against the Poles. On the contrary, he would
avoid anything that might increase tension. For his part,
he was even prepared to make a treaty with the Poles.
" We must be strong first. Everything else will follow
in due course. I shall advance step by step. Never two
steps at once. Remember that, Forster," he added to his
acolyte.

Then followed the conversation on war which I have
already reported.

The hour was late. Hess had come in more than once.
For a moment Hitler left us to ourselves. We looked down
into the valley. Hess explained the surroundings, and
pointed in the direction of Salzburg. He told us that
Hitler looked with unrelenting hatred at the frontier which
closed to him the country of his birth. We sensed that
something more than political and national feelings were
involved here. This was something deeply personal.

Hitler bade us farewell. We took with us some reflections
on our Danzig policy. Danzig was a place with a great
future. In a German Europe it would have a special
mission. It would become a city of teeming millions in
the centre of natural lines of strength. That was Hitler's
opinion. I found the basis of this belief, which ran counter
to the current conception of a dying Danzig, a mere city
of curios, in the ideas of a former adviser of Hitler's, a civil
engineer named Plaichinger, who has remained unknown
because of his early death. I visited him in Munich, and
he expressed similar opinions of a future Great Danzig,
the Antwerp of the Baltic.

We took our leave of Hess. A car was waiting for us
which drove us down to Munich. As we left the Obersalzberg, Goebbels was just getting out of his car. He stumped
heavily on his club-foot up the narrow path from the road
leading to Hitler's mountain abode. He was spinning the
web in which one day the fly, Germany, would be caught.

Chapter III

EASTERN POLICY AND THE NEW
GERMAN ARISTOCRACY

THE first Brown House in Munich was a characteristic blend of unadorned modern office building and garish extravagance. Steel furniture, archives, complicated card-index systems : that was one side of it. The hall of senators, flags, colour symbolism and other kinds of symbolism, bad paintings : that was the other. I had occasion to sit opposite such a painting once for a few hours while listening to a confidential discussion between Hitler and some of his advisers. The picture was called " Triumph of the Movement," or words to that effect. On a tremendous plain, a huge crowd was thronging, as though on the Day of Judgment, through storms and massed clouds towards a brightly shining swastika in the sky. An incredible piece of vulgarity, a kind of Wagnerised National Socialism, this picture hung in what is known as the small conference hall in the second story.

Only a very small circle had been invited here at Darré's instance in the summer of 1932 to discuss the main lines of an " Eastern policy." Darré, the youngest party member under the later " Reich leaders," Hitler's immediate entourage, was specially eager to clarify the future Eastern policy of Germany. It is true that its main outlines were already sketched in *Mein Kampf*. But the political consequences of the agricultural and population policy were not enumerated in that vague and romantically utopian picture. Rosenberg, too, had left all the details undecided.

Darré, as a trained agriculturist, had also accepted responsibility for the practical and scientific accomplishment

of the National Socialist principle of race and racial hygiene.
He was engaged in the elaboration of a huge and detailed
register of the biological heritage of the National Socialist
élite, above all the S.S.   Commissioned by Himmler, he was
working on the pedigree of the new aristocracy—a pedigree
for the planned breeding of a race of *Herren*, on the tested
principles employed by all cattle-breeders' associations.
Darré showed me his filing-cabinets and the register.   At
that time Himmler had just decreed that members of the S.S.
might only marry by special permission, which was not
granted until the couple had undergone searching biological
tests.

"The new aristocracy will arise in this way.   We shall
gather in the best blood only," said Darré, pointing to his
iron filing-cabinets.   "Just as we have again produced the
old Hanover type of horse from sires and dams who had
little of the old purity left, so we shall again, in the course of
generations, breed the pure type of the Nordic German by
means of recessive crossing.   Perhaps we shall not be able
to purify the whole of the German nation again.   But the
new German aristocracy will be a pure breed in the literal
sense of the term."

I looked at the great quarto sheets of the register.

"I want all my peasant leaders to enter the S.S.," Darré
said.   "We shall breed the new aristocracy from the human
reserves of the S.S.   We shall do systematically and on the
basis of scientific, biological knowledge what the old blood
aristocracy of former days did by instinct.   In this transi-
tional era we must replace instinct by rational measures.
We shall in the first instance make use of the peasantry,
insofar as it has the sense to join the movement.   We shall
also make use of the good heritage of all the old blood
aristocracy that has remained pure.   I can visualise the
formation of 'halls of nobility,' where the new aristocracy,
deeply rooted in the soil, will at the same time assume the

mission of leadership among alien races. In other words, these halls of nobility will be situated in the foreign-language districts of our future empire."

Darré, whose second wife was a member of an old German-Baltic noble family, was thoroughly revolutionising the petit bourgeois, socialist conceptions of the party, replacing them by plans for an entirely different type of German agrarian policy. Hitler, who was at that time trying to win over to his views the great landowners east of the Elbe, regarded Darré's ideas with the greatest sympathy. The discussion to which Darré had been invited, with Hitler's approval, dealt in fact with the future Eastern policy as the basis of a new German agrarian and an anti-liberal population plan.

A member of Darré's staff now proceeded to lecture on the problems of space involved in an " Eastern space policy," as Darré called the German Eastern policy. There would have to be, said the lecturer, an alliance of states, such as had in fact begun to develop in the last war. A core of iron, a central great power ; Bohemia, Moravia, Austria as integral parts of it ; then a circle of smaller, dependent titular states : this, the lecturer explained, was the skeleton of the German empire. The Baltic states, a central Poland, severely cut back to strictly ethnographical lines and without an outlet on to the Baltic, a larger Hungary, Serbia and Croatia cut up into their component parts, a diminished Rumania, a Ukraine divided into a number of independent districts, South Russian and Caucasian states : this was the future Reich alliance that was to give Germany the basis of her might. In the north-east, the wedge of Finland, in the south-east, Georgia or Gruziya. But they would all be held together by a common army, a common trade and currency, a common foreign policy.

All this, however, the lecturer continued, would remain

an idle dream, unless a planned policy of colonisation and depopulation were carried out. Yes, a *de*population policy. The great danger for the great white Nordic race was the tremendous biological fertility of the East Baltic races, which, like everything inferior, made up for poor quality by greater quantity, that is to say, by the fecundity of their women. Through the agrarian bolshevism of the post-war period, namely, the splitting up of the large estates among small peasant settlers, this fertility had been increased to an alarming extent. It was necessary to detach the small Slav peasant from the land, and transform him into a landless labourer in order to reduce his fruitfulness. It was necessary to bring agricultural lands predominantly into the hands of the German *Herren* (squire) class. " The large-scale farmer in the Eastern area must always be a German." The alien peasant must again become a labourer, even an agricultural casual labourer for the Reich itself, or an unskilled industrial worker.

Another speaker further elaborated the political aspect of the agricultural problem. It was important that there should be no colonisation within Germany. This was a typically liberal method of evading the real problem. Colonisation always meant settlement in racially alien space, it meant the conquest of new land.

" The settlement notions of a Brüning and company are criminal ! " cried the speaker, excitedly. " They seduce the German people to the Chinese ideal. No internal colonisation ; only genuine colonisation by conquest ! No small peasantry ; only large-scale farming, the creation of a new squirearchy ! "

Even the East Prussian policy of pre-war days had been a total misunderstanding of this great problem, due of course to the spirit of the Kaiser-Wilhelm epoch, which was polluted with liberalism. And this was the result, diametrically opposed to the desired one : an increase in the Slav population and not of the German one. The agrarian bolshevism of systematically destroying the great estates would have to be firmly suppressed. It was necessary to re-create from the dwarfed West German farms large agricultural estates capable of employing horses and machinery. It was necessary to re-create in the states resulting from the Versailles Treaty the ruined German property, above all to transfer the large estates in the whole of the Eastern territory to German hands. An entail law would have to be introduced in Germany which would force the non-inheriting issue to emigrate to the east and themselves become large-scale farmers there. The small farms in Germany would be combined and the agricultural population thus dislodged.

This return to agriculture would never take place in Germany itself, but only in a great, German-ruled area in the east conquered by National Socialism. With the exception of a certain race, the German agricultural labourer would become a farmer himself, or a skilled industrial worker. Casual labourers of alien races would carry out agricultural labour at low wages. With the creation of a modern form of serfdom or, if you wished, slavery, human culture could not be further developed. At the same time, this was the only way in which an agricultural price policy could be followed which would permit German agricultural prices to approach those of the international markets, a thing which would sooner or later be indispensable.

Darré then addressed the meeting himself. Slav fertility must be broken, that was one task. The second was to create and firmly establish a German *Herren*-class. That was the ultimate meaning of the " Eastern space " policy. Instead of a horizontal classification of European races, there must be a vertical one. This meant that a German *élite* was destined to be the *Herren*-class of Europe, and

ultimately of the world. He would give this *élite* the true
Germanic name of *Adel* (aristocracy). But to be called to
this position they must not only be trained mentally,
physically and politically, but also nurtured biologically,
that is, gradually and systematically pure-bred. Unless
this were done, there was a danger that this class, in alien
racial surroundings, open to the temptations of its special
social privileges, would rapidly deteriorate.

A new social structure was therefore necessary in the
Germany and the Europe of the future. It was necessary
to reconstitute a class society, or, more accurately, a
hierarchy. But this could no longer be done within such
limited confines as Germany, but must be applied to a whole
continent, a whole universe. The whole gigantic problem
must be logically planned. In the building-up of a new,
healthy social organism, it was at the same time necessary
to hasten by every means the disintegration of the old,
dying one. The middle class was to be uprooted as well as
the working class. But the mental consequences must also
be faced. It was necessary to have the courage for illiteracy
and heathendom alike. Education and knowledge held
definite dangers for the *Herren*-class. But in another sense
they also endangered the maintenance of a slave class.
The ideal of universal education had long been obsolete.
It was not until knowledge recovered its character of a
secret science, and was no longer universally available, that
it would again exercise its normal function, which was to be
a means of ruling human, as well as non-human, nature.
But this brought us back once more to the importance of
reconstituting a European blood aristocracy, which National
Socialism opposed to the international, liberal, money
aristocracy.

Just as the German peasantry was the eternal blood source
of the German people, and must as such be specially
fostered, so must the new aristocracy be secured for all time

and protected against the dangers of degeneration by being subjected to the most stringent demands of biological selection, and bound in very special ways to agriculture and the soil. It was the special function of aristocracy beyond the borders of German soil to maintain itself as the outpost of German supremacy. The importance of the East German *Junker* class had been just this, that they were the masters, the rulers, of a subject population. This had developed their *Herren*-qualities, and this was why the Prussian *Junker* had been the finest of German types as long as he had remained untainted by liberalism and Jewish blood relationship. The " new aristocracy of blood and soil " must now take a similar mission upon itself, not only in the interest of its class, but quite consciously in the service of the whole nation. Even those of the National Socialist leaders who had no relations with agriculture would one day have to take over a landed estate, an odal* held in fee tail for their kin. Similarly, the political recruits of the movement would in the more distant future be drawn exclusively from these aristocratic families, whose function it was to rule in the German mastery of the world. Gigantic tasks were before us. It would be difficult to perfect their technique in the time left before the ultimate total breakdown.

" My party comrades," Hitler replied to this, " what we have discussed here must remain confidential. I think some of our party comrades might grievously misunderstand it. But Darré is right. We must strike off the egg-shell of liberalism, which unconsciously we still carry on our backs. This is difficult for many of us. We have gathered our ideas from every branch and twig by the wayside of life, and no longer know their origin.

" In the main I approve what has been said about our

* "Among the early and medieval Teutonic peoples, especially Scandinavians, the heritable land held by various odalmen constituting a family or kindred of freeborn tribesmen."—*Webster*.

eastern, or ' Eastern space ' policy. Only one thing, my
party comrades, you must always remember. We shall
never be great statesmen unless we have a nucleus of might
at the centre as hard and firm as steel. A nucleus of eighty
to one hundred million colonising Germans ! My first task
will therefore be to create this nucleus which will not only
make us invincible, but will assure to us once and for all
time the decisive ascendancy over all the European nations.
Once we have succeeded in this, we shall find everything
else comparatively simple.

" Part of this nucleus is Austria. That goes without
saying. But Bohemia and Moravia also belong to it, as
well as the western regions of Poland as far as certain
natural strategical frontiers. Moreover—and this you must
not overlook—the Baltic states, too, are part of it—those
states which for centuries have had a thin upper crust of
Germanhood. To-day in all these regions, alien races
predominate. It will be our duty, if we wish to found our
greater Reich for all time, to remove these races. There is
no excuse for neglecting this. Our age provides us with the
technical possibilities for carrying through such transfers of
population comparatively easily. Besides, the post-war
period brought with it an internal migration of many
millions of people, compared to which our enterprise will
seem a trifle.

" The Bohemian-Moravian basin and the eastern districts
bordering on Germany will be colonised with German
peasants. The Czechs and the Bohemians we shall trans-
plant to Siberia or the Volhynian regions, and we shall set
up reserves for them in the new allied states. The Czechs
must get out of Central Europe. As long as they remain,
they will always be a centre of Hussite-Bolshevik distintegra-
tion. Only when we are able and willing to achieve this
shall I be prepared to answer for the blood-sacrifice of
another young German generation. But at this price I

shall not hesitate for a moment to take the deaths of two
or three million Germans on my conscience, fully aware
of the heaviness of the sacrifice.

" In the Baltic countries," Hitler went on, " the case is
different. We shall easily Germanise the population. They
are peoples who are racially closely related to us and would
have been German long since, had not the prejudices and
social arrogance of the German Baltic barons artificially
prevented it. For the rest, frontier problems as such
interest me very little. If I were to dissipate my energies on
them, we should soon be at the end of our rope, and the
German people would be little benefited. I shall put an
end, too, to the absurdly sentimental views about the South
Tyrol. I have no intention of allowing this problem at any
time to deflect me from the basic line of our policy, namely,
an alliance with Italy. The German people have in their
unhappy history proliferated in every direction like a
cancer. I shall not be persuaded by any memories of our
past, however venerable, to commit a political blunder.
Alsace and Lorraine are in a different class. We shall
never give them up—not because Germans live there, but
because we require these and other parts to round off our
central regions in the west, just as we require Bohemia in
the south and Posen, West Prussia, Silesia and the Baltic
countries in the east and north."

Hitler continued :

" Thus far there are no doubts. In the east and south-
east, I do not follow General Ludendorff nor anyone else ;
I follow only the iron law of our historical development.
When Germany has rearmed, all these small states will offer
us their alliance of their own accord. But we have no
intention of manufacturing a peaceful Pan-Europe in
miniature, with the good Uncle Germany in the centre,
pleasantly shortening the time of his nephews' studies. We
shall not breed our own usurpers. We must once and for

all time create the politically and biologically eternally valid foundations of a German Europe.

" My party comrades, I am not thinking in the first instance of economical matters. Certainly we need the wheat, the oil and the ores of these countries. But our true object is to set up our rule for all time, and to anchor it so firmly that it will stand firm for a thousand years. No political or economic agreements, such as Papen and Hugenberg dream of, will achieve this. These are liberal games, which end in the bankruptcy of a nation. To-day we are faced with the iron necessity of a creating a *new social order*. Only if we succeed in this shall we solve the great historical task which has been set our people."

The classless society of the Marxists, he contended, was madness. Order always meant class order. But the democratic notion of a class order based on the moneybag was equally mad. A genuine aristocracy was not born out of the accidentally successful speculations of bright businessmen. The secret of our success lay in the fact that we had once more placed the vital law of genuine aristocracy at the heart of the political struggle. True aristocracy existed only where there was also true subjection. We did not intend to abolish the inequality of man ; on the contrary, we would deepen it and, as in ancient great civilisations, create insurmountable barriers which would turn it into law. There was no equal right for all. We would have the courage to make this denial the basis of all our actions, and to acknowledge it openly. Never would he concede to other nations equal rights with the German. It was our task to place other nations in subjection. The German people was called to give the world the new aristocracy.

Hitler then went on to show how this new aristocracy was to be created.

" The part played by the *bourgeoisie* is finished—

permanently, my party comrades," he said. "Do not be deceived by any galvanic currents that may for a moment cause their dead muscles to jerk again. But even these ' upper classes justified by history,' this paper aristocracy, these degenerate shoots of ancient noble families, have still one thing left, ' to die in beauty.' The *Herrenklub* members and their associates will not be able by the preposterous methods of their clubs and cliques to halt the march of history. I shall certainly destroy no aristocracy which to-day is still genuine. But where is there any such? If there is any, it will give its support to me. No, my party comrades, we shall not discuss the growth of a new upper class. We shall create it, and there is only one way of creating it : battle. The selection of the new Führer class is *my* struggle for power. Whoever proclaims his allegiance to *me* is, by this very proclamation and by the *manner* in which it is made, one of the chosen. This is the great revolutionary significance of our long, dogged struggle for power, that in it will be born a new *Herren*-class, chosen to guide the fortunes not only of the German people, but of the world.

"Not by hair-splitting and experimentation, but in a single historical occurrence, with the rise of a new *Herren*-class, a new social order will arise as well. We are in the midst of such a process. We stand in the midst of such a revolutionary cataclysm, produced by the abdication of old social powers and the rise of new ones. But the Marxist gentry are mistaken if they think it is the workers who will take the place of the *Junkers* as the new, leading social power. It is the preposterous mark of the cowardice of the surrendering *bourgeoisie* that it sees in the industrial worker the mystic saviour in accordance with a kind of social doctrine of healing. The worker to-day, from the political aspect, is as much a temporary symptom of a dying social order as the nobility and the *bourgeoisie*."

4

He would tell us what the society of the future would look like.

"There will be a *Herren*-class," he said, "an historical class tempered by battle, and welded from the most varied elements. There will be a great hierarchy of party members. They will be the new middle class. And there will be the great mass of the anonymous, the serving collective, the eternally disfranchised, no matter whether they were once members of the old *bourgeoisie*, the big land-owning class, the working-class or the artisans. Nor will their financial or previous social position be of the slightest importance. These preposterous differences will have been liquidated in a single revolutionary process. But beneath them there will still be the class of subject alien races ; we need not hesitate to call them the modern slave class. And over all of these will stand the new high aristocracy, the most deserving and the most responsible *Führer*-personalities. In this way, in the struggle for power and mastery both within a nation and outside it, new classes emerge ; never, as the professors and bookworms would have us believe, through a makeshift constitution, a government decree.

"I fully approve of what our party comrade Darré has said. Our great experimental field is in the east. There the new European social order will arise, and this is the great significance of our eastern policy."

In this connection he wanted to say a final word :

"Certainly we shall admit to our new ruling class members of other nations who have been worthy in our cause. On this point I entirely agree with Darré and Himmler. The racial and biological aspect is only one side of the total process. In fact, we shall very soon have overstepped the bounds of the narrow nationalism of to-day. My party comrades, it is true that world empires arise on a national basis, but very quickly they leave it far behind.

"And this brings me," Hitler said in conclusion, "to the

point we call education or upbringing. As surely as everything we have discussed here to-day must be kept from
burdening the mind of the ordinary party member, equally
surely must we put an end to what is known as universal
education. Universal education is the most corroding and
disintegrating poison that liberalism has ever invented for
its own destruction."

Here Hitler paused deliberately as if to give us a chance of
digesting his astonishing definition of universal education.
He then brought his remarks to a close as follows :

" There must be only one possible education for each
class, for each subdivision of a class. Complete freedom of
choice in education is the privilege of the *élite* and of those
whom they have specially admitted. The whole of science
must be subject to continual control and selection. Knowledge is an aid to life, not its central aim. We must therefore be consistent, and allow the great mass of the lowest
order the blessings of illiteracy. We ourselves, on the other
hand, shall shake off all humane and scientific prejudices.
This is why, in the *Junker* schools I shall found for the future
members of our *Herren*-class, I shall allow the gospel of the
free man to be preached—the man who is master of life and
death, of human fear and superstition, who has learnt to
control his body, his muscles and his nerves but remains
at the same time impervious to the temptations of the mind
and of sciences presumably free."

PART II—1933

CONTEMPORARY EVENTS

Jan. 28. Government resigned.

Jan. 30. Hitler appointed Reich Chancellor ; Vice-Chancellor, von Papen ; Foreign Minister, von Neurath.

Feb. 1. President dissolved Reichstag.

Feb. 27. Reichstag fire.

March 5. Hitler won 288 seats at General Election.

March 8. Jews in many towns forced to close their shops.

March 9. Nazi troops occupied Bavarian Government offices in Munich and demanded resignation of Ministers. Prominent Berlin Jews compelled to resign offices.

March 10. Bavarian Government submitted to Nazis.

April 1. Boycott of Jews enforced throughout Germany for one day.

May 1. Hitler, addressing enormous crowds, intimated that scheme of compulsory labour would be introduced.

May 17. Hitler announced Germany's peaceful intentions and readiness to sign any non-aggression pact.

June 7. Germany accepted final draft of Four-Power Pact.

June 22. " Green Shirts " and " Black Shirts " suppressed.

June 23. Social-Democratic Party suppressed.

June 27. Dr. Hugenberg, leader of the Nationalist party, resigned Ministry of Economic Affairs.

June 29. Centre, or Roman Catholic, Party wound up.

June 30.   Chancellor instructed Minister of Interior to take
            necessary action to promote peace between
            Evangelical Churches and Government.

July 9.   Concordat between Holy See and Germany
            initialled.

Aug. 7.   Britain and France protested against Germany's
            anti-Austrian activities. Germany declared
            interference inadmissible.

Aug. 20.   Government's industrial plan, including
            provision of £25,000,000 for enlargement and
            repair of public buildings and house property.

Aug. 21.   Reichstag Fire Trial of five men opened at
            Leipzig.

Oct. 14.   Germany announced withdrawal from Dis-
            armament Conference and League of Nations.

Nov. 12.   General Election gave Hitler complete rule over
            Germany. No opposition party or programme
            permitted in Reichstag election.

Dec. 1.   Germany became officially a Nazi State, the
            party being identified with the State and no
            other parties allowed to exist.

Dec. 23.   Judgment delivered in Reichstag Fire Trial.
            Van der Lubbe, a Dutchman, found guilty
            and sentenced to death. Torgler, leader of
            German Communist Party, and three Bul-
            garians, were acquitted, but kept in custody.

CHAPTER IV

ANTICHRIST

I REMEMBER in every detail the conversation to be recorded in this chapter. It made an indelible impression on me. From it dates my inner revulsion against National Socialism. For now I began to understand its true nature and aims.

I can still feel to-day the narrow, restricted atmosphere, the smell of new furniture, the meaninglessness of an outworn day. The familiar blend of narrowness and bohemianism, *petit bourgeois* pleasures and revolutionary talk. I can still hear the ubiquitous and abstruse Puzzi Hanfstängel manhandling the piano in the next room. He had just composed a march which seemed to appeal to Hitler's taste —a bastard product of Wagner *motifs*.

A small sofa, a few chairs, a table : Frau Raubal, Frau Goebbels, Forster, Goebbels, and myself sitting in the room. Behind us the " leader," the newly appointed Reich Chancellor. He was leaning across his desk, turning over the pages of documents. Facing him were Julius Streicher and Wagner of Munich. Tea was being served, and small cakes. Frau Raubal, whose manner suggested motherly kindliness, was trying to help a harmless conversation on its way. We were listless. Frau Goebbels, her face in very un-German make-up, was watching Hitler, and I, too, was unable to drag my thoughts away from the conversation that was being carried on behind me and moving me to a growing excitement.

It was late at night. Hitler had been to the cinema—

some patriotic rubbish glorifying Frederick the Great. We
had preceded Hitler to the Chancellery and had waited for
him there. Goebbels had been the first to arrive.

" A magnificent film," he said, " a remarkable film.
That's the sort of thing we shall need."

A few minutes later Hitler came up in the lift.

" How did you like the picture ? " Forster asked.

" A horror—absolute rubbish. The police will have to
stop it. We've had enough of this patriotic balderdash ! "

" Yes, my Führer," Goebbels exclaimed, pushing forward, " it was feeble, very feeble. We have a great
educational task ahead of us."

Prince August Wilhelm of Prussia, who had come back with
Hitler, and was now taking his leave, remarked as he went :

" It's about time some sort of cruelty-to-animals law was
passed against this abuse of historical memories."

The date of this evening is recalled to me by the following
day, which was of special significance. I had dined with
Hitler, after having brought him my report. It was a
momentous day, for the post of *Reichsstatthalter* (lieu-
tenant-governor of the Reich) had just been created. The
sole purpose of this measure was to suppress in time the
independent aims of the provinces. In Bavaria, an independence movement of the greatest danger to National
Socialism had been successful. Had Bavaria made use of
its opportunity, and had Crown Prince Rupprecht, above
all, been firmer, a Bavarian monarchy would have put an
early and decided end to all National Socialist strivings.
The German renaissance would have come from a different
quarter and in an essentially different form.

Our nocturnal conversation arose out of our anxieties
regarding such a development. The two Bavarian *Gauleiter*,
Streicher of Franconia and Wagner of Munich, had brought
us the tale. It was Streicher who gave Hitler his cue in the
conversation. I had not listened to the beginning of it and

became attentive only when I heard Hitler's voice behind me getting louder.

" The religions are all alike, no matter what they call themselves. They have no future—certainly none for the Germans. Fascism, if it likes, may come to terms with the Church. So shall I. Why not? That will not prevent me from tearing up Christianity root and branch, and annihilating it in Germany. The Italians are naïve ; they're quite capable of being heathens and Christians at the same time. The Italians and the French are essentially heathens. Their Christianity is only skin-deep. But the German is different. He is serious in everything he undertakes. He wants to be either a Christian or a heathen. He cannot be both. Besides, Mussolini will never make heroes of his Fascists. It doesn't matter there whether they're Christians or heathens. But for our people it is decisive whether they acknowledge the Jewish Christ-creed with its effeminate pity-ethics, or a strong, heroic belief in God in Nature, God in our own people, in our destiny, in our blood."

After a pause, he resumed :

" Leave the hair-splitting to others. Whether it's the Old Testament or the New, or simply the sayings of Jesus, according to Houston Stewart Chamberlain—it's all the same old Jewish swindle. It will not make us free. A German Church, a German Christianity, is distortion. One is either a German or a Christian. You cannot be both. You can throw the epileptic Paul out of Christianity —others have done so before us. You can make Christ into a noble human being, and deny his divinity and his role as a saviour. People have been doing it for centuries. I believe there are such Christians to-day in England and America—Unitarians they call themselves, or something like that. It's no use, you cannot get rid of the mentality behind it. We don't want people who keep one eye on the life in the hereafter. We need free men who feel and know that God is in themselves."

Streicher or Goebbels made some remark which I did not catch—a question perhaps.

" You can't make an Aryan of Jesus, that's nonsense," Hitler went on. " What Chamberlain wrote in his Principles is, to say the least, stupid. What's to be done, you say ? I will tell you : we must prevent the churches from doing anything but what they are doing now, that is, losing ground day by day. Do you really believe the masses will ever be Christian again ? Nonsense ! Never again. That tale is finished. No one will listen to it again. But we can hasten matters. The parsons will be made to dig their own graves. They will betray their God to us. They will betray anything for the sake of their miserable little jobs and incomes.

" What we can do ? Just what the Catholic Church did when it forced its beliefs on the heathen : preserve what can be preserved, and change its meaning. We shall take the road back : Easter is no longer resurrection, but the eternal renewal of our people. Christmas is the birth of *our* saviour : the spirit of heroism and the freedom of our people. Do you think these liberal priests, who have no longer a belief, only an office, will refuse to preach *our* God in their churches ? I can guarantee that, just as they have made Haeckel and Darwin, Goethe and Stefan George the prophets of their Christianity, so they will replace the cross with our swastika. Instead of worshipping the blood of their quondam saviour, they will worship the pure blood of our people. They will receive the fruits of the German soil as a divine gift, and will eat it as a symbol of the eternal communion of the people, as they have hitherto eaten of the body of their God. And when we have reached that point, Streicher, the churches will be crowded again. If *we* wish it, then it will be so—when it is *our* religion that is preached there. We need not hurry the process."

Hitler paused. Frau Raubal asked me a question about my family, and I failed to catch what followed.

"Let it run its course," I presently heard Hitler say. "But it won't last. Why a uniform religion, a German Church independent of Rome? Don't you see that that's all obsolete? German Christians, German Church, Christians freed from Rome—old stuff! I know perfectly well what is coming, and we shall take care of it all in good time. Without a religion of its own, the German people has no permanence. What this religion will be we do not yet know. We feel it, but that is not enough."

"No," he replied to a question, "these professors and mystery-men who want to found Nordic religions merely get in my way. Why do I tolerate them? Because they help to disintegrate, which is all we can do at the moment. They cause unrest. And all unrest is creative. It has no value in itself, but let it run its course. They do their share, and the priests do theirs. We shall compel them to destroy their religions from within by setting aside all authority and reducing everything to pale, meaningless talk. Shall we succeed? Certainly and irresistibly."

The conversation took a quieter turn. Goebbels sat down at our table, and Hanfstängel came from the other room to join us. The two Bavarian leaders related a few cases of uncompromising resistance from the Bavarian Catholic Church.

"They had better stop deceiving themselves," said Hitler menacingly. "Their day has passed. They have lost."

He would not, he went on, do the same as Bismarck.

"I'm a Catholic. Certainly that was fated from the beginning, for only a Catholic knows the weaknesses of the Church. I know how to deal with these gentry. Bismarck was a fool. In other words, he was a Protestant. Protestants don't know what a church is. In these things you

must be able to feel and think with the people, know what
they want and what they dislike. Bismarck stuck to his
legal clauses and his Prussian sergeant-majors. That was
not enough. And least of all shall I institute a cultural
struggle. That was a blunder. Naturally the monks were
anxious to shine before their poor little woman with the
martyr's crown. But I shall know how to deal with them,
I can guarantee that.

"The Catholic Church is a really big thing. Why,
what an organisation ! It's something to have lasted nearly
two thousand years ! We must learn from it. Astuteness
and knowledge of human nature are behind it. Catholic
priests know where the shoe pinches. But their day is
done, and they know it. They are far too intelligent
not to see that, and to enter upon a hopeless battle. But if
they do, I shall certainly not make martyrs of them. We
shall brand them as ordinary criminals. I shall tear the
mask of honesty from their faces. And if that is not enough,
I shall make them appear ridiculous and contemptible. I
shall order films to be made about them. We shall show
the history of the monks on the cinema. Let the whole
mass of nonsense, selfishness, repression and deceit be
revealed : how they drained the money out of the country,
how they haggled with the Jews for the world, how they
committed incest. We shall make it so thrilling that
everyone will want to see it. There will be queues outside
the cinemas. And if the pious burghers find the hair rising
on their heads in horror, so much the better. The young
people will accept it—the young people and the masses.
I can do without the others."

"I promise you," he concluded, "that if I wished to, I
could destroy the Church in a few years ; it is hollow and
rotten and false through and through. One push and the
whole structure would collapse. We should trap the priests
by their notorious greed and self-indulgence. We shall

thus be able to settle everything with them in perfect
peace and harmony. I shall give them a few years' reprieve.
Why should we quarrel? They will swallow anything in
order to keep their material advantages. Matters will
never come to a head. They will recognise a firm will, and
we need only show them once or twice who is the master.
Then they will know which way the wind blows. *They* are
no fools. The Church was something really big. Now
we're its heirs. We, too, are a Church. Its day has gone.
It will not fight. I'm quite satisfied. As long as youth
follows me, I don't mind if the old people limp to the con-
fessional. But the young ones—they will be different. I
guarantee that."

At the time, I regarded this whole speech as sheer
braggadoccio, and as a concession to the pornographic
Streicher. Nevertheless, it shook me to the depths. I
had not supposed Hitler capable of so much cynicism.
Later I was to remember it many times—at the time of the
currency trials, and then of the immorality trials of
Catholic priests, the purpose of which was to brand them
as criminals in the eyes of the masses and thereby deprive
them in advance of the halo of martyrdom. It was a
cunning and, as has since transpired, long-planned scheme,
for which Hitler himself is solely responsible.

I heard little more after this. The only thing that
interested me further was the Führer's ostentatious contempt for the Protestant church. Hitler by no means shared
the hopes and desires of many militant, anti-Rome
Protestants, who thought to shatter the Roman church
with the aid of National Socialism, and establish an essentially evangelical, German, united church of which Catholics
would be expected to form a subordinate section. I have
spoken many times since then with the Reich Bishop
Müller, who was very nearly my predecessor as President of
the Danzig Senate. His ambitions lay in this direction.

" The Protestants haven't the faintest conception of a church," I heard Hitler saying. " You can do anything you like to them—they will submit. They're used to cares and worries. They learnt them from their Squires. The parsons, when they were invited to the Sunday roast goose, had their place at the foot of the table, amongst the children and tutors. It was even an honour that they were not asked to sit at the servants' table. They are insignificant little people, submissive as dogs, and they sweat with embarrassment when you talk to them. They have neither a religion that they can take seriously nor a great position to defend like Rome."

The conversation ebbed again into unimportant details and mere abuse, and rose only once more to higher levels of interest. Hitler was speaking about the peasantry, claiming that under their Christian exterior, the old eternal heathendom still lurked, and broke out again and again.

" You're a farmer," he said, turning to me. " What can you tell us about it? How are conditions in your district? "

I rose and joined the group. In our district, I said, we had highly rationalised farming where there was little of the old customs left. But no doubt it was true : if you scratched the surface, ancient, inherited beliefs were revealed.

" You see," Hitler returned triumphantly ; " that is what I'm building on. Our peasants have not forgotten their true religion. It still lives. It is merely covered over. The Christian mythology has simply coated it like a layer of tallow. It has preserved the true contents of the pot. I have said this to Darré, and told him that we must start the great reformation. He has suggested means to me, magnificent means ! I have approved them. The old beliefs will be brought back to honour again. In our ' Green Week ' and in the ' Travelling Agricultural Exhibition ' he will allude to our inherited religion in picturesque and expressive language that even the simplest peasant can understand.

" It will not be done in the old way, running riot in colourful costumes and dreaming of a departed, romantic age. The peasant will be told what the Church has destroyed for him : the whole of the secret knowledge of nature, of the divine, the shapeless, the daemonic. The peasant shall learn to hate the Church on that basis. Gradually he will be taught by what wiles the soul of the German has been raped. We shall wash off the Christian veneer and bring out a religion peculiar to our race. And this is where we must begin. Not in the great cities, Goebbels ! There we shall only lose ourselves in the stupid godlessness propaganda of the Marxists : free sex in nature and that sort of bad taste. The urban masses are empty. Where all is extinguished, nothing can be aroused. But our peasantry still lives in heathen beliefs and values.

" The same is true of all other countries, Sweden, France, England, the Slav agricultural countries. The renaissance of heathendom has always broken against the mischief done by the literary, those urban ranks of the totally uprooted, those mental conjurors. Unless we give the masses something in exchange for what we take from them, they will later fall a prey to every kind of swindle. But it is through the peasantry that we shall really be able to destroy Christianity because there is in them a true religion rooted in nature and blood. It is through the peasantry that we shall one day be able to act as missionaries to the urban masses as well. But there is plenty of time for that."

With that the conversation ended. We sat on for a time round the table, where Hitler joined us. Frau Goebbels was solicitous for the well-being of the Führer. It was time to break up, she said.

" You have a hard day behind you, my Führer, and another before you to-morrow."

We took our leave, and I went to my small hotel near the Friedrichstrassen Station.

It was all fulfilled later, even to the last item Hitler had hinted at. Attempts were and are being made to make use of old folk-customs to de-Christianise the peasantry. I have seen pavilions at the agricultural exhibitions subtly planned with this end in view. I have seen a picture-series, prepared with the greatest pedagogical skill, repre-senting the struggle of the Steding peasants against the Church in Bremen. I noted how all visitors reacted, in the midst of the objective representation of our agricultural calling, to the terrible accusations wordlessly raised against the late mediæval Church in regard to her bloodstained repression of surviving heathen beliefs and of the peasant's love of liberty. We agricultural leaders were regularly invited to the new type of godless meetings of the National Socialists, " religious " evenings on which the new religions were paraded. There were Professors Hauer and Wirth and many others. It was clear that these invitations, which were personal ones from Darré, were designed to ascertain how far we might be regarded as belonging to the true *élite* and how serious we were about the total revolution of National Socialism.

In other words, they were a test of our trustworthiness. That was the first step. The second was pressure on us to give up membership in the Church. How quickly the whole process moved became clear to me from the case of an acquaintance of mine, the Westphalian farmer Meinberg, a splendid fellow who was unmistakably solid and loyal. He was a *Staatsrat* (councillor of state) and a leader of the peasantry, Darré's deputy in the Reich Labour Ministry, and a most apt pupil. A new fireplace appeared in his ancient peasant homestead, its walls decorated with runes and heathen maxims. The crosses had disappeared to make room for other sacred symbols. Woden, the ancient huntsman, was in the place of honour. And on the hearth burnt the new, eternal flame. Was Hitler right in saying that the Christian crust was a thin one in our peasants? What happened to us happened also to the men of the SS, especially to the higher ranks—the ranks of the Hitler youth. Thoroughly and systematically, with iron logic, the war of annihilation against Christianity was being waged.

5

CHAPTER V

AT THE DINNER TABLE
(SUMMER OF 1933)

THAT summer I frequently dined with Hitler in his flat. He lived at that time on the second floor of the new Reich Chancellery. His home was good middle-class, one might almost say *petit bourgeois*. The rooms were smallish, the furnishing simple and without refinement. There was not a single piece that revealed anything of good personal taste or artistic value.

Whenever Hitler was in Berlin, he asked people to dine with him. It was considered a high honour to eat at Hitler's table, and there were usually ten to twenty people, at most. The food was simple. In this, too, the party Führer liked to give an impression of modest living on proletarian lines. He frequently expressed his intention of changing none of his previous habits, either in his clothing or in his style of living. As a matter of fact, this did form an agreeable contrast to the extravagant behaviour of some of the new bosses. Hitler retained his old habit of sitting beside the chauffeur in his car ; his clothes consisted of his familiar raincoat seldom surmounted by a hat, while under it he usually wore a civilian jacket with the party uniform trousers, or an ordinary lounge suit.

At dinner, there was soup, followed by a meat course, vegetables and a sweet. Hitler himself ate no meat, but he devoured astonishing portions of the sweet, and his personal cook, an old party member, prepared special vegetable dishes for him. But Hitler placed no vegetarian compulsion

66

on his guests, nor did he refuse them alcohol in the shape of beer. There was a choice between beer and lemonade, and it was amusing to watch newcomers, especially enthusiastic party members, choosing lemonade, with a side-glance at the temperate Führer, in order to make a good impression.

There was always a mixed and varied company at the table. Invariably some outstanding person was present, a film star, an artist or a leading member of the party. There were ladies, too, but usually in the minority. On one occasion I met two strikingly pretty blondes ; Hitler asked one of them to sit beside him, and kept putting his hand on her arm. Sometimes, too, society women were among the guests. It was at one of these gatherings that I made the acquaintance of Hess's sister. She was a handicrafts expert, and had bound Hitler's books for him. A frequent visitor at that time was Prince August Wilhelm of Prussia. Though an enthusiastic Nazi, he shone far more brightly in private conversation than in public speaking or in politics. His behaviour was natural, yet he seemed out of place. In my youth I had often seen him and his younger brother Oskar in the Prussian cadet corps at Potsdam. The princes used to visit us sometimes to play tennis or football. Hitler treated the prince with great courtesy at this time, and there were hopes in conservative quarters that the Führer would make " Auwi " Kaiser.

Then there was that constant visitor, Puzzi Hanfstängel, whose linguistic abilities and knowledge of the world were in great demand ; but his curiously shaped head was more striking than what he had inside it. Goebbels, too, was there quite frequently. He visited Hitler whenever he could, remembering, perhaps, the adage, "Out of sight, out of mind." Brückner, Hitler's tall adjutant, was another frequent visitor, and so was Sepp Dietrich. Everybody of note in the party who visited Berlin was included by Hitler in these dinner-parties.

The tone was informal. Often Hitler was silent, or made only desultory remarks. Again, he would pontificate in a booming voice, and everyone would listen in silence. It was interesting to watch Hitler talking himself into a fury, and to note how necessary to his eloquence were shouting and a feverish *tempo*. A quiet conversation with him was impossible. Either he was silent or he took complete charge of the discussion. Hitler's eloquence is plainly no natural gift, but the result of a conquest of certain inhibitions which, in intimate conversation, still make him awkward. The convulsive artificiality of his character is specially noticeable in such intimate circles ; particularly notable is his lack of any sense of humour. Hitler's laugh is hardly more than an expression of scorn and contempt. There is no relaxation about it. His pleasures have no repose.

At one of these dinners I had, in fact, the opportunity of hearing his views on humour. I was sitting opposite Goebbels, who was on Hitler's left. The two were discussing the National Socialist humorous papers and the significance of wit as a weapon. In humour, too, or what he called humour, Hitler saw only a weapon. It was at this time that, in connection with the *Stürmer* and its Jewish caricatures, he gave utterance to the remark later much quoted in the party, that this was " the form of pornography permitted in the Third Reich." Evidently Hitler took pleasure in these filthy stories.

After dinner, coffee and liqueurs were served in Hitler's small study. There was some smoking too, but not much. Occasionally the coffee would be served on a large terrace rather like a roof-garden, which overlooked the treetops in the gardens of the old Reich Chancellery. Hitler's entire entourage, especially his stepsister, Frau Raubal, who at that time lent his home a housewifely character, were continually worried about his safety. Attempts at assassination were already feared, particularly within the Chancellery gardens, and Hitler had been warned against walking in them. He took little exercise. The terrace was his substitute for a garden.

Hitler's Foot in Latin America

It was on this terrace that, after dinner one evening in the early summer of 1933, I was present at a conversation that was most revealing of Hitler's political opinions about America, and showed how far-reaching were his plans even then, and how mistaken was the belief that National Socialism had political aims only in the east and south-east of Europe. A trusted, leading member of the S.A. had just returned from South America, and Hitler had engaged him in conversation, and asked him many questions. Over the coffee, he took up the thread of the discourse again. Evidently his information was not detailed, and he was merely repeating various notions—highly popular at the time—concerning the land of the future that he had gleaned from certain publications. He was specially interested in Brazil.

" We shall create a new Germany there," he cried. " We shall find everything we need there."

He then outlined broadly all that a hard-working and energetic government could do to create order. All the preconditions for a revolution were there, a revolution which in a few decades, or even years, would transform a corrupt mestizo state into a German dominion.

" Besides, we have a right to this continent, for the Fuggers and Welsers had possessions there. We have got to repair what our German disunity has destroyed ; we must see to it that it is no longer true that we have lost all that we once occupied. The time has passed for us to give place to Spain and Portugal, and be everywhere at a disadvantage."

Von P., his guest, agreed as to the special opportunities
of Germany in Brazil.

" These people will need us if they are going to make
anything of their country," Hitler remarked. They had less
use, he said, for investment capital than for the spirit of
enterprise and for organising ability. And they were fed
up with the United States. They knew they were being
exploited by them, and had nothing to expect from them
for the development of their country.

" We shall give them both : capital and the spirit of
enterprise. We shall make them a third gift : our philosophy," said Hitler. " If ever there is a place where
democracy is senseless and suicidal, it is in South America.
We must strengthen these people's clear conscience, so that
they may be enabled to throw both their liberalism and their
democracy overboard. They are actually ashamed of their
good instincts ! They think they must still give lip-service to
democracy. Let us wait a few years, and in the meantime
do what we can to help them. But we must send our people
out to them. Our youth must learn to colonise. For this,
we have no need of formal officials and governors. Audacious
youth is what we want. They need not go into the jungle,
either, to clear the ground. What we want are people in
good society. What do you know about the German
colony ? Can anything be done along these lines ? "

He turned to von P., who replied that it was very doubtful
whether we ought to keep in touch with good society. In
his opinion we should attain our purpose more quickly by
making use of other classes, such as the Indios and the
mestizos.

" Both, my dear P.," Hitler interrupted impatiently.
" We require two movements abroad, a loyal and a revolutionary one. Do you think that's so difficult ? I think we
have proved that we are capable of it. We should not be
here otherwise. We shall not land troops like William the

Conqueror and gain Brazil by the strength of arms. Our weapons are not visible ones. Our conquistadores, my dear P., have a more difficult task than the original ones, and for this reason they have more difficult weapons."

Hitler asked further questions about German possibilities in South America. The Argentine and Bolivia were in the first line of interest, and it appeared that there were many points where National Socialist influence might make itself felt. Hitler propounded ideas which were much later realised by Bohle on the one hand and Ribbentrop on the other, and took shape in two mutually antagonistic onslaughts of propaganda. Essentially it was a question of personnel. The task of getting a firm foothold in Latin America and squeezing out North America and Hispano-Portuguese influence could only be carried out by new, energetic, unscrupulous representatives of overseas Germanhood.

I turned to Hanfstängel with the suggestion that this seemed to me a most alarming repetition in an aggravated form of the whole pre-war policy. Would it not be wiser not to challenge Britain and America, at least until Germany's position was unassailable? Moreover, this proposed policy was in contradiction to the fundamental rules laid down by *Mein Kampf*. But now for the first time I heard derogatory mention made of this book in Hitler's presence, and concluded from this that it was by no means regarded in the inner circles as the binding pronouncement it was given out to be for the masses. It was Hanfstängel's opinion that sooner or later we should in any case have to face the hostility of the United States and Britain. Germany was ready. Was I still cherishing, he contemptuously asked, illusions about Britain? As for the United States, they would certainly never interfere in Europe again ; he knew that better than anyone, for he knew these gentry and their weaknesses. Britain, he proclaimed, was dead.

Where else, he added, should Germany get the elements of her future world empire if not from the disintegrating empires of Britain and France ? The final struggle with Britain could not be evaded.

" And if you look closer," concluded Hanfstängel, " you will find that everything about Britain in *Mein Kampf* is of purely tactical value. Hitler had good reason to write as he did."

That night I heard mentioned for the first time the general outlines of the future great German overseas Reich. I was amazed to hear that Hitler was reaching out to the Pacific. Above all, he was interested in the former great German island empire, embracing the Dutch possessions and the whole of New Guinea. Japan must not be allowed to grow too big, Hitler remarked. It must be deflected against China and Russia. But Hitler also anticipated a Central African Dominion of Germany as well as a complete revolutionary transformation of the U.S.A. With the break-down of the British Empire, Hitler believed he could also break Anglo-Saxon influence in North America, and substitute for it the German language and culture as a preliminary step towards incorporating the United States in the German world empire.

MEXICO, GERMAN VIRGIN SOIL
(SUMMER OF 1934, AFTER THE JUNE " PURGE ")

This brings me to Mexico, which was actually mentioned in a much later conversation of Hitler's in 1934. Mexico played a special part in Hitler's American plans, which were, however, nothing like Papen's notorious intrigues during the last war to push Mexico into war against the United States. This policy Hitler regarded as sheer stupidity. Here, too, he was prepared to initiate far-sighted schemes and enterprises, the end of which he could not expect to see. His plans presupposed much longer periods of time than his European schemes, and his impatience towards European problems will be understood only if it is seen against the background of his greater plans, for which his European policy was to provide the power basis.

One man has evidently greatly influenced his conceptions concerning Mexico, a man who was a curious mixture of the great industrialist and the eccentric : Sir Henry Deterding of the Royal Dutch. I have made his acquaintance myself. It was in East Prussia, where he was the guest of a friend of mine. He went shooting and pulled some not entirely visible wires. A very agreeable man, incidentally, most stimulating in non-business intercourse. He shared Hitler's interest in the Caucasian oil of the Russians, and was one of the promoters of certain plans for a further partition of Russia. He was interested in the erection of an independent Georgia, a state which, by the way, was once a member of the League of Nations—still is, for all I know. In such hopes, which included the separation of the Russian Ukraine and the establishment of a Volga republic, he was in great sympathy with Hitler. His interest in the establishment of a silver currency was no doubt less of an attraction to the Führer.

Directly or indirectly, Deterding convinced Hitler that Mexico was the best and richest country in the world with the laziest and most dissipated population under the sun. Only the most capable and industrious people in the world, namely, the Germans, would be able to make something of it. This notion fell on very fruitful soil in Hitler's mind. On one of my last visits (it was after the 30th June, 1934, when I saw him to give him a report on Danzig conditions), he spoke of Mexico along these lines. It was at this time that the economic difficulties of the Reich commenced, as did also those of Danzig, the breakdown of whose currency system was then imminent. Hitler's mood fluctuated between blackest depression and uncontrollable rage. On every hand his opponents seemed to be getting the better of him. The *Reichsbank*, which was playing up pessimism for demagogical reasons, claimed that the whole of rearmament was endangered. The Foreign Department was putting restraints on Hitler's temperament at every turn, and working in the old-fashioned style, with no thought of changing either its ideas or its *tempo*. It created a special circle of its own, and Hitler felt hampered on every side. After the terrible blood-bath of June, he was not even sure of his own party. He had to make a great effort not to be completely outmanœuvred.

Among intimate friends, Hitler let himself go. I often heard him shout and stamp his feet. The slightest contradiction threw him into a rage. This was the beginning of the technique by which he would throw his entourage into confusion by well-timed fits of rage, and thus make them more submissive. People began to be afraid of his incalculable temper. The terror of the 30th June and the bloody deeds against patriots and citizens were bearing fruit.

Everywhere, Hitler complained, there were nothing but sterile old men in their second childhood, who bragged of their technical knowledge and had lost their sound common sense.

" If I say : I want to do this or that, Neurath tells me I can't. We'll have everyone up in arms. If I say : Damn your economic science, bring me money, Schacht says he can't, we must first consider a fresh plan."

Hitler then began to dream of all he could do if only he were not surrounded by a lot of indolent old fools who had got stuck in routine. For instance, there was this country Mexico. Who in the Foreign Office would have bothered about it ? This was a matter that must be dealt with in a large way.

" If we had that country," said the Führer, " we should

solve all our difficulties. I have no use for Schacht or
Krosigk ; all they do, day in, day out, is to tell me their
troubles. Mexico is a country that cries for a capable
master. It is being ruined by its government. With the
treasure of Mexican soil, Germany could be rich and
great ! Why do we not tackle this task ? I'll have nothing
to do," he interrupted himself, " with the kind of colonial
propaganda Epp wants. They use that against us anyhow.
We need something new. You could get this Mexico for a
couple of hundred million. Why should I not make an
alliance with Mexico, a defence alliance, and a customs
alliance ? But these official donkeys only pull when they
have the old refuse cart behind them. Because a thing has
never been done before, they think it can't be done now ! "

HITLER ON THE UNITED STATES

About the United States, Hitler had his firm, preconceived opinion which no argument could shake. This
opinion was that North America would never take part
in a European war again, and that, with her millions of
unemployed, the United States was on the brink of a
revolution from the outbreak of which only Hitler could
save her.

In June, 1933, I was present at a dinner-table conversation in Hitler's flat in which he gave expression to this view.
Later, however, I had frequent occasions to hear the same
view expressed. One of the guests suggested that it might
be of decisive importance for Germany to win the friendship
of North America. Certain members of the German
government at that time had publicly emphasised the
unique value of friendly relations with the United States,
and for this reason had some misgivings about the anti-
Semitic policy of the Reich.

" Whose friendship ? " Hitler brusquely interposed.

" The friendship of the Jewish jobbers and moneybags
or that of the American people ? "

He expressed his contempt of the present government of
the United States.

" This is the last disgusting death-rattle of a corrupt and
outworn system which is a blot on the history of this people.
Since the Civil War, in which the Southern States were
conquered, against all historical logic and sound sense,
the Americans have been in a condition of political and
popular decay. In that war, it was not the Southern
States, but the American people themselves who were
conquered. In the spurious blossoming of economic
progress and power politics, America has ever since been
drawn deeper into the mire of progressive self-destruction.
A moneyed clique, which presumes to be good society and
to represent the old families, rules the country under the
fiction of a democracy which has never before been so
nakedly exposed as a mass of corruption and legal venality.
The beginnings of a great new social order based on the
principle of slavery and inequality were destroyed by that
war, and with them also the embryo of a future truly great
America that would not have been ruled by a corrupt
caste of tradesmen, but by a real *Herren*-class that would
have swept away all the falsities of liberty and equality."

That word " equality " seemed to lash him into a fury.
" Equality of whom ? " he shouted.   " Of the descendants
of old Spanish ruling families and of Swedish settlers with
the degenerate masses from Poland, Bohemia, Hungary,
with all the scum of East Baltic and Balkan Jewry ? But I
am firmly convinced that in a certain section of the American
middle class and the farmers, the sound fighting spirit of
colonial days has not been extinguished. We must awaken
that spirit. It has not yet been destroyed. The wholesome aversion for the negroes and the coloured races in
general, including the Jews, the existence of popular justice,

the *naïveté* of the average American, but also the scepticism of certain intellectual circles who have found their wisdom vain ; scholars who have studied immigration and gained an insight, by means of intelligence tests, into the inequality of the races—all these strains are an assurance that the sound elements of the United States will one day awaken as they have awakened in Germany. National Socialism alone is destined to liberate the American people from their ruling clique and give them back the means of becoming a great nation."

Hitler had grown animated. All other conversation died away.

" I shall," he continued, " undertake this task simultaneously with the restoration of Germany to her leading position in America."

" In what sense, my Führer ? " asked Goebbels.

" Have you forgotten that the declaration of German as the national language was lost by only one voice in Congress ? The German component of the American people will be the source of its political and mental resurrection. The American people is not yet a nation in the ethnographical sense ; it is a conglomerate of disparate elements. But it is the raw material of a nation. And the Yankees have failed to create a nation from it ! They have instead kept their noses in their moneybags. To-day this is being avenged. Their difficulties will become insuperable."

" Do you mean," I asked, " that the German-American, rejuvenated by National Socialism, will be called to lead a new America ? "

" That is exactly what I mean," Hitler returned. " We shall soon have an S.A. in America. We shall train our youth. And we shall have men whom degenerate Yankeedom will not be able to challenge. Into the hands of our youth will be given the great statesmanlike mission of

Washington which this corrupt democracy has trodden under foot."

"Shall we not very greatly complicate our own struggle in Europe if we do this ? " interposed Hitler's guest. "Will not the powerful families become our bitterest enemies ? My Führer, I am apprehensive that your great plans will be shattered before they have time to ripen."

Hitler became excited.

"Will you understand, sir, that our struggle against Versailles and our struggle for a new world order is one and the same ; we cannot set limits here or there as we please. We shall succeed in making the new political and social order the universal basis of life in the world. Or else we shall be destroyed in our struggle against a peace-treaty which has in reality never existed, and proved on the very first day of its ratification that the conquerors had accidentally been taken for the conquered, and vice versa."

"Nothing will be easier than to produce a bloody revolution in North America," Goebbels interposed. "No other country has so many social and racial tensions. We shall be able to play on many strings there."

Hitler's guest, with whom I was not intimately acquainted, remained silent, visibly confounded. Hitler observed this and seemed irritated by it.

"North America is a medley of races," Goebbels said. "The ferment goes on under a cover of democracy, but it will not lead to a new form of freedom and leadership, but to a process of decay containing all the disintegrating forces of Europe. The America of to-day will never again be a danger to us."

"It is a mistake to assume that it was a danger to us in the last war," Hitler remarked crossly. "Compared with the British and French, the Americans behaved like clumsy boys. They ran straight into the line of fire, like young rabbits. The American is no soldier. The inferiority and decadence of this allegedly new world is evident in its military inefficiency."

" Nevertheless," Hitler's guest repeated, " I should like to be allowed to express a most humble warning that the Americans ought not to be underestimated as an enemy."

" Who says anything of underestimation ? " Hitler exclaimed angrily, as he rose to lead the way from the table. " I guarantee, gentlemen, that at the right moment a new America will exist as our strongest supporter when we are ready to take the stride into overseas space."

" We have the means of awakening this nation in good time," he added after a pause. " There will be no new Wilson arising to stir up America against us."

THE NEW WEAPON

Only to those who were initiated were the aims and methods of Hitler at that time quite clear. This was by no means the case even with all the leading party members. It was part of Hitler's political shrewdness that he should have discussed his current plans in detail only with a particularly intimate circle, and allowed very few to gain an insight into the wider ramifications of his ideas. Before his seizure of power, the reason for this was largely that his immediate associates, who were of an essentially narrow, lower-middle class mentality, had not the imagination to accept without fear these new ideas which so far exceeded the bounds of a " sensible " nationalism and socialism. The " realists " of the party were already rather scornful of Hitler as a visionary and a crank. That it was these very " crank " ideas of Hitler's which made it possible for him to go his own unusual and eventually self-justifying way was at that time evident to very few.

In all these very nearly insane plans, Hitler thought of the new weapon he was at that time in the process of building up quite inconspicuously, but with great firmness

of purpose, against the resistance of the " experts." I refer
neither to aircraft nor to tanks, but to that " psychological
weapon " of which Hitler had already spoken some time
in 1932, a weapon which he already envisaged with great
clarity and completeness. In this connection, too, I recall a
conversation at Hitler's dinner-table in the summer of
1933, when the Führer was still communicative ; a time
in which the *bourgeois* Cabinet members were publicly
turning up their noses at the Cabinet sittings which under
the new Chancellor had declined into folk oratory or
crystal-gazing rhetoric.

The conversation dealt with the importance of internal
unrest as a weapon. The Ukrainian problem was the
topic of the day in the inner party circles. It was believed
at that time that the question of Poland would be settled
much more quickly than was later the case. Rosenberg
was the driving power behind the scenes, and was seeking
a suitable medium for his revolutionary genius. The
polytechnic of Danzig was at that time a hot-bed of
Ukrainian conspirators, and I myself was commissioned by
certain circles to enter into negotiations with the son of the
former Cossack hetman Skoropadski, who still held a sort
of court in a suburb of Berlin. He believed that his day
would come again. These circles also maintained valuable
social relations with England. National Socialism was
not unwilling to use them for its own purposes, though
Skoropadski was not regarded as a serious political factor.

Hanfstängel elucidated his master's ideas to me as he
saw them. In particular he thought it would be quite
easy to provoke revolt in the Ukrainian part of Poland,
East Galicia, a revolt which would have a decisive influence
on Polish military strength. From my personal knowledge
of Poland, I did not feel equally convinced of this. But
Hanfstängel and Baldur von Schirach, who was sitting
opposite me, did not take my objections very seriously.

Every state, they reminded me, could by suitable methods be so split from within that little strength was required to break it down. Everywhere there were groups that desired independence, whether national or economic, or merely political. The scramble for fodder and distorted ambition —these were the unfailing means to a revolutionary weapon by which the enemy was struck from the rear. Finally, there were the businessmen, whose profits were their all-in-all. There was no patriotism that could hold out against all temptations. Besides, one could always dress these things up. It was really by no means difficult to find patriotic slogans that would cover all such enterprises and would at the same time win over men who were glad to salve their sensitive consciences with some such balsam. And ultimately it was all a question of money and organisation.

I expressed doubts. It seemed to me the real object behind it all must soon become apparent. Besides, such enterprises cost huge sums which Britain could possibly afford for its secret service, but we could not. Moreover, we were notoriously poor conspirators, and in the last war our intelligence service had not functioned at all well.

Hitler's personal photographer, Hofmann, Baldur von Schirach's father-in-law, here began to laugh at me rather contemptuously, remarking that those days had been finished by Hitler. And as for money, for *this* purpose there would always be money. It was true that these conspiracy methods grew costlier as one moved further westward. But that was the only difference. They would succeed everywhere. He guaranteed that. Besides, there were rich people in every country who would themselves find the necessary funds.

Well, I said, somewhat nettled by Hofmann's cocksure manner, no one would ever convince me that this was possible in Britain, for instance. Herr Hanfstängel replied

6

that I had no idea of the possibilities of acting through what is known as good society. I underestimated, too, the imaginative feebleness and psychological backwardness of the English, who would only with difficulty be brought to believe in the possibility of an internal conspiracy. Their very arrogance would prevent them from believing it. They could not imagine that a weapon would be used against them, a *Herren*-race, which only they themselves had a right to use ! And I seemed to have forgotten the ease with which the English reacted to the slogan, " Business as usual."

" Democracy has no convictions," Hanfstängel proclaimed. " Genuine convictions, I mean, for which people would be willing to stake their lives. That is Hitler's fundamental discovery, and it forms the starting-point for his great and daring policies, which will always prove to be right. Fear and personal advantage will in every case, sooner or later, lead to capitulation. In every country there are all the people we shall need to set in motion any desired movement in any level of society or education. Once a beginning has been made, the rest will follow of its own accord. Lack of conviction always results in defeatism : resistance is useless.

" But much is also to be achieved by means of certain convictions with the help of fanatical eccentrics. Sport and religion and love affairs can be used to provide support within the enemy country. From such vantage points, public opinion will then be influenced. It is on public opinion that democracy depends, and public opinion is our greatest help. We shall always be stronger than the democracies in being able to guide their public opinion according to our wish. The money spent for this purpose is certainly not spent in vain. It does not matter if, on this account, we must do with a few army divisions less. The democracies cannot defend themselves against such attacks ; that is in the nature of the matter, for otherwise they would have to become authoritarian themselves. Dictatorships, however, *are* protected against such weapons, and need not fear similar attacks. This creates such an inequality that even considerable differences in military strength are neutralised by it."

In the conviction that the natural powers of resistance and the sound instincts of the democratic nations were being greatly underestimated, I replied that I could well believe that young, unsettled nations, such as those in the east of Europe, might be disintegrated in this way, but not the great, mature, cultural nations. (Here I caught Schirach looking at me with some suspicion.) Besides, I continued, the effectiveness of this new weapon seemed very limited if it was confined to use against the democracies. Surely serious conflict was also possible with non-democratic countries which were immune against this internal disintegration.

" Our only enemies are the democracies," Hanfstängel said with a laugh. " And do you know why ? For the very reason that they are weaker. One must always choose a weaker opponent. That is the secret of success."

And with this piece of cheap wit the conversation ended. It was not until later that I realised this was not a joke. It was, on the contrary, the expression of the very simple and effective tactics used by Hitler.

CHAPTER VI

"YES ! WE ARE BARBARIANS ! "

SHORTLY after the Reichstag fire, Hitler asked me for a
report on the Danzig situation, for there were to be
elections in Danzig as in the Reich. *Gauleiter* Forster
accompanied me. While waiting in the lobby of the
Reich Chancellery, we got into conversation with some of
the Nazi celebrities who were also waiting there. Göring,
Himmler, Frick and a number of *Gauleiter* from the western
provinces were talking together. Göring was giving details
of the Reichstag fire, the secret of which was still being
carefully guarded. I myself had unhesitatingly ascribed it
to arson on the part of persons under Communist, or at any
rate Comintern, influence. It was not until I heard this
conversation that I discovered that the National Socialist
leadership was solely responsible, and that Hitler knew of
the plan and approved it.

The complacency with which this close circle of the
initiated discussed the deed was shattering. Gratified
laughter, cynical jokes, boasting—these were the sentiments
expressed by the " conspirators." Göring described how
" his boys " had entered the Reichstag building by a
subterranean passage from the President's Palace, and how
they had only a few minutes at their disposal and were
nearly discovered. He regretted that the " whole shack "
had not burnt down. They had been so hurried that they
could not " make a proper job of it." Göring, who had
taken the leading part in the conversation, closed with the
significant words :

" *I have no conscience. My conscience is Adolf Hitler.*"

84

There is nothing more extraordinary than that this enormous crime, the perpetrators of which gradually became known in the widest circles, should not have been sharply condemned, even in middle-class quarters. Many people actually condoned this *coup*. Still more extraordinary is the fact that the incendiary himself has actually enjoyed a certain amount of sympathy in foreign countries, even till quite recently. It is true that Göring has always presented a contrast to Hitler. In intimate circles, he has not hesitated to use the coarsest expressions about " that womanish fool." But in decisive crises, he has always stood beside and behind Hitler. It was he who ordered the Reichstag building to be burnt at Hitler's command. He took the responsibility upon himself, just as he did that of the murders on the 30th June, 1934, of the *bourgeois* Nationalists, because he considered Hitler too soft and vacillating. And this is the essential difference between Hitler and Göring, that the former, before he can " act," must always lash himself out of lethargy and doubts into a frenzy. But in Göring amorality is second nature.

We were summoned into Hitler's presence. The conversation was a brief one. It began with conditions in Danzig, and Hitler's difficult position in the Cabinet. But Hitler acknowledged no real difficulties ; it was striking how confident he was of being able to cope with all the constraints and limitations put on him. He reproached Forster for the circumstance that Danzig had not kept pace with the Reich. The first essential was to gain a firm foothold. Everything else would, with the necessary ruthlessness, follow in due course.

" I have been advised against accepting the post of Reich Chancellor under the conditions advanced by the old gentleman [von Hindenburg]," Hitler said. He added scornfully, " As though I had the time to wait till everything falls into my lap of its own accord ! "

He started up from his seat behind the desk and prowled restlessly up and down the small room in which in those days he received visitors.

" I know what I'm doing," he went on.   " I have unlocked the door for you.   It is now the business of the party to go forward to a complete victory."

The first step, he told us, was to create a real power out of the initial victory of National Socialism, which was still hedged about with restrictions.

" The reactionary forces believe they have me on the lead. They will set as many traps for me as they can.   I know that they hope I will achieve my own ruin by mismanagement. . . .   But we shall not wait for *them* to act.   Our great opportunity lies in acting before they do.   And we have no scruples.   I have no *bourgeois* hesitations !   I expect each one of us to become one of a single family of conspirators.   I have had to accept harsh conditions.   I shall observe them as long as I am forced to do so."

Hitler then began to discuss the Reichstag fire.   He asked whether we had seen it yet, and we replied that we had not.

" Go and look at it," he said.   " It is the beacon of a new era in the history of the world."

It certainly provided him with a weapon against the opposition.

" I have sown fear and apprehension in the hearts of those old women Hugenberg and company [the *bourgeois* Nationalist ministers of Hitler's first Cabinet].   They're quite prepared to believe I instigated it.   They take me for the Old Nick himself.   And it's a good thing they do."

Hitler mocked at the involved and technical speeches and objections of his ministerial colleagues.   He shocked them intentionally in his own speeches.   It caused him exquisite amusement to see how indignant they were with him, and how superior they considered themselves.

"They regard me as an uneducated barbarian," he exclaimed jubilantly. "Yes, we are barbarians! We want to be barbarians! It is an honourable title. *We* shall rejuvenate the world! This world is near its end. It is our mission to cause unrest."

He then launched into a verbose exposition of what he called an "historical necessity." Barbarian forces, he claimed, must break into decadent civilisations in order to snatch the torch of life from their dying fires. Then he began to speak of the treatment of Communists and Socialists.

"These people thought I would handle them with kid gloves, that I would be satisfied with speeches," he scoffed. "We are not in a position to dally with humane feelings, nor can I undertake tedious investigations into anyone's good-will or innocence. We must shake off all sentimentality and be hard. Some day, when I order war, I shall not be in a position to hesitate because of the ten million young men I shall be sending to their death. It is preposterous," he continued, growing indignant, "to expect me to look for the real criminals only among the Communists. It is just like cowardly, inconsistent *bourgeoisie* to pacify their consciences with legal proceedings. There is only *one* legal right, the nation's right to live."

Without giving us a chance to say a word in reply, Hitler plunged into a dissertation on the incompetent politics of the *bourgeoisie* and the Socialists.

"I have no choice," he exclaimed. "I must do things that cannot be measured with the yardstick of *bourgeois* squeamishness. This Reichstag fire gives me the opportunity to intervene. And I shall intervene."

He then explained further that he must shock the middle class in order to rouse their fear of the designs of the Communists and their dread of his own severity.

"The world can only be ruled by fear."

The Terror

Hitler dismissed us. His adjutant Brückner had entered. Time was getting on. That afternoon a National Socialist school for leaders was to be inaugurated in a former Social-Democratic school, and Hitler had promised to attend. The interrupted conversation, however, had a kind of sequel later in the autumn. Complaints as to the horrors of the concentration camps had begun to reach Hitler. I remember a particular instance in Stettin, where, in the empty engine-rooms of the former Vulkan docks, respected citizens, some of them of Jewish parentage, were brutally maltreated. Vile things were done in an unmistakable enjoyment of brutality for its own sake. The matter had been brought to Göring's attention, and he had been unable to evade an investigation. In one case, reparation was made.

In those days the routine excuse was that a revolution was taking place in Germany which was extraordinarily bloodless and lenient. It was not justifiable, we were told, to draw general conclusions from a few isolated cases. But the truth was very different. The cruelty, of a nature increasingly refined, dealt out then and later by the S.S. and the S.A. to political opponents was part of a definite political plan. The selection of asocial, abnormal types to guard the concentration camps was carried out with conscious purpose. I had occasion to see something of this myself. Notorious drunkards and criminals were selected from the military organisations of the party and placed in special sub-divisions. It was a typical example of specially selected sub-humans for definite political tasks.

I happened to be present when Hitler's attention was called to the Stettin incident and other similar occurrences. It was entirely characteristic that Hitler was by no means indignant, as one might have expected, at the horrible excesses of his men, but on the contrary roundly abused those who " made a fuss " about these trivial matters.

The occasion was my first experience of Hitler's paroxysms of rage and abuse. He behaved like a combination of a spoilt child and an hysterical woman. He scolded in high, shrill tones, stamped his feet, and banged his fist on tables and walls. He foamed at the mouth, panting and stammering in uncontrolled fury : " I won't have it ! Get rid of all of them ! Traitors ! " He was an alarming sight, his hair dishevelled, his eyes fixed, and his face distorted and purple. I feared that he would collapse, or have an apoplectic fit.

Suddenly it was all over. He walked up and down the room, clearing his throat, and brushing his hair back. He looked round apprehensively and suspiciously, with searching glances at us. I had the impression that he wanted to see if anyone was laughing. And I must admit that a desire to laugh, perhaps largely as a nervous reaction to the tension, rose within me.

" Preposterous," Hitler began in a hoarse voice. " Haven't you ever seen a crowd collecting to watch a street brawl ? *Brutality is respected.* Brutality and physical strength. The plain man in the street respects nothing but brutal strength and ruthlessness—women, too, for that matter, women and children. The people need wholesome fear. They *want* to fear something. They want someone to frighten them and make them shudderingly submissive. Haven't you seen everywhere that after boxing-matches, the beaten ones are the first to join the party as new members ? Why babble about brutality and be indignant about tortures ? The masses want that. They need something that will give them a thrill of horror."

After a pause, he continued in his former tone :

" I forbid you to change anything. By all means, punish one or two men, so that these German Nationalist donkeys may sleep easy. But I don't want the concentration camps transformed into penitentiary institutions.

Terror is the most effective political instrument. I shall not permit myself to be robbed of it simply because a lot of stupid, *bourgeois* mollycoddles choose to be offended by it. It is my duty to make use of *every* means of training the German people to severity, and to prepare them for war."

Hitler paced the room excitedly.

" My behaviour in wartime will be no different. The most horrible warfare is the kindest. I shall spread terror by the surprise employment of all my measures. The important thing is the sudden shock of an overwhelming fear of death. Why should I use different measures against my internal political opponents ? These so-called atrocities spare me a hundred thousand individual actions against disobedience and discontent. People will think twice before opposing us when they hear what to expect in the camps."

No one ventured to put any questions.

" I don't want to hear anything more about this," Hitler said in conclusion. " It's your business to see that no evidence about such cases leaks out. I cannot allow such absurd trifles to break in on my work. Anybody who is such a poltroon that he can't bear the thought of someone nearby having to suffer pain had better join a sewing-circle, but not my party comrades."

CHAPTER VII

COFFEE AND CAKES

IS Hitler unfeeling towards the pain suffered by others? Is he cruel and revengeful? To-day there can hardly be a doubt as to the answer, but a few years ago, everyone who had the opportunity of hearing Hitler's remarkable statements in intimate circles, could not but ask himself this question. Every conversation, however unimportant, seemed to show that this man was filled with an immeasurable hatred. Hatred of what? It was not easy to say. Almost anything might suddenly inflame his wrath and his hatred. He seemed always to feel the need of something to hate. But equally, the transition from anger to sentimentality or enthusiasm might be quite sudden.

In May, 1933, elections took place in Danzig. They turned out more favourably for National Socialism than the Reich elections, which only brought in forty-four per cent. of the votes for Hitler. He sent a telegram to the Danzig *Gauleiter* (" Magnificent, Forster ! ") on receiving from the latter the news that over fifty per cent. were in favour. As a reward, Hitler invited a number of Danzigers to the Reich Chancellery for afternoon coffee and cakes.

There were literally coffee and cakes, " just like mother's," *Streuselkuchen* and *Napfkuchen* (German teacake specialities). And Hitler was the *Hausfrau*. He was in a gay mood, and almost amiable. A few hours earlier he had given Forster and myself a rough outline of his eastern policy. All sentimentality would have to be renounced, and all pretences given up. The National Socialists did not find it necessary, like the Weimar Republic parties, to furnish proof of their patriotism. It was not our business to carry on a noisy patriotic campaign of German national self-assertion. We could afford to proceed to our mission without great gestures.

It was necessary, Hitler impressed upon us, to be astute. German aims were not to be attained in a few days or weeks. We must avoid anything that might give the world cause for suspicion. There was a choice between only two kinds of action : one might pretend or one might be quite sincere in one's aims. He himself was determined to make any treaty that would ease the position of Germany. He was determined to get on with Poland, and it was our task to support him in this. The Danzig problem could not be solved by us, only by him, and even by him only if Germany was strong and feared. The more silently and secretly we carried on our struggle for existence, the better for Germany. It was not our task to solve the Danzig problem or that of the Corridor. This we should have to leave to the Reich. But it would be our business, whenever possible, to clear all difficulties from the path of the Reich.

It was along these lines that Hitler spoke first to Forster and myself, then in a short speech to the other Danzigers. After the speech, we had the coffee and cakes. The conversation carried on by Hitler over the coffee was less statesmanlike. He had just instituted his currency barrier against independent Austria, and thereby begun his attack on that country. He had forced through this measure against the desires of his Foreign Office. It was evident with what satisfaction he took up this struggle, which he regarded as in any case nearly concluded. Flaming hatred burned in his every word—hatred and contempt.

" Austria is rotten with Jews. Vienna is no longer a German city. Slav mestizos have overrun the place. A decent German is no longer respected. Priests and Jews rule the country. These scoundrels have got to be thrown out ! "

Meanwhile, he urged us to help ourselves to cakes. The Danzigers sitting near him listened uncomprehendingly. He continued to outline his future Austrian policy :

" Austria must be renewed through the Reich. This Dollfuss, these paid clerks and nonentities, these absurd dwarfs who imagine they're statesmen and don't see they're the twitching puppets of French and British wirepullers—I shall see that they do not escape their retribution. I know," he continued after a pause, " that we cannot at once burst in with the *Anschluss*. But why do not these men carry on a German policy ? " He would see to it that the whole crew was sent packing.

" We must not deceive ourselves. There is no longer an Austria. The country that calls itself Austria is a corpse. Austria must be colonised afresh from the Reich. It is high time. Another generation, and this country will be lost to Germandom for ever. These people no longer know what it means to be German."

He regarded it as his special task to train Austria to Germandom. He would be a harsh taskmaster in training them to German ways. He would make them sweat, he would drive out their indolence and easygoing habits. There had been enough of softness. And no one need think there was any hope of bringing back those Habsburgs or any such nonsense. But above all the Jews had to be removed. It was a heavy task, but he would accomplish it. It would not be long before Austria was National Socialist.

Hitler hinted at his intentions, and made it clear that everything was ready for a *coup* in Austria. It was evident that he desired such a *coup*, and was positively delighted with the resistance of the Dollfuss government. His excited manner showed that he thirsted for a bloody clash, a conspiracy, some sort of revenge. Perhaps it was his long-desired, yet never attained " March on Berlin " that was revived in this passionate desire for an overthrow of the

Austrian regime. A scorching breath blew from this conversation.   It was not a conversation so much as a passionate
self-interpretation, as indeed, were all Hitler's talks. Meanwhile, the sun shone into the long corridor on the second
floor of the Reich Chancellery where we were drinking coffee.
Our host who was speaking to us thus was the Chancellor of the German Reich. Below, in the courtyard, we could
hear orders being shouted at the changing of the S.S. guard.

" I shall put the screw on this man Dollfuss ! " Hitler
shouted. " He dares to contradict me ! But wait, gentlemen ! You will see them before long crawling on their
knees to me. But," with icy coldness, " I shall have them
put to death as traitors."

Hatred—personal hatred—rang out in his words, revenge
for early years of poverty, for disappointed hopes, for a life
of deprivation and humiliation. For some time there was
an embarrassed silence. Hitler urged his guests to eat
like a hospitable peasant woman. Young S.S. men brought
in fresh dishes of cakes and filled up our cups.

Hitler had mentioned the Viennese Jews, and began to
discuss the Jewish question. The Jews, he said, laughing,
were Germany's best protection. They were the pledge
that guaranteed that foreign powers would allow Germany
to go her way in peace. If the democracies did not withdraw their boycott, he would take from the German Jews
as much of their property as would cover the damage
done to Germany by the boycott.

" We'll show them how fast they'll have to stop their
anti-German propaganda ! The Jews will yet make
Germany's fortune ! "

Everybody laughed. Hitler went on to say that there
must, of course, come a time when there would be nothing
left to take from the Jews. But then he would still hold
their lives in the palm of his hand : their precious Jewish
lives. The company burst out laughing again.

" Streicher," Hitler continued, laughing himself, " has suggested that in the next war they should be driven ahead of our attacking defence lines. They would be the best protection for our soldiers. I shall consider the suggestion."

The party shouted with laughter at this " witticism," and Hitler, stimulated by his success, went into detail on the measures he would take to expropriate the Jews slowly, but relentlessly, and to drive them out of Germany.

" Everything we plan will be carried out," he snapped. " I shall not permit anyone to talk me out of it."

What followed covered essentially the measures actually taken in 1938. Truly, everything had been planned and considered long beforehand. It was anything but merely the rabid response to an unhappy murder.

At that time (1933), after the first pogrom, Hitler was compelled slightly to water down his attacks on the Jews. But for that very reason he seemed to think it important not to allow anti-Semitism to slacken. I have since heard Hitler many times express his views about the Jews. I shall return to the subject in a later chapter. Here I wish only to draw a picture of the extraordinary contrast between the peaceful, typically *petit bourgeois* coffee-table, with party members from the provinces, as it were, and the talk of the host, the Chancellor of the great German people : talk that revolved round death, revolt, gaol, murder, robbery. No word of enthusiasm, of intellectual encouragement, or of interest in the personal affairs of his individual guests.

" What do I care about personal happiness or personal affairs ? " Hitler had, on one occasion, cried impatiently. " Do as you like, do as you please ! "

Envy, primitive hate and the craving for power : this was the wisdom that Hitler gave his followers along their political path.

CHAPTER VIII

ENRICH YOURSELVES !

HITLER knew very well that the ordinary person
cannot live on hate and revenge alone. This man,
who was quite consciously making use of the worst human
instincts, knew the weaknesses and desires of his people
very thoroughly.

"Don't marry till I am in power," he used to advise
his lieutenants, the *Gauleiter*, the Reich leaders and others
who looked upon their posts as secure and permanent
jobs, and expressed a wish to live prosperous, comfortable
lives.

"Occupy positions," was Hitler's slogan as soon as he
came to power. To seize everything available in the way
of jobs was the rule everywhere. "Gather ye roses while
ye may," sang from below the croaking voice of the bibulous
Dr. Ley, leader of the Labour Front. "Enjoy life and
enrich yourselves," came the jovial order from above.

"We are no spoil-sports. Fires need fuel," was the
whisper going round the corridors outside Hitler's offices.
"Building up one's own position," was the motto of the
first few months after the seizure of power.

"I give my men every freedom," Hitler said, in the
course of a dinner-table conversation. "Do anything you
like, but don't be caught at it ! "

It was Hitler himself that egged on his men quite intentionally to make the most of their opportunities. They
needed no second bidding. It was then that I heard the
curious expression : " planned corruption." Certainly this

corruption *was* planned, and not merely condoned. There were people who hoped this would quickly bring about the downfall of National Socialism. But Hitler knew he had to let his men " get something out of it." Instead of the " night of long knives," they obtained middle-class positions ; instead of a genuine revolution, they at least reaped the advantages of one : jobs for careerists.

It is nothing new for a revolution to help its sons to enrich themselves, but in Germany this was done with such shameless haste that it made one dizzy to watch. One, two, or four houses, country estates, palaces, pearl necklaces, antiques, valuable tapestries and paintings, dozens of motor cars, champagne, farms, factories—where did the money come from ? Had not all these people been poor as church-mice, up to their eyes in debt ? They all had official posts, three, six, a dozen at a time, and always there was room for one more. There were posts of all kinds, honorary directorships, and dividends, loans and bonuses. Everyone was anxious to help : every bank and business enterprise required the protection of a party member.

The Führer, however, waived his claims to the Chancellor's salary, thus setting a good example. He could well afford to do so. Overnight he had become the richest publisher in the world, worth millions, and the most widely read author—read under compulsion. He could afford to complain about Göring's excesses and extravagance. He complained demonstratively, thereby reassuring opinion in certain quarters. Hitler was " most unhappy " about Göring's recent development, Forster told me at that time. " We must keep strictly to our promise that there should be no salaries over a thousand marks a month." It was all very well for Forster to talk. He had five separate posts. His income amounted to about a dozen times the stipulated sum. Eventually he became

7

the owner of extensive house property in Danzig. Two years earlier he had arrived in Danzig with an empty cigar-box.

Matters were no different in Berlin. A newly appointed secretary of state had his apartments furnished at the State's expense for ninety thousand marks, as the department concerned in the Reich Finance Ministry complained to me. Göring had gold tiles laid in the bathroom of one of his many official apartments. Hitler ordered the complainants to pay to the recently appointed *Reichstatthalter* (Reich Lieutenant-Governors) salaries hitherto unheard-of in the German bureaucratic hierarchy. They paid. And the ordinary citizen, when he saw the parade of super-luxurious cars outside the public buildings, whispered : " The new bosses are going up fast."

Hitler expressed his views on this state of things with his usual candour. It was by no means a situation that he had perforce to tolerate because it was too strong for him. On the contrary. I had just attended a so-called " Führer conference " in the former Prussian Upper House, in which Hitler had developed the political programme of the immediate future. It was not a very informative speech. Afterwards, however, I had occasion to hear him speak in a closer circle.

He was being reproached, he said angrily in his guttural voice, for having instituted unwarrantable prosecutions for corruption against the former rulers and their accomplices, while his own men were filling their pockets.

" I have answered the fools who venture to use such language to me," he said. " I have asked them to tell me how I could otherwise meet the justified desires of my party comrades for some recompense for their years of inhuman struggle. I have asked them whether they would prefer me to let my S.A. men loose to loot in the streets. I could still do this, I said. I had no objections. And it would be more wholesome for the people to endure a really bloody revolution for some weeks. I had refrained only out of consideration for them and their *bourgeois* love of comfort. But I could easily make up for it ! They very quickly ceased making their foolish reproaches ! " Hitler laughed.

" It is necessary to throw them into a fright now and again. I owe that to my party comrades," he added after a pause. " They have a right to demand it. After all, my party comrades have also fought to rid themselves of their personal difficulties. Preposterous not to admit it frankly. It is a duty of friendship that I should see that they all have a livelihood. My old fighting comrades have earned it. In making Germany great, we have also a right to think of ourselves. We are above clinging to *bourgeois* notions of honour and reputation. Let these ' well-bred ' gentry learn that we do with a clear conscience the things they do secretly with a guilty one."

Growing angry, he began to shout.

" Are we to pull their cart out of the mud, only to be sent home with empty hands ? They would like that, wouldn't they ? How can I hold the power unless I have every post occupied by my men ? They ought to be glad we don't shoot them, as they do in Russia ! "

This was something very close to controlled, planned corruption. But Hitler had more in his mind than this. He knew that there is nothing so binding as crimes committed in company. I found out later how the party, to make certain of unreliable members, forced them to commit punishable acts in its interests in order to keep them under complete control. The same principle underlay the sharing out of the long-desired spoils. The " inner conspiracy " of the party *élite* was thus a circle of those who were all in the secret. Everyone was in the power of everyone else, and no one was any longer his own master. This was the desired result of the slogan : " Enrich yourselves."

It is of interest to note that well-founded rumours were already spreading to the effect that each of the leading party members, and everyone else who was able to, was placing money abroad in order to ensure himself against all eventualities. Besides the money, there was usually also deposited in a bank safe or with a solicitor a dossier of incriminating material, the publication of which might have disastrous results for a number of important personages of the National Socialist movement. These dossiers were intended as a sure protection for the possessor against intervention by the party or the civil authorities. In other words, sheer gangster methods were used by the leading party members *without exception* to secure, not only their own futures after the downfall of the regime, but also their present lives and positions. It is difficult to conceive the extent of the universal, unparalleled and uncontrolled corruption that had so suddenly broken out in Germany.

A *Gauleiter* (whose name I do not wish to mention because he is one of the naturally decent party members, and may therefore in a coming downfall of the regime still play an important part) told me quite frankly that he had no choice but to make use of the same methods. If he did not, he would very soon not only be deprived of his position, but above all instantly murdered. He gave me the friendly advice to acquire incriminating evidence about my opponents, for instance, *Gauleiter* Forster. The moment I had this in my hands, I might regard my position as assured. Without it, I was eternally condemned to a subordinate position. Incriminating material and property abroad— these alone made one invulnerable. He, at any rate, had both, and he was planning to send his wife abroad, as she could best watch his interests there.

This friend of mine has, in fact, contrary to all expectations, been able to hold a position bitterly disputed for years.

Profession of Cynicism

The remarkable feature of these early self-revelations is the quite candid cynicism with which the position was discussed in party circles. I must return to a dinner-table conversation in Hitler's home during this same early summer of 1933. The conversation opened with a reference by Goebbels to the National Socialist humorous journal, *Die Brennessel* (The Stinging Nettle). Goebbels mentioned some caricatures on the so-called *Zwickelerlass*, that extraordinary decree promulgated by the then Chancellor von Papen, who had assumed responsibility for the maintenance of public decency by instructions as to the kinds of bathing-suits it was permissible to wear. Goebbels made some sharp comments about the antediluvian moral conceptions of the reactionaries, and their spurious Germandom. He castigated their attempts to stigmatise short hair in women and the use of make-up as un-German. It was high time, he said, to stop the pettifogging activities of these people, who confused National Socialism with provincialism, and diluted the spirit of battle with the tracts of religious sisterhoods.

" I can imagine our S.A. men laughing if somebody were to try to explain to them that their struggle had taken place in order to make German girls wear their hair in long plaits and to stop their smoking ! "

Hitler, who had up till then sat in morose silence, now joined in the conversation, and soon talked himself into a rage.

" I detest this prudery and moral snooping," he cried. " It has nothing to do with our struggle. These are the stale notions of reactionary old women like Hugenberg, who can only imagine a national rejuvenation by means of virtuous customs and severity. ' League of Virtue ' and ' Christian-German table-companions,' ' replacing the material losses of the nation by spiritual gains '—I can't

remember all their empty patriotic rubbish. Our uprising
has nothing to do with *bourgeois* morals. We are an
uprising of the strength of our nation. The strength of its
loins, if you like, as well. I shall not spoil the fun for any
of my lads. If I demand the supreme effort from them,
then I must also give them the right to carouse as *they*
please, not as it suits a lot of church-going old women.
Heaven knows my boys are no angels, and they are not
expected to be. They are sturdy yeomen, and must remain
so. I have no use for hypocrites and virtue-peddlers. I
am not interested in their private lives any more than
I will permit any snooping about my own private life.
The party has nothing to do with revivalist meetings or
nonsensical talk about moral renewal from the spirit and
the history of our people. We are after something entirely
different. Let that old goat, Hugenberg, go to the S.A.
and try to tell them such things ! I need men who will
not stop to think if they're ordered to knock someone down !
I don't care a tinker's damn if they knock down something
on their own account as well."

I have since heard this opinion expressed many times by
members of all sections of the party, down to the pettiest
official. The teachings of Hitler had a prompt effect. In
Danzig at that time, we were compelled to accept a few
nasty cases of assault and violence, but they were child's
play to what went on daily in the Reich. The road to
destruction was paved, not with good, but with thoroughly
evil intentions. There spread through the party a cynicism
which only shortly before would have been inconceivable.
There were two things everyone in the party, big or small,
strove for : apart from the collection of loot and the enjoyment of unrestrained licence, immunity for the past and
security for the future. The universal aim was to have a
share in everything, to take no risks, to keep one's head
above water, and above all not to sink down again into the

anonymous, powerless mass. The lobbies were all crowded
with job-hunters. Quite openly they made their demands.
" The Führer said so," they would announce naïvely.
" All the old fighters are to have jobs and bread. We
haven't fought to go empty-handed."

Someone asked me for the post of councillor of state.
He was not interested in the post itself or the salary, but
the pension. He wanted security for all time. What
sorry fighters they were ! Wretched little *petits bourgeois*
whose fear of the future flickered in their eyes !

" I won't get down again ! " one of them screamed at
me angrily. " Perhaps you can wait. You're not sitting
on a bed of glowing coals ! No job, man, no job ! If I
have to go through that again, I'll turn to crime. I'll stay
on top no matter what it costs me. We can't get on top
twice running ! "

Small men and criminals—these were the " old guard "
of Hitler. They were all trying to consolidate their positions,
and they were all able to refer to the Führer. No one, up to
those in the highest posts, quite trusted the peace. No one
believed much in the millenium of the National Socialist era.
An eminent bank president admitted to me openly that
having risked his skin once in a world war, he had no
intention of doing so again, or, indeed, of risking anything.
He would do as all the others did. He would not expose
himself. He had no desire to make personal sacrifices.

It was an evil competition in cynicism. The old upper
classes wanted to remain on top. Bared of any shame or
dignity, they clung to their positions, followed all the party
doings they were told to follow—anything not to lose their
positions. The greatest blame for the men's rapid loss of
courage must be placed on the women. Unwilling to give
up their luxurious cars, to be turned out of their palatial
residences, they dinned into the men's ears the thought of
the future, and of their children's future. The new social

classes, on the other hand, pushed upwards ruthlessly, by every means. Never before has there been such corruption, such lack of stamina, in Germany ! And why have not all these people been purchased ? They could all have been had for the asking, all, both old and new. They are still to be had. It would have been cheaper than war.

MONEY IS NO OBJECT

Apart from this, money was no object.

" There is plenty of money, as much as we want. But *they* don't want to spend it ! " *Gauleiter* Forster shouted at me as early as the autumn of 1933.

This was on the occasion of my expressing certain doubts as to the possibility of carrying through the " plans for the creation of employment," which included the erection of new theatres and swimming-pools, and extravagant improvements in city streets and hygienic services. None of these desperadoes had the slightest conception of the value of money, least of all Hitler himself. In the first place, they did not even know the difference between currency and capital. On the basis of their master's primitive ideas, they had concocted a money theory, the central plank of which was that you could " create " as much money as you liked as long as prices were fixed.

In consequence, I became engaged in a stubborn dispute with the party, which Hitler had to arbitrate. His decision was as might have been expected. But were his notions really so primitive ? I began to suspect something quite different, namely, that Hitler quite consciously and intentionally planned to destroy the economic power of certain classes of society. The harshness with which he refused any attempt at an open devaluation was in marked contrast to the ease with which he not only tolerated, but actually encouraged, concealed inflation. Hitler regarded the new policy of expenditure and concealed inflation as a most effective means of redistributing wealth and changing the personnel of the ruling class. It is possible that the connection was not quite clear to him, but with the instinctive peasant cunning peculiar to him, he evidently sensed the right thing.

Hitler distrusts everyone who tries to explain political economy to him. He believes that the intention is to dupe him, and he makes no secret of his contempt for this branch of science. He does not understand it, but he feels that an essentially simple matter has been made needlessly complex. He is convinced that labour, money and capital are related in a manner to be ascertained by practice alone ; if the speculators and Jews are excluded, then a sort of economic *perpetuum mobile* remains. Ultimately the thing to do was to make people believe in you, whether by suggestion or by force.

" For pity's sake," an officer of the ministry advised me as I was on my way to see Hitler, " don't suggest devaluation or any complicated investigation into the means of creating employment."

I found Hitler impatient and hostile. He had been informed of my business with him. Already at that early period, he disliked hearing anything not calculated to strengthen his own convictions.

" I sent Köhler to you to Danzig," he said as he received me. " Haven't you seen him ? "

Köhler was an alleged expert in economics.

" I have seen him," I replied, " but we didn't agree."

" Why not ? " asked Hitler.

I tried to explain to Hitler that throughout our discussion, this so-called economist had failed to understand that Danzig was not a town of the German Reich, but of another country with its own independent currency. He had not understood that for us, the German *Reichsmark* was a foreign currency, and that our own currency was bound by certain rules of backing. I mentioned that we had already a state bank of our own for creating fluid credit, which, strictly speaking, was an inflatory measure.

Hitler's face darkened.

" Inflation ! What do you mean by inflation ? Don't talk to me about inflation. All you need is to keep the confidence of the population. Everything else is nonsense."

I attempted to explain to him the method of meeting the balance of payment of the Danzig state. Hitler broke into my remarks angrily.

" Details don't interest me. Don't make absurd difficulties for Forster. If he wants to build, then in heaven's name, find the money. It *must* be found. Understand ? "

" Forster knows what he's doing," he added in a calmer tone. " We must get the unemployed off the streets. The quicker we do it, the more effective it will be. We cannot afford the luxury of a long wait. The whole of the responsibility rests on Forster. The party must therefore see to it that something is done. Don't make difficulties for him—help him instead."

I replied that I was doing all I could, but we had to make regular statements of the backing available for our currency. There was a Pole on the board of directors of our issuing bank.

" When must you produce your statement ? " Hitler asked.

I told him.

" And you can't help yourself ? " he cried, turning on me. " I shall give instructions that before the required date you are to be provided with the bills of exchange you need. You can return them again later. You don't need forty per cent. backing. You can go down to twenty, or even ten."

That, I tried to say, would be open——

" Fraud ! " Hitler broke in. " What do you mean by
fraud ? What do you mean by backing ? Confidence.
The people have confidence in us even without backing.
We are their guarantee, not money or bills of exchange.
Our word is valid, not bank rules ! Bills of exchange or
money can be valueless to-morrow. Do you understand ?
We are the guarantee. Don't raise stupid objections. Are
you going to be a realist in politics, or a theoretician ? You
recoil before unconventionality ? I shall take the responsibility. Do you consider my word of less value than your
absurd rules ? "

Hitler paused a moment.

" Now don't make any further difficulties," he presently
went on more calmly. " The money is here. There will
always be money. As long as the German people work,
I am not afraid. Talk to Funk," he advised me. " He is
very clear-headed. Don't let anyone impose on you."

His tone became friendlier. " Why do you make things
so difficult for yourself ? " he asked. " You stumble over
threads. Where should we be if we had formal scruples ?
I simply disregard these things. I am prepared to commit
perjury half-a-dozen times a day ! What difference would
it make ? "

He was growing more excited again. I did not know
what to reply. What, indeed, could I have replied ?

" Don't falter over trifles ! " exclaimed the Führer.
" Follow my example ! "

He sensed my inner resistance, and became very friendly.
He stopped pacing the room and continued :

" What choice have we ? Is an easy conscience more
precious to you than the rise of a new Germany ? We have
no right to think of ourselves and our *bourgeois* immaculate-
ness. We have only one mission. Do you think I don't
know that if things don't go as we hope, we shall be cursed
to our very graves ? I walk a dizzy path. Shall I be held

back by paper rules ?   Only vain people take themselves so
seriously that they posture and say : I can't take it on my
conscience !   Do you imagine *you* can't take on your conscience what I can take on mine ?   Do you consider yourself
better than me ? "

Lammers entered the room.   Hitler had again talked far
beyond the allotted time. I was dismissed.   Outside in
the great lobby, acquaintances were waiting, among them
Count Schwerin-Krosigk, the Finance Minister.   He knew
my troubles.   The subject had not yet been exhausted by
this interview with Hitler.   A year later it was to be a
contributing cause of my resignation.

Chapter IX

AFTER LEAVING THE LEAGUE OF NATIONS
(October, 1933)

GERMANY had left the League of Nations. I was present at Geneva when this momentous decision—the first of Hitler's abrupt political surprises—was taken. On my return to Berlin, I went to call on Hitler. It seemed necessary to draw his attention to the dangers of the situation. In the universal tension, the slightest mistake on our part might precipitate a " preventive " war on Germany. That, at least, was my impression. Hitler was of a different opinion. I found him in high spirits, full of expectancy and eagerness. He greeted me with the words,

" These people want war. Let them have it—but only when it suits me."

I replied that we had certainly heard indignant cries of *C'est la guerre!* in the lobbies and corridors of Geneva. Hitler waved his hand contemptuously.

" They don't dream of making war. Goebbels has reported to me already. A pretty crew they are ! They'll never act. They'll just protest. And they will always be too late."

Hitler asked if I had anything to report of my impressions. I replied that Germany's position seemed to me a precarious one. Certainly that of Danzig would become extremely difficult. I could not see that resignation from the League had been absolutely necessary. Surely continued membership would have afforded us many opportunities of educating and influencing foreign opinion. With an active political

programme in which were included some of the aims of the
League itself, such as the minorities principle, the strong,
strategic position of the Reich must soon have led us to
numerous successes. The newly elected South African
President of the League, for example, had spoken with a
good deal of understanding of the national discipline now
instituted by certain nations. I had gained the impression
that the sympathies which the new Germany might have
expected in British circles had not been promoted by this
abrupt resignation.

" What sort of chap is Simon ? " Hitler broke in.
" Is it true he's a Jew ? "

I replied that I had never heard anything of the kind
about the British Foreign Secretary.

" I've been told he's a Jew, and wants to destroy
Germany."

This seemed to me extremely unlikely, I said. I had,
on the contrary, gained the impression that Sir John was the
very man who wanted to clear up relations with Germany.

" And what about Boncour ? " Hitler inquired.
Goebbels had already brought back a description of him.
" What sort of man is he ? I understand he has flowing
hair and poses as a radical."

He gave me no opportunity to reply, but went on at once.

" These people will not prevent Germany's rise. I have
had to put an end to all this haggling—once and for all."

Nevertheless, I persisted, we should now have to pass
through a most critical period. I took the liberty, on the
strength of the past summer's experiences, to urge the need
for the strictest discipline in all party organisations. Only
if all " incidents " were avoided could we hope to escape
danger. Without a doubt our resignation from the League
was increasing the risks for German rearmament, and
awakening premature suspicion of our new national policy.

Hitler got up and paced the room in silence for some

minutes.   Then, without looking at me, he embarked upon self-justifying monologue.

" I had to do it.   A liberating deed was necessary—one that should be universally comprehensible.   I had to tear the German people out of this clinging network of dependence, vain talk and false conceptions in order to restore our liberty of action.   I am not merely an opportunist.   Perhaps the difficulties have for the moment been increased.   But that is counterbalanced by the increased confidence this deed has won me among the German people.   They would not have approved of our going on like a debating society, doing what the Weimar parties had been doing for ten years.   As yet, we have not the means of revising the frontiers, but the people believe we have.   The people want to see something done ; they want no more cheating and swindling.   It was not something approved by hair-splitting intellectuals that we needed, but a bold deed— a clear and honest ' no ' to lying intrigues—a tangible proof of our firm will to a fresh start.   This is the only sort of action, be it wise or not, that the people understand—not this eternal, sterile arguing and haggling,which never leads to any result.   The people are tired of being led by the nose."

I did not know what to reply.   It might be a novel, foolhardy policy, but it had the advantage of being emphatic, with the emphasis of simple, elemental decisions.   It was on such simple decisions, easily understood by everyone, that Hitler's long series of internal and external successes rested.   He seemed to know instinctively the proper psychological moment at which to produce them.   But just as one was prepared to admit that the party Führer was unquestionably right in his judgment, his inordinate loquacity would again cause one to doubt the sanity of the man.   I know that many of his visitors have come away from an interview with him in a similar state of perplexity.

Forgetting time and place, Hitler continued to talk,

leaping from one subject to the next, with neither commas nor full stops, discursiveness personified.

" The era of democracy is over, inexorably finished," he exclaimed. " We have been drawn into a movement which will carry us along with it whether we like it or not. If we resist, we shall be annihilated. If we stand aside, we shall die off. It is a choice between taking action or being destroyed. Democracy is no longer the suitable political medium for the great decisions of the coming years. It is the happy fortune of Germany to have cast off this outworn political form in good time. This alone assures us supremacy over the Western European nations. Our opponents are destroying their development with the toxins of their own decaying organisms.

" It is my historical achievement to have recognised this. My policy only seems dangerous ; it is not really so. Success will be mine because I have fathomed the weaknesses, including Marxism, of all the spurious great men of democracy and liberalism. We shall triumph by the same inexorable logic of fact in our foreign policy as in our home policy. I shall attain my purpose without a struggle, by legal means, just as I have come to power—simply because the inner logic of events demanded it, because there was no other power left in Germany that could have saved us from chaos. The opposition to us is dismally helpless, incapable of acting because it has lost every vestige of an inner law of action. The secret of National Socialist success is its recognition of the irrevocable passing of the *bourgeoisie* and their political ideals."

He paused for a moment, then continued.

" Democracy is a poison which distintegrates the body of the nation, and its action is the more deadly the more naturally strong and healthy the nation it infects. In the course of time, the old democracies have become more or less immune from this poison, and might have gone on vegetating under its influence for another decade or so. But for Germany, a young, unspoiled nation, the poison is instantly fatal."

The German people, he resumed, had had to be rescued from all dangerous and contaminating contact with this political pestilence, democracy. They would have perished otherwise.

" To-day we do not yet know what the end will be. We are only at the beginning. But we desire revolution. We shall not retreat. Fully conscious of what I was doing, I burnt all bridges in my foreign policy. I will compel the German people, who are hesitating before their destiny, to walk the road to greatness. I can attain my purpose only through world revolution. For the German people, there is no other way. Relentlessly they must be driven to their greatness, or they will fall back into timid renunciation."

Under the feeble governments of the last years, he continued, Germany had been all but isolated in a void round which the nations had grown increasingly active. Had this state of affairs persisted, Germany would have been crowded into the background, to sink to an inglorious slavery from which she would never again have escaped.

" In new geological ages, the whole structure of the earth is changed by gigantic avalanches, piling up new mountains and creating canyons, plains and oceans. So also will the entire European social order be uprooted in mighty eruptions and collapses. In such times of world upheaval, it is a law of elementary self-preservation to be hard as the primeval rock, lest one be overwhelmed and buried. The only hope for Germany of resisting this increasing pressure is to intervene actively in the inexorable development of a new era."

Only by accepting the inner law of the new world order, he contended, could the German people become the world people who would give their name to the coming era.

Hitler grew calmer as he spoke, and added with a certain

8

degree of modesty that National Socialism had perhaps
given its name to the great German upheaval more or less
by accident.   The leading role of National Socialism, which
could never more be struck from the historical register of
the nation, was due to its timely and accurate recognition of
this great world transformation, into the cosmic maelstrom
of which all of us were being drawn.

After this vast survey, Hitler returned to the more
prosaic problems of every day.   He accepted unreservedly
my view that Germany must provide no excuse for any other
country to proceed against her.   It was necessary, he
considered, that all arbitrary acts should be avoided, and
that an absolute national discipline should make any
" incidents " impossible.   Apart from this, he was prepared,
he said, to make any agreement that would publicly
guarantee him a measure of rearmament.

" I am willing to sign anything.   I will do anything to
facilitate the success of my policy.   I am prepared to
guarantee all frontiers and to make non-aggression pacts
and friendly alliances with anybody.   It would be sheer
stupidity to refuse to make use of such measures merely
because one might possibly be driven into a position where
a solemn promise would have to be broken.   There has
never been a sworn treaty which has not sooner or later
been broken or become untenable.   There is no such thing
as an everlasting treaty.   Anyone whose conscience is so
tender that he will not sign a treaty unless he can feel sure
he can keep it in all and any circumstances is a fool.   Why
should one not please others and facilitate matters for
oneself by signing pacts if the others believe that something
is thereby accomplished or regulated ?   Why should I not
make an agreement in good faith to-day and unhesitatingly
break it to-morrow if the future of the German people
demands it ? "

" I shall make any treaty I require," Hitler repeated.

" It will never prevent me from doing at any time what I regard as necessary for Germany's interests."

This view of treaties leaving me speechless, Hitler began to announce his Polish policy. After asking me to persuade Marshal Pilsudski to come and see him, he expressed his willingness to sign a pact, however far-reaching, with Poland too. He was at this time most anxious to improve his relations with that country. At the same time, his views about Poland were positively naïve. It was no wonder that he relied on the " expert " advice of *Gauleiter* Forster in all eastern questions. Forster, who was a Bavarian by birth, spoke of the Poles in the most contemptuous terms, the mildest of which was " lice." As long ago as September, 1933, on returning full of arrogance from the first great party conference at Nürnberg, he suggested to me that we should reverse the recently instituted " reconciliation policy " with regard to the Poles, and make war on Poland instead. Germany was now so strong, he claimed, that she could conquer Poland in a few days.

Hitler seemed to dislike being reminded of his special disciple's foolish estimate of the position. He changed the subject at once, and began again to paint a picture of vast perspectives. He hinted that mistakes like that made by Forster in a moment of warm enthusiasm were reparable. But no one would ever attain a conception of the greatness of our task by reasoning alone ; it had to be felt and experienced. He had no objection to such enthusiastic impulses, since they showed him who were the true revolutionaries.

" The Germans are ponderous and slothful. They lack the revolutionary temperament. National Socialism is the first genuinely revolutionary movement of the Germans— not Marxism, not the men of '48, not the miserable little Weimar Republicans. I like my comrades to yearn for the impossible."

He returned to the question of the League. It was corrupt and rotten, like everything in the democracies. There would be no resistance there. At best they were just a lot of officials, worried about their maintenance rights. Incidentally he would now more than ever speak the language of the League. He would not find it difficult.

" And my party comrades will not fail to understand me when they hear me speak of universal peace, disarmament and mutual security pacts ! "

PART III—1934

Jan. 26.   Germany concluded peace pact for ten years with Poland.

Jan. 30.   Bill passed to remodel the constitution.

Feb. 25.   Oath of absolute obedience to Hitler taken by over 1,000,000 Nazi officials.

March 27. Large increases shown in financial estimates for navy, army and air force.

May 29.   In debt talks at Berlin Germany obtained six months' moratorium. Dawes and Young loans excluded from its operations.

June 14.   Official announcement that for six months there would be no payment abroad of interest or sinking fund charges on any of Germany's medium and long-term foreign loans, including Dawes and Young loans.

June 30.   Shooting (without trial, or arrest) of many prominent Nazi leaders, including former Chancellor, General von Schleicher, and his wife, and Captain Roehm, leader of Storm Troops. Brown Army suppressed.

July 2.   Executions in suppression of the revolt officially stated to number 90.

July 13.   Hitler stated that 77 lives had been taken on his orders on June 30. Declared action necessitated by discovery of plot to assassinate himself and Vice-Chancellor von Papen. Reichstag approved action and thanked Hitler.

Aug. 2. Death of President von Hindenburg. Hitler became President, the Cabinet uniting the office with that of Chancellor.

Aug. 3. Entire German Army took new oath of allegiance to Hitler as " Leader and Chancellor."

Aug. 26. Speaking at Coblenz, Hitler inaugurated his campaign for the recovery of the Saar.

Sept. 10. German note to Great Powers, objecting to proposed Eastern " Locarno " pact of mutual assistance.

Oct. 17. Law passed requiring all Ministers to take personal oath of loyalty to Hitler.

Oct. 31. Official announcement of death sentence for alleged treason on unknown number of un-named persons.

Nov. 5. Hitler appointed a Commissar to control prices and fight profiteers and speculators.

Nov. 9. Minister of Interior banned discussion of Church affairs in the press.

Dec. 3. Agreement reached that Germany should pay to France 900,000,000 francs for Saar mines in event of plebiscite resulting in return of territory to Germany.

Dec. 22. Main body of British troops, with Swedish, Italian and Dutch contingents, reached Saarbruecken to keep order during plebiscite.

CHAPTER X

HITLER'S FOREIGN POLICY

IT was not till later that Hitler allowed me a more
intimate insight into his foreign policy. The time
was the beginning of 1934, and Hitler had just returned to
Berlin from a mid-winter visit to Berchtesgaden. I had
not yet had any opportunity of reporting to him on the
results of my visit to Marshal Pilsudski. Hitler received
me very cordially, expressing his appreciation of what I
had " done in the interests of the German Reich." He
listened to my report, making no criticisms at first. Now
and again he would ask a question.

The conclusion of the German-Polish pact, in spite of
all the criticism it aroused in *bourgeois* Nationalist and
army circles, meant a considerable improvement. It
might have been the beginning of a broad German policy
of federation. In the opinion of the self-styled initiates,
the pact was merely a temporary measure, until Germany
was strong enough to recapture the once Prussian districts
of Poland without fear of intervention from the Western
powers. But this was more probably said to reassure party
members than because it represented the true intentions
of Hitler. The camouflage he made use of in international
affairs was also employed against his own party members.
As for me, I considered it possible that Hitler might be
influenced towards a moderate policy of economic and
political penetration of Central Europe, and I saw signs of
this in his Polish policy. Hitler was chiefly interested in my
report because he wished to draw from it conclusions as to further implications of the pact. At length he asked me bluntly:

" Will Poland remain neutral if I take action against
the West ? "

This was a question for which I was not prepared ; it
seemed to me at the time without practical significance.
I therefore answered with some hesitation that this must
depend on the extent to which the reduced tension between
Germany and Poland could be developed into a genuine
identity of interests and political co-operation. I begged
him not to overlook the fact that we had only just escaped
the menace of a preventive war. The new relations would
require time to mature. It was therefore too early to
answer his question. Generally speaking, however, I had
the impression that the circles close to the Marshal were
prepared to see the sphere of Polish interests in the East and
North-East rather than in the West.

Hitler agreed.

" But what will be Poland's attitude when I force through
the Austrian *Anschluss* ? "

I replied that I believed it was in the interests of Poland
for German expansionist ambitions to be deflected from
Polish territory as long as possible. How far these were
mere tactical moves, and how far based on weightier considerations I could not judge. I could only say that as
early as July of the previous year, I had been asked in
Warsaw the embarrassing question why our slogan was
not *Drang nach dem Westen*, instead of *Drang nach dem Osten*.
In the West there were biologically dying peoples, but in
the East there were young, growing ones. The population
was denser in the west of Poland than in the eastern districts
of Germany.

" That is true," Hitler replied. " If I conquer Slav
territory, I expose the German people to the danger of
gradually losing their identity in the preponderance of
Slavs."

He walked up and down in silent thought. I seized

this opportunity of outlining for him my own views of a possible great German policy in the East. My idea was that the frontiers should not be tampered with, but that an identity of interests should be created across them by a tightening of the economic and political relations among the Central and South-Eastern European states, leading gradually along peaceful lines to a sort of federation. I felt there was every reason to hope for the assistance of Great Britain in such a peaceful expansion of Germany. The conditions for such a policy existed not only in Poland, but above all in Germany, for the very reason that she was known as a nationalist state. Germany would have a great future, I urged, if, instead of a rigorous revisionist policy, she were to carry out a policy of peaceful alliances. Certainly I had received from my conversation with Marshal Pilsudski the impression of a very real desire on the part of Poland for a permanent understanding with the Reich.

Hitler had allowed me to talk on. Whether or not he was really listening, I do not know. But at this point he broke in.

" Naturally," he remarked, " I should prefer an eastern policy of agreement with Poland rather than one directed against her."

Again he fell silent, then resumed :

" At any rate I shall give the Poles a chance. They have men who seem to me to be realists, and they have as little use for democracy as we have. But of course they will have to be generous in their views. Then I shall be so as well."

Hitler asked me whether Poland would be prepared to yield certain districts to Germany in return for others. I replied that it would not be wise to open negotiations with such demands, though it might be possible to discuss them later. Hitler did not reply to this.

" The struggle against Versailles," he said, " is the means, but not the end of my policy. I am not in the least interested in the former frontiers of the Reich. The re-creation of pre-war Germany is not a task worthy of our revolution."

" Do you plan to attack Russia with the assistance of Poland ? " I asked him.

" Perhaps," he returned.

" I rather thought your previous remarks implied that," I said.

" Soviet Russia, however, is a difficult problem.   I doubt if I shall be able to start anything there."

I replied that perhaps Poland might be induced to surrender western territory against compensation in the east, which should be of considerable value to Poland.   However, she would not be content with White Russian districts alone.   She would want a coastline on the Baltic as well as districts that would give her an outlet to the Black Sea.

" I think the gentlemen will have to give up their pretensions to Ukrainian territory," Hitler interrupted me.

I replied that perhaps these considerations were a little premature, as it was necessary to find out first whether any co-operation was possible at all, and if so, how far it could be carried.   I did not doubt that Poland and Germany had a powerful common interest in pushing back Soviet Russia from Europe, but I was afraid Poland had little understanding of the German-Ukrainian policy.   On my very first visit to Warsaw, I had been asked to use my influence to see that Rosenberg's plans for a Ukraine under the German government were dropped.   If Poland were to relinquish certain interests in the west, then I could not but believe she would lay claim to the Ukraine herself, as well as Lithuania, and perhaps even Latvia.   For Polish politicians to dream of a Greater Polish Empire extending from the Baltic to the Black Sea, and from Riga to Kiev, was surely something more than mere patriotic romancing.   These were realistic hopes based on geopolitical considerations.

" I have little use for a military might and a new Polish great power on my frontiers," Hitler broke in abruptly. " A war with Russia would not be in my interest."

In that case, I replied, Poland would hardly be likely to surrender any of her western territory.

" Then I shall force her. I have it in my power to force her to neutrality. It would be a simple matter for me to partition Poland."

I asked Hitler what he meant.

" All our agreements with Poland have a purely temporary significance. I have no intention of maintaining a serious friendship with Poland. I do not need to share my power with anyone."

He paced the room in silence for some minutes.

" I could at any time come to an agreement with Soviet Russia," he said at last, as he paused and faced me. " I could partition Poland when and how I pleased. But I don't want to. It would cost too much. If I can avoid it, I will not do it. I need Poland only so long as I am still menaced by the West."

" Do you seriously intend to fight the West ? " I asked.

He stopped and looked at me.

" What else do you think we're arming for ? " he retorted.

I said that I thought this would surely call forth a hostile coalition against Germany which would be too strong for her.

" That is what I have to prevent. We must proceed step by step, so that no one will impede our advance. How to do this I don't yet know. But that it will be done is guaranteed by Britain's lack of firmness and France's internal disunity."

Hitler then began to talk about his favourite subject, the pacifism of Britain and France. I have heard him many times reiterate his unshakable conviction that Britain was quite incapable of waging another war, and that France, in spite of her magnificent army, could, by the provocation of internal unrest and disunity in public opinion, easily be brought to the point where she would only be able to use her army too late or not at all. I objected that we might find ourselves grievously mistaken in our belief in the impotence of Britain and France.

Hitler laughed scornfully. He would not live to see Britain again at war with Germany.

" Britain *needs* a strong Germany. Britain and France will never again make common cause against Germany."

" Do you intend to break through the Maginot Line," I asked, " or will you march into Holland and Belgium ? If you do the latter, you will certainly bring Britain in on the side of France."

" If they have time to come in," Hitler returned. " Besides, I shall neither break through the Maginot Line nor enter Belgium. I shall manœuvre France right out of her Maginot Line without losing a single soldier."

I must have looked sceptical, for Hitler added triumphantly :

" How to do it is my secret ! Of course," he continued after a pause, " I shall do everything in my power to prevent co-operation between Britain and France. If I succeed in bringing in Italy and Britain on our side, the first part of our struggle for power will be greatly facilitated. Anyhow, we don't for a moment pretend to believe that this degenerate Jewish democracy has any more vitality than France or the United States. It will be my mission to see that at least an effort is made to inherit this disintegrating empire peacefully, so that conflict can be avoided entirely. But I shall not shrink from war with Britain if it is necessary. Where Napoleon failed, I shall succeed. To-day there is no such thing as an island. I shall land on the shores of Britain. I shall destroy her towns from the mainland. Britain does not yet know how vulnerable she is to-day."

"But supposing Britain, France and Russia make an alliance?"

"That would be the end. But even if we could not conquer then, we should drag half the world into destruction with us, and leave no one to triumph over Germany. There will not be another 1918. We shall not surrender."

"But that stage will never be reached," Hitler continued, restraining his mounting excitement. "It could only happen if I failed in all my undertakings. In that case I should feel I had wrongly usurped this place. Certainly I shall never blame accident for any mistakes I may make. But fortune follows where there is a firm will."

I remarked that the lesson for Germany of the last war seemed to me to be this : That it was unwise to rouse all nations against us by our too ambitious political aims, and thus be left in the end without allies. It seemed to me that the only practicable method for Germany must be the attainment, by political means, without the use of force, of successive, limited objectives.

Hitler lost patience with me.

"If Germany is to become a world power, and not merely a continental state (and it must become a world power if it is to survive), then it must achieve complete sovereignty and independence," he shouted. "Do you understand what that means? Is it not clear to you how tragically mutilated we are by the restriction and hemming-in of our vital space, a restriction which condemns us to the status of a second-rate power in Europe? Only nations living independently in their own space and capable of military defence can be world powers. Only such nations are sovereign in the true sense of the word.

"Russia is such a state," he went on, "the United States, Britain—but only by artificial means, not at all from the nature of its populated areas. France is such a state up to a point. Why should we be worse off? Is this an unavoidable inferiority ?   It is necessary that in spite of our diligence and efficiency, in spite of our industries and our military skill, we should always remain second to Britain, second to France, though we are greater than both of them together ?   This is why I must gain space for Germany, space big enough to enable us to defend ourselves against any military coalition.   In peacetime we can manage.   But in war the important thing is freedom of action, for in war one is mortally dependent on the outside world.   Our dependence on foreign trade without even an ocean coastline would condemn us eternally to the position of a politically dependent nation.

" We need space," he almost shrieked, " to make us independent of every possible political grouping and alliance. In the east, we must have the mastery as far as the Caucasus and Iran.   In the west, we need the French coast.   We need Flanders and Holland.   Above all we need Sweden. We must become a colonial power.   We must have a sea power equal to that of Britain.   The material basis for independence grows with the increasing demands of technique and armaments.   We cannot, like Bismarck, limit ourselves to national aims.   We must rule Europe or fall apart as a nation, fall back into the chaos of small states. Now do you understand why I cannot be limited, either in the east or in the west ? "

I asked him whether he was not trying to fly in the face of nature.   Was he not trying to do by force something that could only succeed by a policy of alliances ?

" What about Britain ? " Hitler shouted at me.   " Didn't Britain get her Empire by theft and robbery ?   Was that a ' policy of alliances ' or was it force ? "

I replied that every age has its own methods, and that I thought success very unlikely with methods by which a century and a half ago it had still been possible to found a colonial Empire.

But Hitler would have none of this.   Banging his fist on the table, he cried at the top of his voice :

" You're wrong, sir, quite wrong !   One thing is and remains eternally the same : force. Empires are made by the sword, by superior force—not by alliances ! "

This was not the first time, he went on more mildly, but still with strong disapproval, that he had noticed in me an evident tendency towards mistaken ideas about political forces.   I was indulging, he told me, in pacifist day-dreams. I should remember, once and for all, that all this palaver and pact-making had no permanency.

" Germany's future," he said, " lies, not in alliances, but in her own strength."

I reminded him that Bismarck's Reich could not have been founded without his policy of Prussian customs unions.

" And without the victories of '66 and '70, that union policy would no more have led to anything than did the chattering of the men of '48 in the Cathedral at Frankfort ! " Hitler retorted.

I suggested that perhaps the modern constitution of the British Empire provided a suitable example.   We needed something like a Statute of Westminster for the states of Central and Eastern Europe, a voluntary federation under German leadership.   This seemed to me more in line with our present position and our future development.

" So," Hitler replied, " you consider the British Empire in its present shape a proper model for what National Socialism is to achieve for the future of Germany !   Certainly not !   This modern Empire shows all the marks of decay and inexorable breakdown because there is nowhere in it the courage of firm leadership.   If you no longer have the strength to rule by means of force, and are too humane to give orders, then it's time to resign.   Britain will yet regret her softness.   It will cost her her Empire.   Even if an old ruling class may be able to vegetate for another decade or so without any real leadership, a new Empire can never rise otherwise than by blood and iron, by a firm will and brutal force."

He paced the room in great excitement.

" In the centre I shall place the steely core of a Greater Germany welded into an indissoluble unity. Then Austria, Bohemia, and Moravia, western Poland. A block of one hundred million, indestructible, without a flaw, without an alien element, the firm foundation of our power. Then an Eastern alliance : Poland, the Baltic states, Hungary, the Balkan states, the Ukraine, the Volga basin, Georgia. An alliance, but not of equal partners ; it will be an alliance of vassal states, with no army, no separate policy, no separate economy. I have no intention of making concessions on sentimental grounds, such as re-establishing Hungary, for example. I make no distinction between friends and enemies. The day of small states is past, in the west as well. I shall have a Western Union too, of Holland, Flanders, Northern France, and a Northern Union of Denmark, Sweden and Norway."

Hitler was silent for a little, lost in the contemplation of his vision.

" There will be continual changes in the power relationships," he presently resumed. " But, after a certain point, these changes will all work in favour of Germany. There will be no such thing as neutrality. The neutrals will be drawn into the sphere of influence of the great powers. They will be absorbed. These things will not all take place at the same time. I shall proceed step by step, but with iron determination."

With prodigious self-sufficiency, Hitler dilated on these plans, which at the time were all the more astonishing since they seemed to lack the slightest hope of realisation. In 1934 they were madness ; in 1940 they will perhaps be fact. It is not surprising that a man who has been able to

realise so many of his dreams should be drunk with powe
and believe himself a god.

It is of no interest to pursue these plans in further detail.
In part they have been realised, like the Austrian *Anschluss*
and the dismemberment of Czechoslovakia ; in other
instances, the exact opposite of the original plan has
happened. The lightning war, the surprise attack, the
sudden turn from west to east, the unexpected blow to the
north—all these were to have been the irresistible measures
of open warfare, while the revolutionary disintegration of
the enemy from within would have represented the subtle
methods of psychological attack.

Hitler's imagination ranged over the entire world. He
would attack Britain at all its weakest points, India no less
than Canada. He planned the occupation of Sweden as
well as Holland. The latter country, in particular, seemed
to him a valuable jumping-off ground for air and under-
water attacks on England.

" In less than eight hours we shall break through to their
coast," he told me, in a tone of malignant triumph. A
situation might arise, he explained, in which he might risk
a great war. In that case, he would remain on the defensive,
and leave it to the enemy to take the first aggressive step.
On the enemy's doing so, he would then seize on Holland,
Denmark, Switzerland and the Scandinavian states, improve
his strategic positions, and propose peace under certain
guarantees.

" If they don't like it, they can try to drive me out. In
any case they will have to bear the main burden of attack."

On my suggesting that another blockade of Germany
would bring defeat, he laughed derisively.

" The day of Britain's might at sea is past. Aircraft and
the U-boat have turned surface fleets into the obsolete
playthings of the wealthy democracies. They are no longer
a serious weapon in decisive warfare."

9

One other item in this conversation with Hitler seemed to me remarkable, and that was his view of Italy.   He spoke of Fascism with almost hostile contempt, as a half-measure.

" The Italians can never be trained to become a warlike people, nor has Fascism ever understood the real meaning of the great upheaval of our era.   Of course we can make temporary alliances with Italy ; but ultimately we National Socialists stand alone, as the only ones who know the secret of these gigantic changes, and therefore as those chosen to set their seal on the coming age."

It would be a bad day for Germany's future, he continued, if she had to rely on a nation like Italy in her hour of need.

Hitler accompanied me to the door, talking as he went :

" We must keep our eyes open.   Under more favourable conditions, it is our task to carry to a victorious conclusion the war that was interrupted in 1918.   If I succeed in that, everything else will accomplish itself with the elemental power of an inner necessity.   What lay behind us was a truce ; before us lies the victory we threw away in 1918."

Hitler dismissed me with expressions of cordiality, but I had a feeling that I had lost ground with him.   However, he thanked me once more for my efforts in Poland.

RUSSIA, FRIEND OR FOE ?

(SPRING, 1934)

I learned of Hitler's plans for Russia on a later occasion.   In the spring of 1934 I asked for an interview with him in order to report on the Danzig negotiations with Poland.   They had reached a critical stage.   Since the conclusion of the German-Polish agreement there was a chance that Germany might be able to influence Poland in Danzig's favour.   It was natural in this connection to discuss our relations with Soviet Russia, which had always taken an interest in the maintenance of the Free City's independence. At certain critical moments Russia had even exerted unmistakable pressure on Poland. I had endeavoured to strengthen this interest in my conversations with Kalina, the Soviet representative in Danzig at that time, in order to leave our backs free during our negotiations with the Poles. We had not confined ourselves to purely economical questions, but had touched on the problem of Danzig itself, and the need for granting the Free City, the " most western of the Baltic states," a greater measure of independence. This was a plan which greatly interested Kalina.

We did not, however, reach the point of signing a Soviet-Danzig agreement, on the basis of which Danzig was to have built a number of merchant ships for Russia. The latter country was at that time drawing away from Germany as well as from Danzig. Kalina told me the reasons ; he had the good sense to speak quite candidly.

" Your National Socialism," he told me over an early luncheon, " is certainly revolutionary, but what have you done with this revolutionary force ? Your Socialism is only a decoy for the masses. You are carrying out a chaotic, unplanned revolution without a conscious aim. This is not revolution in the sense of a social advance of human society. You want power. You are abusing the the revolutionary strength of Germany. You are exhausting it. For us, you are more dangerous than the old capitalist powers. The German people were on the road to liberty. But you will disappoint them. You will leave behind you a dejected, suspicious people, incapable of productive labour. One day the masses will fall away from you. At that time, perhaps, we shall be able to work together. We shall conclude a pact with the German people when they have corrected their mistake. That day will surely come ; we can wait."

But it did not take as long as this for relations between
Soviet Russia and National Socialist Germany to be renewed.
Actually they had never quite broken down, not even where
the party was concerned. Goebbels was not the only one who,
during the years of struggle, had been well-nigh exultant
over the close relationship between National Socialism
and Bolshevism, though he was not so indiscreet in public.
There were a number of *Gauleiter* who saw in a German
pact with Russia the only political solution that could spare
us many dangerous deviations from our path. Hitler
himself remained sceptical for a number of reasons, none of
which were ideological in character, all being purely
practical. He never attempted the rejection of any agreement on grounds of principle, never, that is to say, among
the inner circle of party members.

" Go to Moscow," Hitler returned as I explained to him
certain plans to facilitate the Danzig-Polish negotiations,
which were threatening to become bogged. " Go to
Moscow ; I have no objections. But you won't enjoy your
stay much. They're a lot of quibbling Jews. You never
get anywhere with them."

I mentioned that I had also discussed these plans with
Gauleiter Koch, of Königsberg.

" Yes, Koch's got a good head," said Hitler. " But I'm
worried about him."

Koch was a friend of the disgraced Gregor Strasser who,
as a potential rival, was mortally hated by Hitler. I took
good care not to enter into a discussion of the rivalries
between the East Prussian party cadres. I told him
instead about Koch's " planning centre." A young Professor von Grünberg had devised some fantastic " plan
landscapes " of the future, which were drawn up at his
institute. There were plans of means of transport, power
stations, electric lines, roads, railways, and canals.
Accurately planned economic " landscapes " covered the

whole of the East as far as the Black Sea and the Caucasus. These plans showed Germany and Western Russia as a huge economico-political block, on a German basis, of course, planned and ruled by Germany. There was no Poland in this " planned landscape," still less a Lithuania. It represented a huge continental space which was to stretch from Vlissingen in the West to Vladivostok in the Far East.

" Unless we get that, the whole revolution is only a flash in the pan," Koch had told me when I expressed my amazement at the breadth of his plans.

" Koch runs a little too far ahead of reality," Hitler said in reference to these plans. " He's trying to persuade me that an alliance between Germany and Russia will instantaneously remove all our difficulties. He wants me to ally myself with Russia against Poland. There is no reason why I shouldn't make a pact with Russia if that will improve my position. So far he is quite right. That is by no means impossible, and to a large extent, it will depend on Poland when this happens. But Koch is also wrong. In this way we shall never attain what is necessary for us. We shall never be a great, world-conquering entity. On the contrary, we should then distrust each other more than ever, and the end of such a pact would be the decisive battle that cannot be escaped. Only *one* can rule. If *we* want to rule, we must first conquer Russia. After that, Koch can go on carrying out his ' planned landscapes.' Not before."

I explained that I had not meant an alliance between Germany and Russia, but simply a temporary arrangement as a tactical cover for our rear. I quite agreed that a hard-and-fast alliance was not without its dangers for Germany.

" Why ? " Hitler asked sharply. " I've said nothing like that."

Surely, I suggested, there would be considerable danger of the Bolshevisation of Germany.

"There is no such danger, and never has been," Hitler returned. "Besides, you forget that Russia is not only the land of Bolshevism, but also the greatest continental empire in the world, enormously powerful and capable of drawing the whole of Europe into its embrace. The Russians would take complete possession of their partners. That is the real danger ; either you go with them all the way, or you leave them strictly alone."

Then if I understood him rightly, I said, he drew a line of distinction between Russia as an empire and Russia as the home of Bolshevism. But it was not quite clear to me why an agreement as between sovereign states should not be possible between the Reich and Russia. It seemed to me that the only difficulty would be Russia's Bolshevism, which would always be a danger for us.

"It is not Germany that will turn Bolshevist, but Bolshevism that will become a sort of National Socialism," Hitler replied. "Besides, there is more that binds us to Bolshevism than separates us from it. There is, above all, genuine, revolutionary feeling, which is alive everywhere in Russia except where there are Jewish Marxists. I have always made allowance for this circumstance, and given orders that former Communists are to be admitted to the party at once. The *petit bourgeois* Social-Democrat and the trade-union boss will never make a National Socialist, but the Communist always will."

I raised cautious objections, pointing out the obvious danger of a planned permeation of party organisations by Communist agents. Most of those who had transferred their allegiance from the one party to the other were engaged as Comintern spies. Hitler rejected these suggestions rather sharply. He would accept the risks, he said.

"Our spirit is so strong, and the power of our magnificent

movement to transform souls so elemental, that men are remodelled against their will."

He feared internal unrest no more from the German Communists than from the Russian agents of the Comintern. If he were compelled to make a pact with Russia, he would still have his own second revolution in the background, a revolution which would protect him against all infection from Communist-Marxist chimeras.

" A social revolution would lend me new, unsuspected powers. I do not fear permeation with revolutionary Communist propaganda. But Russia, whether she is to be a partner or an enemy, is our equal and must be watched. Germany and Russia are in an extraordinary fashion complementary to each other. They are made for each other, I might almost say. And the danger for us is that we may be absorbed, that we may lose our identity as a nation. Have you not noticed that Germans who have lived a long time in Russia can never again be Germans ? The huge spaces have fascinated them. After all, Rosenberg is rabid against the Russians only because they would not allow him to be a Russian."

I remarked that it was curious how many young people— young Conservatives, young Prussians, young soldiers and civil engineers—saw the safeguarding of the future in an alliance with Russia. Evidently, Hitler did not like to hear this.

" I know what you mean—all this chattering about ' Prussian Socialism ' and so on. Just the thing for our generals, playing at political games of war. Because a military alliance of this kind seems convenient to them, they suddenly discover that they're not in the least capitalist, in fact that they suffer from a kind of anti-capitalist nostalgia ! They are quite happy with their half-knowledge, and think of their Prussian Socialism as a kind of drill-ground discipline in economics and personal liberty. But the matter isn't as simple as that. I can understand that the engineers are delighted with their ' plans,' but this isn't such a simple matter either. They seem to think it is just a question of exchanging raw material for engineering technique. The engineers, by the way, that they've got over there now are peculiarly rotten."

" These beliefs in a supernational workers' state," he continued, " with production plans and production districts can only come out of the misguided, over-rationalised brains of a literary clique that has lost its sound instincts. It's all convulsive, false, and a public danger because it obstructs National Socialism. Perhaps I shall not be able to avoid an alliance with Russia. I shall keep that as a trump card. Perhaps it will be the decisive gamble of my life. But it must not be made the subject of hole-and-corner literary gossip, nor played too soon. But it will never stop me from as firmly retracing my steps, and attacking Russia when my aims in the west have been achieved. It is naïve to believe that our rise will always move along a straight line. We shall change our fronts from time to time—and not the military ones alone.

" But for the time being we may retain the doctrine that Bolshevism is our deadly enemy. We shall endeavour to go on from the point at which our armies in the last war left off when the armistice was signed. It is still our task to shatter for all time the menacing hordes of the pan-Slav empire. Under the shadow of this supreme power, Germany would not be able to rise. Let us not forget that the Slav East is more fertile than all the rest of Europe. We must meet this danger, which threatens to engulf all Europe. We cannot in any way evade the final battle between German race ideals and pan-Slav mass ideals. Here yawns the eternal abyss which no mutual political interest can bridge. We must win the victory of German race-consciousness over the masses eternally fated to serve and obey. We alone can conquer the great continental space, and it will be done by us singly and alone, not through a pact with Moscow. We shall take this struggle upon us. It will open to us the door to permanent mastery of the world. That does not mean that I will refuse to walk part of the road together with the Russians, if that will help us. But it will be only in order to return the more swiftly to our true aims."

CHAPTER XI

HITLER'S FOREIGN POLICY—*continued*

OBLIGATION TO DEPOPULATE

WAS this really Hitler's Russian programme?
At that time, I had still no inkling that in fact
Hitler might have no definite political aims at all, but
simply rode on the crest of every favourable opportunity,
prepared to surrender everything he had ever fought for,
solely in order to strengthen his power. Perhaps he had
improvised everything he said about Russia, simply to have
something to say, to enhance his importance. He has always
been a *poseur*. He remembers things he has heard and has
a faculty of repeating them in such a way that the listener
is led to believe that they are his own. Perhaps he told a
visitor who followed me the exact opposite of what he
presented to me as the result of profound political study.

Hitler's politics consists in an unscrupulous opportun-
ism which discards with perfect ease everything that a
moment before has passed as a fixed principle. His past
continues to haunt him—his past as a paid political agent
prepared to accept every advantage offered him, flirting
with Marxism to-day, and accepting money from the
promoters of a Bavarian restoration to-morrow. Such a
political attitude is characterised by two things : first, an
unbelievable capacity to tell falsehoods, and second, a quite
disarming *naïveté*, a total innocence of promises and assertions made only a moment before. Most of these National
Socialists, with Hitler at their head, literally forget, like
hysterical women, anything they have no desire to remember. Everyone who has had dealings with Hitler has
had the same experience that I had over and over again :

when reminded of some former statement he would either stare in blank amazement, or would curtly declare that he had never said anything of the kind.

Only people who indulge in such mental acrobatics are capable of risking elevating into a policy a series of radical changes of front. Only thus could a man believed to be the high priest of a rigid philosophy completely and cynically deny his entire past for the sole purpose of remaining in power.

In the conversation on foreign policy recorded in the last chapter, Hitler made some other remarks that are worth remembering. For example, he referred again to the danger of too great an infusion of Slav blood into the German people. The national character, he declared, would unquestionably be altered by it.

" We have far too much Slav blood in our veins already. Have you never noticed," he asked me, " how many people in high positions in Germany have Slav names ? " It appeared that someone who had studied this question had told him that only half a century ago the position was quite different. His informant had made a special investigation amongst Prussian judges and barristers, and people in comparable stations. The same person told me that there was a disproportionately high percentage of people with Slav names among criminals.

" What conclusion can one draw from this ? " asked Hitler. " That an asocial, inferior section of the nation is gradually moving up to a higher social class. This is a great danger to the German people. They lose their character, an alien people takes possession of their language. The nation as a whole is still the German nation. But the German spirit lives in it as in a strange house. The true German is merely a tolerated stranger in his own nation. The Jews have already done their share in bringing this about."

Hitler paused, but I said nothing.

" The least we can do," he continued, " is to prevent this alien blood from rising higher in the national body. I admit that this danger will not be diminished if in the near future we occupy regions with a high proportion of Slav population, which we shall not be able to get rid of very quickly. Consider Austria, consider Vienna ! Is there anything German left there ?

" *We are obliged to depopulate*," he went on emphatically, " as part of our mission of preserving the German population. We shall have to develop a technique of depopulation. If you ask me what I mean by depopulation, I mean the removal of entire racial units. And that is what I intend to carry out—that, roughly, is my task. Nature is cruel, therefore we, too, may be cruel. If I can send the flower of the German nation into the hell of war without the smallest pity for the spilling of precious German blood, then surely I have the right to remove millions of an inferior race that breeds like vermin ! And by ' remove ' I don't necessarily mean destroy ; I shall simply take systematic measures to dam their great natural fertility. For example, I shall keep their men and women separated for years. Do you remember the falling birth-rate of the world war ? Why should we not do quite consciously and through a number of years what was at that time merely the inevitable consequence of the long war ? There are many ways, systematical and comparatively painless, or at any rate bloodless, of causing undesirable races to die out.

" And by the way," he added, " I should not hesitate a bit to say this in public. The French complained after the war that there were twenty million Germans too many. We accept the criticism. We favour the planned control of population movements. But our friends will have to excuse us if we subtract the twenty millions elsewhere. After all these centuries of whining about the protection of the poor and lowly, it is about time we decided to protect the strong against the inferior. It will be one of the chief tasks of German statesmanship for all time to prevent, by every means in our power, the further increase of the Slav races. Natural instincts bid all living beings not merely conquer their enemies, but also destroy them. In former days, it was the victor's prerogative to destroy entire tribes, entire peoples. By doing this gradually and without bloodshed, we demonstrate our humanity. We should remember, too, that we are merely doing unto others as they would have done to us."

The Northern Myth

It is astonishing that both in and outside Germany, National Socialism should have been misunderstood for so many years. The reasons for this are various, but I may mention one of them. No sufficiently sharp distinction was made between the true aims of the movement and the popular ideas and misconceptions about it. It was a long time before even those of the so-called initiates who did not belong to the inner circle of demigods began to guess what the stakes really were.

In the old Hanseatic city of Lübeck, there was a so-called " Northern Society," the purpose of which was to foster the cultural and personal relations between Germany and the Northern States. This society, like all similar organisations, had been " co-ordinated " (*gleichgeschaltet*), and the National Socialists made use of the society's solidly established reputation to shift valuable connections and sympathies in the Northern States to themselves. From what had been the slightly romantic instrument of a valuable cultural mission, the society became the tool of insidious propaganda and crass espionage, without the majority of its members either in the Reich or in the North having the slightest suspicion of what was going on.

In keeping with old Hanse traditions, a Danzig " guild "
was going to be held at which I was asked to preside, and
early in the summer of 1934 there was a ceremonial inauguration at Lübeck. Rosenberg and the Minister of
Education, Dr. Rust, took prominent part in the celebration. There were speeches, meetings, the ceremonial
inauguration of a literary hostel for northern visitors, a
flowery oration by Blunck, the president of the Reich Board
of Literary Production (*Reichsschrifttumskammer*), and a nocturnal organ concert in the old Marienkirche, the church
of St. Mary. In short, the whole procedure was provincially
peaceful and sleepy. The well-known industrialist
Thyssen, who was also officiating, complained to me of
the waste of time, the phrase-mongering, and the futile,
uninspiring speeches. For example, Werner Daitz, one of
our foreign envoys, was continually mouthing the expression " the economics of greater European space." Or there
was the local *Gauleiter* Hildebrandt, formerly an agricultural
labourer, rising to make a speech which was mere confused
gibberish. Statements were solemnly made that the
original culture of mankind had not arisen round the
Mediterranean at all, but on the shore of the Baltic,
created by the Nordic races. The Baltic was the home of
heroism and Aryan racial culture, and the Mediterranean
was the seat of racial decay and Semitic degeneration.

A great deal of this sort of nonsense was spoken. The
public, according to its cultural background, was either
disgusted or naïvely enthusiastic. In the former category
were members of old senatorial families who had lost their
influence. But, precisely because the whole thing appeared so
silly and sentimental, hardly any of us guessed that this was
a subtle performance behind which lurked a serious purpose.

Here is the explanation :

In the conversation already recorded, Hitler had said
that in a future war there would be no neutrals. And he

added that the Northern States belonged to Germany quite as much as did Holland and Belgium. In the next war, one of his first measures must be to occupy Sweden. He could not leave the Scandinavian countries either to British or Russian influence.

I suggested that the military subjugation of this vast, and to a large extent wild, peninsula must entail a disproportionate drain on our resources. To this Hitler replied that there was no question of occupying the entire country, but only the important ports and industrial centres, above all the iron-ore mines.

" It will be a daring, but interesting undertaking, never before attempted in the history of the world," he pointed out. " Protected by the fleet, and with the co-operation of the air force, I shall order a series of unexpected individual exploits. The Swedes will nowhere be prepared to put up a sufficiently strong defence. But even if one or other of these exploits should fail, the overwhelming majority of strategic points will be held."

On my expressing surprise, he added that to ensure the political success of this enterprise, it would be absolutely necessary to possess a close network of supporters and sympathisers in Sweden. Such a *coup* would lead to the permanent incorporation of the Northern States into the Greater German system of alliances only if the sympathisers gained for National Socialism could force an alliance by overthrowing their government. He was convinced, he said, that the Swedes would no more wage war now than they had done in 1905, when Norway broke away from the Swedish-Norwegian Union.

" I shall in every possible way make it easy for them to adhere to this determination," he explained, " more especially by declaring that I have no hostile intentions. I should tell them I did not wish to conquer them, but wanted only an alliance that was entirely natural and would certainly also be openly desired by Sweden if she were not, out of fear of Russia and Britain, withdrawing into a perfectly suicidal neutrality. I should explain that I came to protect them, and so give the friendly elements in the country the opportunity of deciding according to their own free will."

I must admit that when I first heard this, I refused to take it seriously. But I believe it ought to be so taken. One thing, however, is certain : Hitler is not interested in the pure Aryan blood of the Scandinavians, nor in the northern myths of Viking heroism. He is interested in the iron-ore mines. The President of the *Reichsschrifttumskammer*, Herr Blunck, and our Swedish friends are playing gratuitous parts in a play the background of which they have never seen.

The World Propaganda Troupe

The various German organisations in different parts of the world are all in the same position. Largely without their knowledge, their functions are all being terribly distorted. Only history will show how great an accumulation of trust and belief has been wantonly destroyed. All these overseas German communities have become the breeding-ground of a mushroom growth of propaganda, flourishing in the dark, which has run through all the stages up to effective espionage. Every German, whether still a German national or a citizen of the country in which he was living, was impressed into the service of this enormous machine. Every organisation that did not explicitly state its aims as being anti-Nazi was more or less the agent of a system of political propaganda and espionage centre that far exceeded all legal and legitimate limits.

Hardly any of the participants understood the nature of the growing movement. All we could see was the internecine struggles of the various cliques for powerful and lucrative posts. For years this vulgar quarrelling went on in all the overseas German associations. It was an un-

dignified scramble of all the political sections, old as well
as new, under the banner of loyalty to the Führer, for the
favour of the leading circles in the Reich, that is, of the
men who held the country's purse-strings, and were in a
position to dispense honours and recognition to the ambitious. Unfortunately there were all too many such in the
new Reich. There were at least seven party organisations in
charge of overseas German societies used for propaganda and
intelligence. Not one of them had the well-being and preserva-
tion of the German spirit at heart. They were all committed
to the task of making Germandom abroad the instrument
of a gigantic, world-embracing system of secret service.

The German communities abroad were permeated with
jealousies and quarrels, and there was so much confusion
and disagreement that outsiders looked on in amazement
and scorn. They were inclined to regard this " struggle for
power " as a purely German concern, and, in their contempt for its pettiness, to overlook its essential menace.

We too—myself and some of my friends in the German
diplomatic service abroad—failed to understand the
dangerous game played at Hitler's orders by unscrupulous
party members. The spirit of overseas Germandom, indispensable to our reputation and our standing in the world,
was being jeopardised. I emphasise this point because this
abuse of the representative German spirit has called forth
great indignation abroad, and threatens to destroy something that may never be restored again. If every foreigner
all over the world is regarded with suspicion as the possible
agent of a hostile power, then we shall soon be back in a
state of general barbarism. It is necessary therefore to
point out that certainly the great majority of Germans have
quite unconsciously and unwillingly been made use of by
the National Socialist machine. The blame should be laid
exclusively at the door of Hitler and one or two of his
lieutenants, especially Hess.

10

It was with Hess, the Führer's deputy, that I had frequent conversations about the Germans in Poland. Through my personal relations, I had some knowledge of the German colony there. I was repeatedly asked for explanations and on one occasion, had to act as mediator between the opposing lines of interest. Hess himself was a sort of supreme authority with regard to the new function within the National Socialist struggle to be given to Germans living abroad. I knew nothing of this function, and acted in good faith, believing that I was merely reconciling adherents of the older order with the newer elements.

I was present at a meeting of overseas Germans. The speeches themselves were not startling. But in conversation with the new representatives, members of the Hitler Youth, of Rosenberg's organisation, the SS, and other party cadres, it became clear to me what game was really being played. Later, when I was informed of the true aims of the " German Academy" in Munich, of which I became a temporary member, I understood the criminal use that was being made of German nationals abroad in the interests of world revolution.

Not long after this, I had occasion to hear Hitler's own views. Early in the summer of 1934, a conference of a small circle of people took place in Berlin, attended by some of the older school of representatives of Germans abroad, and a number of younger people who had not hitherto occupied responsible positions. There were present also representatives of the great German societies in other countries. One of the older representatives (long since fallen into disfavour) has asked me to attend because of my many years of preoccupation with the problem of minority rights and cultural autonomy. He expected me to exercise a restraining influence on the new elements. But there was no question of anything of the kind. The conversion of the minority pacts into a real European minority law for the whole of Europe, and a new and permanent European order without another war of revenge—things for which we had been hoping for more than a decade—were completely ignored. The discussion turned on economic questions, on the support of newspapers, the removal of distasteful committee members, the transfer of property—in short, the quarrels of the cliques. But the climax of the meeting was a short address by Hitler.

"Gentlemen," Hitler began, after each one had been presented to him personally, and had the privilege of " looking into his eyes," " gentlemen, you have been entrusted with one of the most essential tasks. You are needed for something more than the fostering and strengthening of the German spirit which has engaged you so far. You must also train it into a fighting company. You are not out to gain parliamentary rights and limited privileges for the German spirit. Such rights might even be a hindrance rather than a help. You have therefore no longer to do your best, according to your lights, but to obey orders. What may seem to you advantageous may, from a higher point of view, be injurious. My first demand from you, therefore, is blind obedience. You are not the judges of what is to be done in your district. Neither shall I always in be a position to explain to you in detail what my intention is. Your obedience is the fruit of your trust in me. This is the reason why I have no use in our circles for representatives of the old parliamentary system. Such gentlemen will have to resign. They have tried to solve the problem in their way. Now we have no further use for them. If they will not give up their posts willingly, you are to remove them by any means necessary. The policy of the overseas German groups is no longer to be debated and voted upon, but to be determined here by me, or by my deputy, Party Comrade Hess.

" As the front line of our German fighting movement, you will make it possible for us to complete the occupation of our positions, and to open fire. You have all the functions that we older men carried out in the last war. You are the army's outposts. You will have to prepare definite enterprises far in advance of the front. You will have to mask our own preparations for attack. You must regard yourselves as at war. You will be subject to martial law. To-day you are perhaps the most important section of the German nation. The nation and myself will always be grateful to you for whatever sacrifices you may have to make for the future Reich."

Hitler knew how to appeal to young people, and in fact they glowed with enthusiasm, and spoke afterwards of this meeting as something that would affect their whole lives. Hitler then began to handle tactics. He was not disposed to take it too seriously, he said, if there were transient disagreements among certain groups and factions. The party had thriven not only on external struggles, but on internal ones as well. It was futile to worry about such rivalries. Wherever there was life there was also struggle. For other reasons, too, he did not consider it desirable that there should be only one privileged society in every country. By all means let there be tension and differences of opinion. This might even prove useful as a means of masking their true aims from the authorities.

"It is a good idea," he said emphatically, "to have at least two German societies in every country. One of them can then always call attention to its loyalty to the country in question, and will have the function of fostering social and economic connections. The other one may be radical and revolutionary. It will have to be prepared to be frequently repudiated by myself and other German authorities. I want to make it quite clear, too, that I make no distinction between German nationals and Germans by birth who are citizens of a foreign country. Superficially we shall have to make allowances for such citizenship. But it will be your special task to train all Germans, without distinction, unconditionally to place their loyalty to Germandom before their loyalty to the foreign state. Only in this way will you be able to fulfil the difficult tasks I shall give you. I must leave to your discretion the means by which you train your fellow-Germans to this new discipline. It will not always be possible without friction. For me, success is the only criterion. The means are of no interest to me. But whoever opposes you should know that he has nothing more to expect from the German Reich. He will be outlawed for all time. And in due course he will reap the fruits of his treacherous attitude."

Hitler concluded his address as follows :

" It will depend on you, gentlemen, whether we reach our goal with comparative ease and without bloodshed. You must prepare the ground. Germany will spread its might far beyond its borders in the east as well as in the south-east. You, too, gentlemen, will have the same duties overseas. Forget all you have learned hitherto. We do not seek equality, but mastery. We shall not waste time over minority rights and other such ideological abortions of sterile democracy. When Germany is great and victorious no one will dare to give any of you the cold shoulder. It is your mission to win this leading role in the world for Germany. If you succeed, then you too will be called to leadership, unhampered by agreements and legal red tape. It will be your task to lead these conquered countries in the name of the German people. You shall be my viceroys in the countries and amongst the people who to-day persecute and oppress you. What has been our handicap—the splitting, the century-long impotence of the German Reich, leaving millions of the best Germans to emigrate and become the cultural fertiliser for other countries —this is now our pride. Just as the Jews became the all-embracing world power they are to-day only in their dispersal, so shall we to-day, as the true chosen people of God, become in our dispersal the omnipresent power, the masters of the earth."

It was a period of suspense ; the storm of the 30th June, the German St. Bartholomew's night, was approaching. Indignant at this criminal nonsense, I seized the opportunity not long after of speaking to my friend, who was going abroad as the accredited representative of the Reich, about the consequences of this policy. We walked up and down in the Tiergarten for hours, discussing the possible means of liberating the German people from this adventurer.

It was not long before the party leadership began to show suspicion of me. Hess's head office sent me a telephone message in which I was curtly forbidden to take any further part in problems connected with Germans abroad, above all, the Germans in Poland. Soon after this, a telegram of congratulation which I had sent to the former Chancellor von Papen on the occasion of his famous Marburg speech, was passed on to the party leaders instead. The speech seemed an announcement of a counter-revolution against Hitler, and was greeted with relief by those of us who could see where Hitler was leading the country. Papen was still our great hope. However, I shall return to this later.

I had one further opportunity of speaking on the problem of the Germans abroad. This was shortly before my resignation in the autumn of the same year. A meeting of the representatives of overseas Germandom had concluded their conference with an excursion to Danzig. Most of them were my guests, and it was my function to deliver an address of greeting. I spoke in contradiction to Hitler's opinion, emphasising my view that outside the Reich, only a National Socialism adapted to the particular conditions of Germandom in the country in question was possible. I spoke of my hope of a " purified " National Socialism. The word was understood and placed me on the black books of Berlin. Even the oldest and most respected representatives of our overseas interests capitulated, and went on disputing with the youngsters the honour of being regarded as the most enthusiastic supporters of National Socialism.

One more opportunity I had of acting on behalf of the Germans abroad, at least of those in Eastern Europe. I had just returned from Geneva, where, in the League, the Polish Foreign Minister, Colonel Beck, had publicly repudiated the clauses of the Versailles Treaty safeguarding minority rights—a grave error on the part of Poland. No less a person than Clemenceau himself, in a letter to Paderewski, the first Polish president, had explained that the safeguarding clauses, as an integral part of the Peace Treaty, were a prerequisite for establishing the sovereignty of the new Poland. I spoke at the time to the German Foreign Minister, Baron von Neurath, pointing out the dangers of this development. It was moving in the wrong direction, turning history backwards. Neurath, who was in a position to know better, denied this.

The conversation proved to me that he, too, was prepared to repudiate all treaties and standards of justice as irrelevant in the decisive struggle for power. These minority treaties, he claimed, had hardly benefited even the minorities themselves. He could accomplish more for the Germans in Poland in a few private talks with Beck than all the discussions in the League of Nations. I replied that nevertheless there was value in the mere outlines of a new justice, even if for the present it had no practical results.

I went on to ask if and when Germany intended to return to the League. Neurath shrugged his shoulders and said with a laugh that much water would run under the bridges before that happened.

Chapter XII

A DANGEROUS GAME

BARON VON NEURATH is not a member of that Prussian aristocracy of the sword which is so much decried as lacking all culture, but a representative of South German aristocracy, which is regarded as measuring up to European standards of culture. One day in the spring of 1934 I was invited to lunch with him. With characteristic joviality he slapped me on the shoulder, saying,

" Let it run its course. In five years, no one will remember it."

I had hinted to him my apprehensions that Germany was rushing headlong into a gigantic smash-up. Neurath entirely disagreed. Cheerfully sanguine, he made light of all difficulties and doubts. Was he only pretending optimism, or was he really convinced of an imminent change in affairs ?

The choice in 1934 was between continuation of the revolution and a real restoration of order. Up till then, each man had interpreted the German revolution in the light of his own political aims and desires, but it had become suddenly clear, at least to the thoughtful and intelligent, that this German upheaval really *was* a revolution. But whither was it leading ? Evidently to an indescribable destruction of everything that had hitherto been accepted as the basis of all national and social order. Could we look on any longer with our hands folded ? Was it not necessary to put an end to it and, even at the risk of another *coup*, to drive out the whole gang of brown-shirts ?

But would this be possible without a civil war ? And

could Germany afford civil war at this juncture ? Although the thinking members of Conservative and Liberal circles, of the intelligent middle classes, had begun to understand what they had done by placing Hitler in power, the formerly Socialist masses of the working-class and the black-coated workers were unreservedly in favour of National Socialism. Perhaps, in fact, it was amongst the masses in this very year of 1934 that National Socialism was strongest. Could one, at the moment of the greatest mass popularity of National Socialism, undertake a *coup* to remove Hitler for reasons not understood by the masses ?

These were thoughts which many " anxious patriots " in every political camp shared with me. From the early days of 1934, the desire had been growing to put an end, cost what it might, to the evil spell which must bring Germany to its ruin. But no hope of any feasible solution seemed to offer.

Suddenly the Roehm affair became acute. The *Reichswehr* (the army) understood the dangers threatening it from the new revolutionary nihilism. The army leaders saw, unhappily only from their technical point of view, the imminent disintegration of military discipline, and the extreme dangers of the recently instituted rearmament. Perhaps the *Reichswehr* was ready to put an end to this situation.

I knew Roehm only slightly. In the spring of 1933, soon after the party's accession to power, Forster had introduced us to each other. We had driven out to the Hotel Fasanenhof in Charlottenburg, where Roehm usually stayed when he was in Berlin. We met him with his adjutant, whose bedroom adjoined his. Roehm was dissatisfied. He had not been made a minister. The entire meaning of the National Socialist revolution seemed lost to him.

" We've just beaten up the game for the generals," he grumbled.

Could not Forster use his influence with the Führer on
Roehm's behalf?   The entire National Socialist revolution
would be bogged if the S.A. were not given a public, legal
function, either as militia or as a special corps of the new
army.   He was not inclined to be made a fool of.   At a
later date, I had the opportunity of speaking to him in
greater detail at Kempinski's well-known wine-restaurant in
the Leipzigerstrasse in Berlin, where he usually lunched.
We discussed the new defensive power of the State, and
who ought to command it, who, in fact, ought to create
it, the *Reichswehr* generals or he—Roehm, who had made
the party possible in the first place.   Apart from his special
weakness, Roehm was unquestionably a pleasant companion,
gifted, and a competent organiser, but, generally speaking,
an adventurer whose right place was in the colonies, as
far away from Europe as possible.   In his reproaches
against the *Reichswehr* he was unjust and embittered.   He
resented the arrogant reserve of the *Reichswehr* officers.
Ardently desirous of action, in the consciousness of being
able to accomplish something great, he confided to me in
a few disconnected sentences his dream of the future.   We
were sitting in the great windowed dining-hall.   His scars
were scarlet with excitement.   He had drunk a few glasses
of wine in quick succession.

" Adolf is a swine," he swore.   " He will give us all away.
He only associates with the reactionaries now.   His old
friends aren't good enough for him.   Getting matey with
the East Prussian generals.   They're his cronies now."

He was jealous and hurt.

" Adolf is turning into a gentleman.   He's got himself
a tail-coat now ! " he mocked.

He drank a glass of water and grew calmer.

" Adolf knows exactly what I want.   I've told him often
enough.   Not a second edition of the old imperial army.
Are we revolutionaries or aren't we ?   *Allons, enfants de la*

patrie! If we are, then something new must arise out of our *élan*, like the mass armies of the French Revolution. If we're not, then we'll go to the dogs. We've got to produce something new, don't you see? A new discipline. A new principle of organisation. The generals are a lot of old fogeys. They never have a new idea.

" Adolf has learnt from me. Everything he knows about military matters, I've taught him. War is something more than armed clashes. You won't make a revolutionary army out of the old Prussian N.C.O.'s. But Adolf is and remains a civilian, an ' artist,' an idler. ' Don't bother me,' that's all he thinks. What he wants is to sit on the hilltop and pretend he's God. And the rest of us, who are itching to do something, have got to sit around doing nothing."

He filled his glass, with wine this time, and went on :

" They expect me to hang about with a lot of old pensioners, a herd of sheep. I'm the nucleus of the new army, don't you see that? Don't you understand that what's coming must be new, fresh and unused? The basis must be revolutionary. You can't inflate it afterwards. You only get the opportunity once to make something new and big that'll help us to lift the world off its hinges. But Hitler puts me off with fair words. He wants to let things run their course. He expects a miracle. Just like Adolf! He wants to inherit an army all ready and complete. He's going to let the ' experts ' file away at it. When I hear that word, I'm ready to explode. Afterwards he'll make National Socialists of them, he says. But first he leaves them to the Prussian generals. I don't know where he's going to get his revolutionary spirit from. They're the same old clods, and they'll certainly lose the next war. Don't try to tell me! This is where you're letting the heart of our movement rot."

He was full of abuse of the Prussian officers. Too

scared to put their noses outside the door. Coddled cadets, that had never seen anything but the military academy and the war office. But *he* was a revolutionary, a rebel ! He nearly burst into tears. The restaurant was nearly empty by this time. The adjutant took him away.

I had very little to do with Roehm after that. This outpouring seemed to me, albeit partly inspired by strong drink, to reveal the tragedy of a man who had creative talents of a sort, a man who, in spite of everything, was a rebel, as he himself said, and knew how to die. On Christmas Day, 1933, he deprived me of my rank in the S.A. because I reported the gross insubordination of a highly-placed S.A. leader to General von Brauchitsch, who was at that time O.C. in East Prussia. I saw Roehm only once more, shortly before he was murdered. He ignored me.

I mention all this because a conversation with Hitler in February of 1934 showed me not only the Führer's superiority to his entourage, but also the dangerous game he was playing, a game which, when he was close to being deposed, saved him—at the cost of his friend, it is true—and made him one of the commanders of the newly created army. He seemed to have betrayed the revolutionary ideas of this friend, but it was only a seeming betrayal.

At that time everything was still fluid. Hitler had to adapt the realisation of his " gigantic " plans to the difficult conditions of internal and external politics, and could take only small, cautious steps forward. He therefore felt an uncontrollable craving to assure himself of the greatness of his historical significance by continually returning in discussion to his world-embracing plans. With regard to the current difficulties, Hitler told me he would conclude any pact that would allow Germany an army of four hundred thousand men, or even three hundred and sixty thousand. Then at least he would be rid of this worry, and able to form the core of his future mass army openly, prepared to take the next step without risk on the first politically favourable opportunity.

I guessed from this that he would regard a pact on the German limitation of arms merely as a temporary facility for himself and the army, and not as a permanent regulation. He mentioned the difficulties of keeping such matters secret, and the rapid pace of rearmament. Inevitably the quality would suffer from such speed. He would therefore welcome a temporary pause in armament. He had gradually received the impression that perhaps the responsible generals had " bitten off more than they could chew," and he feared a disaster in case, during the present transformation of the professional army of the *Reichswehr* into a people's militia, the need should arise of defending Germany by force of arms. He had had different plans, plans that would have made it possible for Germany to raise a mass army at once. It would then have been possible, under the protection of this army, to undertake systematic improvement and training according to the gradually increasing demands of modern technique. He had, however, submitted to the judgment of the generals and "the old gentleman" (Hindenburg), who had stubbornly insisted that he was the supreme authority, and the only real expert, and would have the final decision.

I asked whether this plan included the general arming of the S.A. and S.S., and whether it had been definitely discarded.

" This plan is discarded," Hitler replied. " Enthusiasm and willingness are not enough. The arming and equipment of a great army is a serious and difficult problem. My S.A. men are disappointed. They have reproached me in terms which I have had to reject as unjustified. What did they imagine, I asked them. Could I recommend that Germany should have two mutually independent armies ? One might proceed on the principle of calling up men according to age. If this principle were accepted, it could not be arbitrarily forsaken. Or there was the principle of recruiting and voluntary service. My party comrades would surely understand that this principle, which possibly satisfied Britain, was not sufficient for us. And how could I combine the two principles ? Were the party members to give voluntary service and be bound to the army for a specially long period ? Or were all the members of the S.A. to belong to a special military *élite*, or was I to use them as a sort of people's militia ? If so, they would be lacking in the reserves of the regular army, and there would be an incredible amount of confusion. No, I must say the arguments of my S.A. men have not convinced me. I have every intention of keeping to my agreement and my obligations to Hindenburg and the army."

After a pause, Hitler continued :

" The day of the mass army is not past. Germany must return to universal conscription, and as quickly as possible train as a military reserve the classes of men who have not yet served. Of course, in view of the increasing importance of mechanised units, an ever larger part of the army will have to be professional soldiery serving for a long period. But the best of these professional troops cannot be selected on the basis of their revolutionary feeling or their status in the party, but solely on their technical qualifications. I can't seriously be expected to draw the material for my military *élite* from the bow-legged and knock-kneed S.A ! I couldn't do so even if I separated the S.A. reserve and the active S.A. men ! "

It was not difficult to recognise in this the arguments of the army leaders who were resisting Roehm's aspirations.

" The revolutionary feeling," Hitler continued, " which is so much on the lips of some of our party comrades, who seem to think they have a monopoly of it, is in fact a decisive factor, the importance of which I shall never overlook.

We cannot simply take up the pre-war traditions where we left them. In accordance with our doctrines, we must create something entirely new. If the army leadership were to continue artifically to shut itself off from the National Socialist spirit, I should certainly not tolerate it. In that case, I should intervene at the proper moment. But for the present it is necessary to master the technical problems. They must not be complicated by other questions."

Hitler seemed to be reasoning with himself :

" You mustn't be impatient. I have really every reason to be impatient myself, but I suppress the feeling. For yourselves you make things easy, but for me you make them hard," he quoted unconsciously from the *Meistersinger*. Then he lost himself in the greatness of his task, which would not end with the creation of a vast army and the production of the required armaments. The spirit alone was the decisive factor, the spirit of unity, which filled officers as well as men. It would all be incomplete and soon decay again if he did not succeed in imbuing the new army with the new, revolutionary spirit. He would therefore never renounce the thought of making the army the carriers of the same ideas as the party. The spirit of the army was the essence of the people's mass spirit. There must be no contradictions here. He would sooner have a technically imperfect instrument with the right enthusiasm than a technically flawless one which lacked soul and spirit.

" But," he added, " I shall attain what I consider indispensable by slow and determined degrees. We shall see which of us has the tougher will and the greater patience, the generals or myself. My aim is to get a specially trained and technically first-rate corps, shock troops consisting of long-serving party comrades, which will at the same time represent the National Socialist spirit in the national

defence. The mass of the conscripts, on the other hand,
will sink more and more to the level of second-rate troops
with the function of a well-trained militia whose essential
task will be defensive. The road is difficult and circum-
stantial. I must walk it because we have something more
to establish than the army alone. But I shall never renounce
the aim of firmly incorporating it in the National Socialist
state as its strongest member outside the party itself."

Hitler's judgment was not always so detached and
moderate. Three months later, in the closest circles of
the party leadership in Berlin, I heard the demand being
raised for an exclusively National Socialist professional
army. Without it, National Socialism ran the risk of being
crowded out by reaction. I was told that Hitler made
assertions which completely contradicted what I have just
quoted. The new army must be built, he said, from purely
National Socialist elements. He could grant no monopoly
to the old *Reichswehr*. In the preparation of universal
conscription, it would be necessary firmly to resist all the
attempts of the reaction to seize control of the army, and
thereby of Germany. The subtle plans of the reaction
were now clear. By way of universal conscription, the
party was to be compelled to disband the S.A. and S.S.
The party would then be defenceless, and handed over for
good or evil to the generals.

If Hitler had really said this, then it plainly showed the
influence of the men round Roehm, and the fact that the
internal crisis had become acute. It meant that they had
torn him out of his lethargy. Later I heard Hitler in
person, in the course of a visit I paid him in company with
other Reich leaders. Hitler was on the point of dismissing
us, but was still deep in his explanations.

" It is madness," he said violently, " to attempt to
make revolutionary wars with a reactionary army."

Evidently he had accepted the opposition of his entourage,

and constituted himself its radical mouthpiece—a thread-bare tactic that he loved, and by which he had repeatedly circumvented troublesome objections.

" I shall refuse to approve the plan for universal conscription. The German people is at the present stage incapable of satisfying the needs of conscription without jeopardising the constructive work of National Socialism."

Without previous National Socialist training, Hitler insisted, indiscriminate arming of the German people would be well-nigh a crime. A professional army must first be created, and none but the party organisations might be called upon to complete it. If he was told that these organisations lacked the necessary training, then he replied that revolutionary *élan* was worth twice as much as lifeless military drill.

He Leads Us into Destruction

What had happened to cause Hitler, driven into a corner, to speak the language of the radicals in the party ? Evidently the crisis had sharpened. A decision was unavoidable. But what was Hitler's aim ? Was he simply drifting with the tide ? Was he not the man he made himself out to be ? The more the broad masses began to believe in Hitler, the deeper grew the doubts of the old revolutionary guard. Was this the National Socialist revolution ?

" Hitler dead would be more valuable to the movement than Hitler alive," was the sentiment beginning to circulate among the initiates.

" Away with the clown ! " cried the radicals. There were demands for the second revolution, the true revolution. Hitler was only the precursor, the St. John, of the movement. The true leader was still to come. Was his name Roehm ? Just as Lenin and the true Russian revolution followed Kerensky, so perhaps Hitler was merely the soon-to-be-

forgotten precursor of the real German revolution that was
still to come.

Hitler must be removed, some said. Hitler must be
kidnapped, rescued from the claws of his reactionary
friends, said others. In the spring of 1934 the danger of
reaction became intensified.

" Unless Adolf breaks through, he's finished," the S.A.
were saying.

" Adolf belongs to us ! " clamoured those who still felt
some loyalty for him. There was perhaps no one with less
popularity among the revolutionary S.A. than Adolf Hitler.

But was he any more fortunate with his " reactionary "
friends ? That same spring I had addressed a group of
heavy industry magnates at the Essen Mining Syndicate
(*Essener Bergwerksverein*), and at a social gathering after the
meeting I found them in the blackest depression regarding
the political situation. The general complaint in private
conversation was : " He's leading us to ruin." Some
time later the present Commander-in-Chief, General von
Brauchitsch, was in Danzig as my guest. On a visit to the
German Consul-General, he spoke of his serious apprehensions about the general situation. In the interests of
the state, the army could no longer tolerate it, and would
seek unqualified changes.

Hitler was isolated.

What, actually, was the aim of the second National
Socialist revolution ? Hitler knew his party members
very well.

" There are people," he said, " who believe that Socialism
means simply their chance to share the spoils, to do business
and live a comfortable life."

Unhappily, this conception had not died out with the
Weimar Republic. He had no intention, like Russia, of
" liquidating " the possessing class. On the contrary, he
would compel it to contribute by its abilities towards the

building up of the new order. He could not afford to
allow Germany to vegetate for years, as Russia had done, in
famine and misery. Besides, the present owners of property
would be thankful that their lives had been spared. They
would be dependent and in a condition of permanent fear
of worse things to come. He had no intention of changing
this practical arrangement for the sake of continual bickering
with so-called old soldiers and over-ardent party members.

Hitler had told me this in connection with a discussion
on the raising of a " structure of graded ranks " (*ständischer
Aufbau*), an abortive effort to build up a corporative economy
and constitution which Hitler very soon relinquished.

He knew perfectly well that every phase of a revolution
meant a new set of rulers. The flood-tide of a second revolution would wash new men to the top. Would it not mean
the end of Hitler and his immediate associates ? Was it
at all possible to keep the reins in one's hands, once the
revolt of the proletarian masses was unchained ? In spite
of his armchair battles, Hitler was afraid of the masses.
He was afraid of his own people.

" Irresponsible elements are at work to destroy all my
constructive labours," he said. " But I shall not allow
my work to be shattered either by the Right or the Left."

He gave out that treacherous elements within the party,
agents of Moscow and of the German *bourgeois* Nationalists,
were together plotting the " second " National Socialist
revolution in order to overthrow him.

He had received information that Roehm had intentions of kidnapping him—a suspicion which kept cropping
up every time Hitler hesitated to strike at the right moment.
On the other hand, it was certain that he must eventually
—unless his antagonists were exceptionally stupid—have
become the secret captive of the Conservative circles, to be
employed as the taskmaster of the revolutionaries, the
tamer of that wild beast " the masses."

Hitler for a long time felt tempted to place himself at the head of the radicals of his party and demand a second revolution, thereby retaining at least a semblance of leadership, and possibly even regaining, after some time, the real leadership. Intense struggles for power were at that time going on in the inner circles, very little of which ever came to the ears of the public. But it is to be assumed that the outcome was not an accidental one. For it proved that Hitler, in his insight and his far-sightedness, is infinitely superior not only to his party clique, but also to his Conservative opponents and the leaders of the *Reichswehr*.

DISSOLUTION OR OPEN REVOLT?

In the background, one man was waiting : Gregor Strasser, Hitler's great antagonist within the party. Once again the same alignment took place as in the autumn and winter of 1932, when the party was threatened with a split, when General von Schleicher conceived his plan to make the trade unions and the social wing of the National Socialist movement the mass foundations of his government. This solution, premature in 1932 and distasteful to the big industrialists, seemed now, after the universal muddle created in a year and a half of the National Socialist regime, the only possible alternative both to a fierce revolution of the S.A. and the sterile mass demagogy of Hitler. It would have provided the permanent form of a new constitution, supported by the *Reichswehr*.

Everything happened again exactly as in 1932 : the contemptible cowardice of the National Socialist civil servants, who tried to find cover in every direction, and the sentimental speeches of Hitler's inner circle, proclaiming eternal loyalty to the Führer. " Hard times are coming. We must remain true. Perhaps we shall have to start from the bottom again." The same thing in 1934 as in 1932.

The indolence and softness Hitler displayed betrayed the questionable greatness of the " leader." Was this really the heaven-sent liberator of Germany ? A man who complained of the ingratitude of the German people in the sobbing tones of a down-at-heel music-hall performer ! A weakling who accused and sulked, appealed and implored, and retired in wounded vanity ("—if the German people don't want me ! ") instead of acting.

The same thing had happened during the critical winter of 1932-33, and now we had it once more, with a slightly different colouring, as a premonition of the great decision to come.

In Danzig and in most of Northern Germany, Gregor Strasser had always been more esteemed than Hitler himself. Hitler's nature was incomprehensible to the North German. The big, broad Strasser, on the other hand, a hearty eater and a hearty drinker too, slightly self-indulgent, practical, clear-headed, quick to act, lacking bombast and bathos, with a sound peasant judgment : this was a man we could all understand.

I had been present at the last meeting of leaders before our seizure of power, in Weimar, in the autumn of 1932. Gregor Strasser gave the meeting its character. Hitler was lost in a sea of despondency and accusations on the top of the Obersalzberg. The party's position was desperate. Strasser was calm, and with assurance and quiet confidence, succeeded in quenching the feeling that the party was at its last gasp. It was he who led the party. To all practical purposes, Hitler had abdicated.

Was not the position essentially the same as that of 1932 and 1933 ? The difference was merely that Roehm now stood on the one hand, preparing his radical revolt, but on the other, in the background, Strasser, the potential successor, the exiled, the disgraced, the hated rival. Hitler knew that if he took Roehm's side, the *Reichswehr* would restore Strasser and split the party. Strasser, the man who had spoken of the anti-capitalist nostalgia of the German people, would return and, together with Conservative, Liberal and Socialist sympathisers, create the new order in Germany. Positions were reversed : Hitler, the friend of heavy industry, became the rebel, the street-corner agitator of proletarian mass revolution, while Strasser, the anti-capitalist, became the friend of generals.

Hitler made his decision. He made it out of hate and jealousy. The 30th June broke. He struck down more than the rebellious S.A. He struck down General von Schleicher. He struck down Gregor Strasser.

CHAPTER XIII

PAST THE CIVIL WAR

THE blood-bath might have been greater. A secret plot had been made to murder Hitler and place the blame for his death on the middle class. This was to be the signal for a real " night of long knives."

It is a matter of indifference whether Roehm had really intended a " betrayal," or had merely played with the idea of a second revolution, and then dropped it. It was a repetition of the Wallenstein* tragedy in the new German gangster republic. Nevertheless, there was something of genuine tragedy in the dark events of June 30th, when more than a thousand party members were shot without trial, and many others, innocent of any crime, were simply murdered. The speech by which Hitler tried publicly before the Reichstag to justify his act was in every detail an unprecedented collection of falsehoods and abominations. It was this " justification " which turned an act of qualified self-defence into a crime. True, it silenced the opposition, but at the same time it inflicted a wound that has never since ceased to fester and to poison the life of the people.

A few days after this speech, I had to see Hitler on a matter—of merely passing interest—concerning Danzig. Others present at the meeting were Schwerin-Krosigk, the Minister of Finance, von Neurath, the Foreign Minister, and Forster, the Danzig *Gauleiter*.

" Why don't you let the poor man get some rest ? " Neurath asked, unwilling that Hitler should be disturbed at this juncture. However, the conference did take place,

---

* Famous German general of the Thirty Years' War, murdered by some of his officers.—Translator's note.

and it was evident that it was not Hitler who had been
defeated in the recent conflict. The two *bourgeois* Conservative Reich ministers were anxiously servile in their
manner towards the Reich Chancellor. This was something
very different from the once much-contemned fawning on
the former monarch. This was abject fear of the hangman.
A friend of mine, a high official of one of the ministries,
had warned me when I talked to him about the chaotic
state of affairs, in which there seemed no hope of a solution.

" For heaven's sake be careful," he begged me. " The
walls have ears."

Fear stalked the corridors of the Foreign Department—
fear of fresh violence, of the outbreak of open revolution,
of the sudden shots of the Gestapo. Every time a door was
suddenly opened the staff saw on the threshold their
potential executioners, ready to shoot them down without
a word. They were all conscious of the same guilt, at
least in thought and desire. They had all had the same
hope concerning this sallow-faced man who roared at them
ferociously and never wanted to listen, but only to lecture
others. They all hoped that at last they were to be delivered
from him. And then, instead of hope, came this deep fear
and restraint. What would become of the individual,
what would become of Germany ? Hitler had given orders,
through his closest intimates, that no mention must be made
of what had happened to von Schleicher and his other
bourgeois Nationalist opponents, otherwise he would at once
proceed to open revolution. Those circles which had
forced him to mete out bloody justice, instead of allowing
him time to settle matters peaceably, according to his wish,
would then bear the responsibility for Germany's destruction in civil war, and her occupation by hostile foreign
troops.

All this I heard less in outspoken words than in whispers
and stammers. Everyone felt that the 30th June had been

no solution. And "the old gentleman," Hindenburg, already too aged to have a clear conception of things, the hand of death already descending upon him, " stood by " in East Prussia, waiting for his end.

They had all disappeared like rats in their holes, all these Nationalist opponents who only a few days before had been importantly discussing their plans to overthrow the government, and had already distributed Cabinet posts and instituted proceedings against the embezzlers of public funds.

" Don't expose yourself and us to ruin," I was implored by friends in Berlin with whom, only a few weeks earlier, I had discussed the reconstruction of Germany—with whom, to put it bluntly, I had conspired. Many people refused to receive visitors, and lived in retirement. Whoever was able to do so travelled, concealed himself, slept every night in a different place.

The most difficult thing to understand was the attitude of the army. They had got their wish : Roehm was removed. The independence of the *Reichswehr* was assured. That was enough for them. They had no use for civil unrest. They reserved the right to make a special investigation into the shooting of the two generals, von Schleicher, the former Reich Chancellor, and von Bredow. They allowed their one opportunity of shaking off the National Socialist yoke to go by. Without political insight, uncertain and vacillating in everything except their military calling, they were anxious to return as quickly as possible to ordered and regular activities. This failure of the high officials and officers, and also of the big industrial and agricultural interests, was symptomatic of their further attitude. They were no longer capable of any statesmanlike action. In every crisis, they would again be in the opposition, but would always recoil before the final step, the overthrow of the regime.

With his peculiar intuitive gifts, Hitler at once sensed the vacillation of his *bourgeois* antagonists. But at first he too had little of the demeanour of a victor. With swollen, distorted features, he sat opposite me as I made my report. His eyes were lifeless. He did not look at me, but sat playing with his fingers. I had the impression that he was not listening. At length, however, after asking me one or two questions, he made his decision along the lines I suggested. All the time, I felt that disgust, weariness and contempt filled his mind, and that his thoughts were far away.

After we had taken our leave, he suddenly recalled Forster and myself.

"Just a moment, Rauschning," he said, in a clearer tone, as though he were just rousing himself. Then to Forster, "Just a moment, I want to ask you something more."

I wondered what he was going to say, but it was soon evident that all he wanted was not to be left alone.

"Tell me more about Danzig. Have you got rid of your unemployment? How is the new motor road doing? Are you getting on all right with the Poles?"

Forster cut me short, and complacently related all that had been done, and all that could be done if only Danzig had not such currency difficulties. Hitler made an effort to seem interested, but I could see that he was not listening at all. His eyes were expressionless, and gazed fixedly into the distance. Then he looked at the floor. Forster had finished with a question, but there was no reply. A pause ensued.

Hitler rose and began to walk up and down. Some time before this, he had transferred his office to a large new room, hung with tapestries and paintings; here he paced the long floor-space between the door and his desk, his hands clapsed behind him.

There were rumours that since the bloody occurrence he had been able to sleep only in snatches. At night he prowled restlessly up and down. Sleeping tablets either did not help, or he would not take them, for fear of being poisoned. It was alleged that he had started out of his short, uneasy sleep in convulsive fits of weeping, and had been sick repeatedly. Wrapped in blankets, and shaking with ague, he had remained sitting in a chair, believing he was poisoned. One moment he wanted everything lit up and the rooms full of people, and the next he could not bear to see anyone, fearing even his most intimate friends. The only one whose company he still tolerated was Hess. Buch, the executioner, was said to inspire him with a positive horror, but he dared not show it. As a matter of fact, his nerves had, it was alleged, completely deserted him at the crucial moment, and everything had been done without his knowledge, though in his name. For a long time he had not known the whole terrible truth, and even then was not informed as to the full extent of the executions.

" I am determined to pursue the absolutely legal path, and no one shall persuade me otherwise," he now began his self-justification. " All the representations that were made to me, all the difficulties ahead of us—I saw them long before these officious pessimists did, and made allowance for them. I have not been surprised by anything that has happened. With the same unalterable certainty, I shall attain the gigantic aims of our revolution. I don't need the assistance of critics and busybodies who want to make their own licentiousness the law of our development. These people take pleasure in prophesying to me daily the certain shipwreck of our movement, and in exaggerating the difficulties inherent in the initial stages of every great achievement. They would encourage me and themselves in our difficult struggle much more by emphasising the positive instead of the negative side of our great work. I know far better

than they that we have not the power yet. But *my* will is
the final one. Whoever fails to obey my orders will be
destroyed. Nor shall I wait until their insubordination is
already evident to all the world. I shall strike as soon as
I have so much as a suspicion of their disobedience. Firm
and unwavering, I shall continue on my path."

Hitler gave himself up to such generalities for some time.
Suddenly his mood changed.

" With the old gentleman at death's door, these criminals
make such difficulties for me ! " he cried indignantly. " At
a time when it is so important to decide on the successor
to the Reich presidency, when the choice lies between
myself and one of the reactionary crowd ! For this alone
these people deserve to be shot. Have I not emphasised
time and time again that only the inviolable unity of our
will can lead our venture to success ? Anyone who gets
out of step will be shot. Have I not implored these people
ten, a hundred, times to follow me ? At a moment when
everything depends on the party's being a single, close
entity, I must listen to the reactionaries taunting me with
the inability to keep order and discipline in my own house !
I must accept the accusation that the party is a hotbed of
insubordination, worse than the Communists ! I must
hear them say that matters are at a worse pass than they
were under Brüning and Papen ! I must listen to *their*
ultimatum—these cowards and poltroons !   I, I ! " he
screamed.

" But they're mistaken," he went on in a quieter tone.
" I am by no means at the end, as they think. They're
all mistaken. They underestimate me because I have
risen from below, from the ' lower depths ' ; because I
haven't had an education, because I haven't the ' manners '
that their sparrow brains think right ! If I were one of
them, I suppose I should be a great man, even now. But I
don't need them to assure me of my historical greatness.

The insubordination of my S.A. has deprived me of a great many trump cards. But I hold plenty of others. I am in no embarrassment because of an occasional stroke of bad luck. The foul plan of these men will not succeed. They can't pass over me when the old gentleman dies. They can't put up anyone as vice-regent without my consent. And I will not give it to them. The people don't want a Hohenzollern monarchy. Only *I* could induce them to accept it. Only *I* could make them believe that a monarchy is necessary. But I *will not* do it. They're at their wits' end, these miserable busybodies, these second-rate clerks. Have you noticed how they tremble before me, how anxiously they try to please ?

" I have spoiled their plans. They thought I would not dare ; they thought I was afraid. They saw me already wriggling in their net. They thought I was their tool. And behind my back they laughed at me and said I had no power now, that I had lost my party. I saw through all that long ago. I've given them a cuff on the ear that they'll long remember. What I have lost in the trial of the S.A. I shall regain by the verdict on these feudal gamblers and professional card-sharpers, the Schleichers and company.

" If I call on the people to-day, they will follow me. If I appeal to the party, it will respond, more closely knit than ever. They will not succeed in splitting my party. I have destroyed the ringleaders, as well as the potential ringleaders that have been lying in ambush. They have tried to estrange me from the party in order to make me a weak-willed tool in their hands. But I stand here stronger than ever before. Forward, Messrs. Papen and Hugenberg ! I am ready for the next round."

It was thus that Hitler kept his courage up. He dismissed us—a man who had just dosed himself with the morphine of his own verbiage.

THE SECOND REVOLUTION

Hitler had prophesied correctly. His great *coup* was successful. He became the successor of Hindenburg, who died in Neudeck in August—died too soon, or too late. Few know what lies behind the army's oath of allegiance to Hitler. I am not one of those few. Before the removal of Hindenburg's body to the Tannenberg war memorial, I saw it lying in Neudeck on a plain iron bedstead, in a small simply-furnished room. Neudeck was a modest example of the East Prussian manor-house as I had known it from my childhood. How different from the clamorous objectivity of the modern building, or the self-indulgent luxury of the new rulers ! It was the same type of country house as Kadinen, one of the favourite seats of the former Kaiser. Family traditions bound me to the Neudeck estate, my great-grandfather having returned from the Napoleonic wars more than a century ago as an adjutant of the brigade of von Beneckendorf and von Hindenburg. I had been received in audience by the aged Field-Marshal early that same year in Berlin. His memory was beginning to fail him, and at times he did not recognise his visitors. I myself found him unusually well, and we had a long conversation about Danzig.

That summer at Neudeck, already doomed, he had still on occasion been cheerful and in good spirits. A Japanese prince who visited him was still able to amuse him with stories of exotic customs. He could laugh and make innocent jokes—something of which his Reich Chancellor Hitler was incapable. He had received Hitler's report on the executions of the 30th June, and thought everything had been dealt with in the most satisfactory way. He had even consoled Hitler when the latter complained of the difficulty of his task. There could be no birth without blood, he told him. And the new, great German Reich could not be born without the spilling of some blood.

On his death-bed, between the lucid moments and the fancies of the dying Field-Marshal, something must have happened which we do not yet know. One thing is certain : Hindenburg died with the command to his successor to reinstate the Hohenzollern dynasty. He could imagine a secure future for Germany only under the guidance of the old, hereditary dynasty which had won the mastery of Germany through a consistent, historical development.

His son Oskar greeted me after my final view of the old Field-Marshal. There was no time for anything but the most perfunctory salutations. The property was closely guarded by the S.S.

I attended the funeral ceremony at Tannenberg, and noted the execrable taste of the funeral oration, which Hitler concluded with the blasphemous suggestion that the aged and devout Christian was entering Valhalla.

Hitler had succeeded. The second revolution was postponed, but he was the master of Germany, and increasingly tightened his hold.

Shortly after the funeral, Hitler spoke in a circle of his intimates, about the second revolution, and his views were circulated among the initiated members of the party. It was in this way that they came to my ears ; I was not present at Hitler's private celebration of his official recognition as " Führer " of the German Reich.

" My Socialism," he is reported to have said, " is not the same thing as Marxism. My Socialism is not class war, but order. Whoever imagines Socialism as revolt and mass demagogy is not a National Socialist. Revolution is not games for the masses. Revolution is hard work. The masses see only the finished product, but they are ignorant, and should be ignorant, of the immeasurable amount of hidden labour that must be done before a new step forward can be taken. The revolution cannot be ended. It can never be ended. We are motion itself, we are eternal

revolution. We shall never allow ourselves to be held down
to one permanent condition."

What he had done, he said, would remain incomprehensible to many people. But he had been justified by
success. Within six weeks, his opponents in the party had
already been shown that the events of June 30th were
necessary and correct.

" Externally," he went on, and these, I was told, were
his exact words, " I end the revolution. But internally it
goes on, just as we store up our hate, and think of the day
on which we shall cast off the mask, and stand revealed
as those we are and eternally shall remain."

He was not yet, he continued, in a position to tell them
all that he had in mind. But they could rest assured that
Socialism, as the Party understood it, was not concerned
with the happiness of the individual, but with the greatness
and future of the whole people. It was an heroic Socialism
—the community of solemnly sworn brothers-in-arms
having no individual possessions, but sharing everything
in common.

But the first task was to create order, to re-arm and
prepare for the war that was unavoidable, and that meant
the bringing about of the best possible social and economical conditions for preparedness for battle. The German system from thenceforth would be that of the fortified military
camp, and all thoughts of self and private needs must go.

" And," he added, " the S.A. must prepare for a period
of purgatory. But the time is coming when I shall fully
recompense it and restore it to the highest honours. Because they too," and at this point his voice is alleged to
have been choked with sobs, " they too have died for the
greatness of our movement. They wanted everything for
the best, but in their own stubborn way. Therefore they
were doomed to err, and succumbed to the verdict under
which all those must fall who do not learn to obey."

CHAPTER XIV

A NEW SOCIAL ORDER, A NEW ECONOMY

HITLER'S conception of a social and economic order for the German people was something quite different from a permanent " military camp order." That is, if he had any conception at all. At all events, the party propagandists had orders to expound a National Socialist programme, and Feder, the civil engineer, was ordered to publish official pamphlets, one of which outlined the " structure of graded classes " in the Third Reich. Soon after the party's accession to power, the wildest plans were set afoot to " order " the country's economy. The promising slogan " The good of all before the good of one " was in the opinion of some, to inaugurate the establishment of an economic system in which the economic usefulness of the individual subject was to be as far as possible eliminated. Others believed that by State management of the country's economy, an equalisation of interests would follow because the true function of economy would be seen to lie in the satisfaction of the needs of State and people, and not of the individual.

More easily said than done. Did this mean the corporative state ? Did it mean totalitarian planned economy ? Or was it state socialism ? The first necessity was to act. The aim would then gradually define itself. So an enormous amount of organisation was begun on all sides. The highly developed and sensitive organism of German economy was broken into by people who had no knowledge whatever of organisation, and all conception of order was turned topsy-turvy. This feverish organising called forth revolt on every side.

In agriculture, the difficulties were not too great. Also, though there was still a partial free market system, the " Reich working-class " could, up to a point, realise the ideas of a corporative order. But the moment trade, the professions and industry were touched, there arose an impenetrable tangle of difficulties. What was the real aim ? What was meant by " an economy of bare essentials " (*Bedarfsdeckungswirtschaft*) ? One was faced by phrases and slogans which, when analysed, suddenly dissolved in mist.

But there were other people, intelligent and quite realist, who found that certain machinery was being created in the " class " organisations of the country's economy by means of which a considerable influence could be exerted on industrial undertakings. This " structure of graded classes " was the most suitable instrument for the control of economy. It would not do, these people maintained, to allow the national economy to become one great body, self-determining according to its own needs. In that case, it would even more than heretofore absorb and put itself in the place of the State. If that was the meaning of the corporative state, then National Socialism could have nothing to do with it. No, not the organisation, but the control of economy ; the subordination of economy to the guidance of the National Socialist party : this was the aim of these people, who recognised no specific economic laws, but held that the national economy could without harm be made subject to rules independent of its own terms of reference. To these people, the " structure of graded classes " was a means of gaining control. The only organisation they were interested in was that of an instrument of control over economy.

Unquestionably the prevalence of unemployment did make some sort of intervention in industry necessary. But could this really increase production ? Were these measures not merely temporary ? But if the purpose of organisation

was not the increase of production and the internal adjust-
ment of the various branches of economy, but, on the
contrary, the subordination of economy to the State, or possibly
even to a mere party, what became of economy itself?

In Danzig, too, we had these problems to deal with on
a smaller scale. Here, too, an immense amount of organising was being done. I personally thought it possible to
develop new forms of a certain degree of protectionism
that would have improved our situation with regard to the
Poles. In fact, I was not averse to the idea of a really
corporative state and a new type of mercantilism. Forster,
on the other hand, was ambitious to be the first to complete
the graded class structure in order to gain Hitler's praise.
He sent for one of the young men engaged in this field, no
other, in fact, than the author of the above-mentioned
pamphlet about the " structure of graded classes." The
young man arrived in Danzig with a bodyguard of five
companions, ready to lay the foundation-stone of his life-
work.

In the meantime, it soon became evident that Danzig
was the least promising place for economic experiments,
since a seaport with international shipping, and without a
customs department of its own, did best in allowing its
economy to develop as freely as possible, and in avoiding
complications and regulations which could only cause
foreign shipping to be withdrawn to some more favourable
port. I saw, therefore, that the best thing we could do was
to put the whole " graded class structure " on the shelf.

This gave rise to a serious conflict with the party, all
the more since the whole elaborate plan of the new economic order had no other effect than that of simply
subordinating economy to the orders of the party.

I refused to accept this as binding. There were a great
many complaints on every side, and Hess, Hitler's deputy,
summoned me to an interview. In his laconic fashion,

which gives an impression of profound thoughtfulness, but is in reality nothing more than the diffidence and uncertainty of an immature mind, Hess could find no solution, merely uttering a few mild reproofs. Eventually I was sent for to speak to Hitler.

" What's your trouble ? " he asked. When I explained to him my apprehensions as to this type of economic order, he was amazed. He had not the slightest intention of encouraging this nonsense. Did not Forster know that he had long since discarded the " structure of graded classes " ? I replied that I had known nothing of that either ; if I had, it would have spared me much trouble and needless annoyance. Hitler, in his characteristic fashion, at once plunged into a self-justification of his decision, and in this connection outlined along general lines his creed of Socialist ideas, a topic on which at that time he was very fluent.

" Do you intend to repudiate the corporative system of economy altogether ?" I asked.

" At the present time I can see no meaning in this term at all," he returned. "And I am convinced you cannot either. Mussolini has for years been working at the realisation of a new economic order which he calls by this name. But he has got no further. That is to say, he has not yet found the essential, crowning principle, the keystone supporting the arch. You know, it's not a good idea to try to force such things. One should never build elaborate structures. These things must grow, and what's more, they must grow up from below. If you construct something from above, it will be a dead body that never fills with life-blood. Do you know how an artist creates ? In the same way the statesman must allow not only his own thoughts to mature, but even more the driving forces of the nation itself. He may stimulate here and there, he may regulate and guide the forces, and he may even shut them all down again if he sees that the true forces have not yet arisen. But he cannot artificially bring forth anything. Nothing is more false than to cloak an immature nation with plans from above, however well-thought-out they may be. There is only one thing that can be done, and that is to keep alive the creative unrest that holds the true artist in constant tension. This must never be allowed to become stunted."

" Then the graded class structure, or the corporative state, or whatever you want to call it," I replied, " is, according to your statement, not mature enough to be realised yet. But surely the present state of chaos cannot remain either ? "

" Brooding over these matters is of no use," Hitler returned. " No matter what you attempt, if an idea is not yet mature, you will not be able to realise it. I know that as an artist, and I know it as a statesman. Then there is only one thing to do : have patience, wait, try again, wait again. In the subconscious, the work goes on. It matures, sometimes it dies. Unless I have the inner, incorruptible conviction : *this is the solution*, I do nothing. Not even if the whole party tried to drive me to action. I will not act ; I will wait, no matter what happens. But if the voice speaks, then I know the time has come to act.

" The same thing applies to the party members, to the people. If they do not understand a measure, then it must be dropped. It will have to be tried again later, continually tried again. The right time will arrive in the end. They will grasp it, carry it out, as though they had never had any other intention.

" Naturally," he went on, " I had to allow the party to become familiar with the theory of graded classes. I had to discover experimentally just how mature it was, and whether it could be carried any further at this juncture. I shall never act according to preconceived ideas. It is a matter of course that before I put something into practice, I must convince myself that it is feasible. And I must have men who will carry it out. For example, I have given my party comrades a task to perform. Very well ; if they can master it, then they are the right men for it ; if not, others must do it. But if I find no one, then this too is an un-mistakable sign that the time is not yet ripe.

" There is a rigid relation between a problem and the men to solve it. If the men are not available, then the problem has not yet matured, and the time is not ripe. It is no use calling for a ' strong man ' then. But if the time is ripe, the men will also be found. I cannot realise my ideas without the men for the job.

" In these last months," he concluded complacently, " I have not been able to find the men to give the graded class theory its suitable form in practice. Very well, then—we must postpone the task, and return to it on another occasion."

The time seemed to me ripe, I interjected, to attempt some sort of synthesis between free, economic liberalism and a totally controlled Bolshevik economy.

" Is there such a thing ? " Hitler inquired. " Don't allow yourself to be deceived by cut-and-dried theories. Certainly I know less to-day about these matters than I thought I knew a few years ago."

It seemed to me that an aimless organisational fever was less likely to dispel confusion than a preliminary serious theoretical examination.

Hitler grew impatient.

" Can't you remember," he said, " that I must keep the people occupied ? They all want to help. They are filled with glowing enthusiasm. I must offer them something. Very well, let them try their hand. The graded class structure, after all, is not so important that they can do much harm in it. Something useful is bound to result from all this activity."

What then did all his previous explanations mean ?

That there was no intention of finding a new economic order for Germany by experiment, but only a desire to keep the mass of the party members occupied, and their attention turned away from more important matters? Certainly not. The motives behind Hitler's policy and his personal decisions are always of a complex nature. Without a doubt one very strong reason for the re-organisation of the national economy was the desire to distract the party's attention. But it would be a mistake to regard this as the only reason, though Hitler's memory had indeed the quality of retaining only those motives which might later serve him well as a means of self-interpretation.

In this connection I might mention that Hitler has never occupied himself with the minor details of a problem, with two exceptions : foreign policy and the army. What is known as the mastery of material was quite unimportant to him. He quickly became impatient if the details of a problem were brought to him. He was greatly averse to " experts " and had little regard for their opinions. He looked upon them as mere hacks, as brush-cleaners and colour-grinders, to use the terms of his own trade.

" You must keep free of red tape," he advised me on this same occasion. " You have other people to attend to such things. You must keep your vision clear. Very evidently you pay too much attention to details. You mustn't fall into the unhappy habit of the former Chancellor Brüning, who prepared every law for publication with his own hands. So typical of the man ! That's why he had no strength left for great decisions. Don't lose yourself in the false ambition to deal with details. Don't formulate the laws yourself."

I replied that I had indeed worked in detail on the laws planned for the " graded class order," since the matter became decisive and dangerous only in its details. I could not see how that could be avoided if one was not to be entirely dependent on the experts, and in the end was reduced to making decisions on an emotional basis.

"That is exactly what you should do," Hitler interrupted with animation. "Trust your instincts, your feelings, or whatever you like to call them. Never trust your knowledge. Let me tell you one thing : the experts never have the true instinct. You must never seek it in them, but only in yourself, and in your party comrades. The more you talk to your party comrades, the more things become clear to you, too, the more they are simplified. You must think more clearly, more simply, when you try to explain something to a party comrade. You must get rid of all complicated, learned expressions. That is the salutary effect of our constant interchange of ideas with party comrades, with the people themselves—not with delegates who are strangers to the people, as in the democracies. Experts are caught in their routine like the spider in its web, incapable of spinning anything but eternally the same web. To them you must simply give orders, and you will see how, quite suddenly, they will bring you an entirely different plan from their original one. Experts are always capable of thinking something diametrically opposed to their first opinion. In short, if we are in earnest about it, we shall find that the experts will always provide us with the material we require."

I must confess that I was disappointed at Hitler's stubborn rejection of any discussion of details, since it was just the details that I felt were important. But evidently the whole question of the "graded class structure" no longer interested Hitler. A decision one way or the other was not to be had from him. This was not the first time that, when difficulties arose, he simply pushed aside everything he had just planned, and lost all interest in the pile of wreckage that remained behind. He ignored all difficulties that threatened to be troublesome to him, and refused to be reminded of them.

Once more it was his gift of simplification, which he himself pointed out as his special characteristic, that proved his superiority to his entourage.

EXECUTOR OF MARXISM

" I am not only the conqueror, but also the executor of Marxism—of that part of it that is essential and justified, stripped of its Jewish-Talmudic dogma."

I had asked Hitler whether the crux of the whole economic problem was not the extent to which private economic interests might continue to be the motive force of the national economy. There were party members who passionately denied the possibility of this, and expected a more radical social revolution than moderate Marxism, at any rate, had ever intended.

"I have learnt a great deal from Marxism, as I do not hesitate to admit," Hitler went on. " I don't mean their tiresome social doctrine or the materialist conception of history, or their absurd ' marginal utility ' theories and so on. But I have learnt from their methods. The difference between them and myself is that I have really put into practice what these peddlers and pen-pushers have timidly begun. The whole of National Socialism is based on it. Look at the workers' sports clubs, the industrial cells, the mass demonstrations, the propaganda leaflets written specially for the comprehension of the masses ; all these new methods of political struggle are essentially Marxist in origin. All I had to do was to take over these methods and adapt them to our purpose. I had only to develop logically what Social Democracy repeatedly failed in because of its attempt to realise its evolution within the framework of democracy. National Socialism is what Marxism might have been if it could have broken its absurd and artificial ties with a democratic order."

" But surely," I objected, " what you are describing is not distinct from the Bolshevism and Communism of Russia."

" Not at all ! " Hitler cried. " You are making the usual mistake. What remains is a revolutionary creative will that needs no ideological crutches, but grows into a ruthless instrument of might invincible in both the nation and the world. A doctrine of redemption based on science thus becomes a genuine revolutionary movement possessing all the requisites of power."

" And what is the aim of this revolutionary will ? " I inquired.

" It has no fixed aim. Do you find that so difficult to understand ? " Hitler asked me.

I replied that such a viewpoint certainly seemed to me rather novel and unusual.

" We are a movement," the Führer replied. " Nothing could express our nature better. Marxism teaches that a vast upheaval quite suddenly changes the world. The millennium falls from the skies like a seventh heaven. After that world history ceases. There is no further development. Everything is in order. The shepherd tends his flocks. The end of the world has come. But we know there is never a final stage, there is no permanency, only eternal change. Only death is unchanging. The past is eternal. But the future is an inexhaustible fount of possibilities of further development."

I had not, I admitted, seen matters from such a lofty point of view.

" It is the only point of view from which it is possible to see them at all," Hitler retorted. " In my youth, and even in the first years of my Munich period after the war, I never shunned the company of Marxists of any shade. I was of the opinion that one or other of them showed promise. Certainly they had every freedom to unfold their potentialities. But they were and remained small men. They wanted no giants who towered above the multitude, though they had plenty of pedants who split dogmatic hairs. So I made up my mind to start something new. But it would have been possible at that time to transform the German working-class movement into what we are to-day. Perhaps it would have been wholesomer for Germany if there had been no split over this matter. Really, there was not much to prevent the German workers from throwing off their mistaken conception of a democracy, within the framework of which their revolution could be fulfilled. But of course that was the decisive, world-historical step reserved for us."

After reflecting for a moment, Hitler resumed :

" You ask whether private economic interests will have to be eliminated. Certainly not. I have never said anything of the kind, nor have I deputed any of my subordinates to say so. That would be as mad as an attempt to abolish sexual intercourse by decree. The instinct to earn and the instinct to possess cannot be eliminated. Natural instincts remain. We should be the last to deny that. But the problem is how to adjust and satisfy these natural instincts. The proper limits to private profit and private enterprise must be drawn through the state and general public according to their vital needs. And on this point I can tell you, regardless of all the professors' theories and trades-union wisdom, that there is no principle on which you can draw any universally valid limits. The needs of a state, varying according to time and circumstances, are the sole determining factor. What may be necessary to-day need not be so to-morrow. This is not a question of theoretical suppositions, but of practical decisions dictated by existing circumstances. Therefore I may—nay, must—change or repudiate under changed conditions to-morrow what I consider correct to-day.

" There is no ideal condition of permanent validity. Only fools believe in a cut-and-dried method of changing the social and economic order. There is no such thing as equality, abolition of private property, just wage, or any of the other ideas they've been splitting hairs over. And all the distinctions that are made between production for consumption and production for profit are just pastimes for idlers and muddle-heads."

" What about the programme of land reforms, the rescue from ground-rent serfdom and nationalisation of the banks ? " I asked.

Hitler gesticulated impatiently. " Are you worrying about that programme, too ? " he asked. " Need I explain its meaning to you ? Anybody who takes it literally, instead of seeing it as the great landscape painted on the background of our stage, is a simpleton. I shall never alter this programme ; it is meant for the masses. It points the direction of some of our endeavours—neither more nor less. It is like the dogma of the Church. Is the significance of the Church exhausted by the dogma ? Does it not lie much more in the Church rites and activities ? The masses need something for the imagination, they need fixed, permanent doctrines. The initiates know that there is nothing fixed, that everything is continually changing. That is why I impress upon you that National Socialism is a potential Socialism that is never consummated because it is in a state of constant change."

THE MYSTIC TRIANGLE

Even a man like Hjalmar Schacht, the great economic wizard, declares that he never leaves Hitler's presence without feeling uplifted and strengthened by the great perspectives Hitler unrolls, giving him a sense of the significance of his work. If even the astutest of economists

feels thus, then how could I feel otherwise? Generalities
propounded with every evidence of profound conviction
have at times the effect of a revelation. There is not always
a clear distinction between simplicity and foolishness.

Could I make use of anything I had just heard in my
daily struggle with the small minds of the party? Hitler
had given me to understand that he regarded me as worthy
of being admitted to his innermost thoughts—such as he
had not disclosed even to his *Gauleiter*, who had shown
himself incapable of understanding them. Did this not
place me under obligations, compel me to keep this knowledge from the masses, and even to be tolerant of the uncomprehending desires of these masses, not to mention the
Gauleiter themselves? Or, on the other hand, was this
appearance of confidence a mere deception, one of Hitler's
many tricks by means of which he kept people subservient?

I asked Hitler the meaning of the triangle he had drawn
for Ley, of the Labour Front, and a number of *Gauleiter*,
in order to make the future social order clear to them.
Evidently Hitler did not remember. Forster had not been
able fully to explain it to me, I told him, but had been
much impressed by it nevertheless. He said it made everything quite clear.

"Oh, yes, I remember," Hitler replied. "This is what
you mean : one side of the triangle is the ' Labour Front,'
the social community, the classless community in which
each man helps his neighbour. Everyone feels secure here,
each one gets assistance, advice and occupation for his
leisure time. All are equal here.

"The second side is the professional class. Here each
individual is separate, graded, according to his ability and
quality, to work for the general good. Knowledge is the
criterion here. Each is worth as much as he accomplishes.

"The third side represents the party, which, in one or
other of its many branches, embraces every German who

has not been found unworthy. Each one in the party shares the privilege of leading the nation. Here the decisive factors are devotion and resolution. All are equal as party comrades, but each man must submit to a grading of ranks that is inviolable."

This, I agreed, was roughly what Forster had tried to explain to me, but he had been only partially successful. There had been some mystic significance as well, the first side at the same time representing the will in man, the second, what is usually called the heart, and the third, the intelligence.

Hitler laughed at this. There was no need to labour the comparison, he remarked. He had only meant to show how each individual, in all his feelings and activities, must be included in some section of the party.

" The party takes over the function of what has been society—that is what I wanted them to understand. The party is all-embracing. It rules our lives in all their breadth and depth. We must therefore develop branches of the party in which the whole of individual life will be reflected. Each activity and each need of the individual will thereby be regulated by the party as the representative of the general good. There will be no licence, no free space, in which the individual belongs to himself. This is Socialism—not such trifles as the private possession of the means of production. Of what importance is that if I range men firmly within a discipline they cannot escape ? Let them then own land or factories as much as they please. The decisive factor is that the State, through the party, is supreme over them, regardless whether they are owners or workers. All that, you see, is unessential. Our Socialism goes far deeper. It does not alter external conditions ; no, it establishes the relation of the individual to the State, the national community. It does this with the help of one party, or perhaps I should say of one order."

I could not help remarking that this seemed a novel and harsh doctrine.

Quite true, Hitler replied, and not everyone was capable of understanding it. For this reason, he had felt it necessary to popularise his ideas by means of the diagram.

Then doubtless he would not approve, I suggested, of the kind of state landlordship, or state ownership of the means of production, the dream of some of the most ardent social and economic workers of the party?

Hitler again registered impatience.

" Why bother with such half-measures when I have far more important matters in hand, such as the people themselves ? " he exclaimed. " The masses always cling to extremes. After all, what is meant by nationalisation, by socialisation ? What has been changed by the fact that a factory is now owned by the State instead of by a Mr. Smith? But once directors and employees alike have been subjected to a universal discipline, there will be a new order for which all expressions used hitherto will be quite inadequate."

I replied that I was beginning to understand what new and tremendous perspectives this opened.

" The day of individual happiness has passed," Hitler returned. " Instead, we shall feel a collective happiness. Can there by any greater happiness than a National Socialist meeting in which speakers and audience feel as one ? It is the happiness of sharing. Only the early Christian communities could have felt it with equal intensity. They, too, sacrified their personal happiness for the higher happiness of the community.

" If we feel and experience this great era thus," Hitler concluded, " then we shall not be disturbed by details and individual failures. We shall know then that every road leads us forward, no matter how much it seems to go in another direction. And above all, we shall then maintain our passionate desire to revolutionise the world to an extent unparalleled in history. It gives us also a special, secret pleasure to see how the people about us are unaware of what is really happening to them. They gaze fascinated at one or two familiar superficialities, such as possessions and income and rank and other outworn conceptions. As long as these are kept intact, they are quite satisfied. But in the meantime they have entered a new relation ; a powerful social force has caught them up. They themselves are changed. What are ownership and income to that ? Why need we trouble to socialise banks and factories ? We socialise human beings."

CHAPTER XV

IS HITLER A DICTATOR?

THE conflict of views between myself and the National Socialist party in Danzig continued. I was pressed to make a *de facto* change in the constitution by treating the opposition with brutality. Meanwhile, continual excesses against the Polish minority were obstructing a policy of settlement with Poland. Economically, the party was recklessly extravagant. I was completely isolated in the Government, since my colleagues, with an eye to their careers, preferred to meet the wishes of the party than to expose themselves personally by raising purely objective considerations. Matters went so far that, outside the official deliberations of the Government, secret special sessions were being held without me, in which Government decisions were in part annulled. Although conditions in Danzig were on a much smaller scale, they did involve problems similar to those calling for solution by the National Socialist dictatorship of Germany. The same conflict and confusion reigned in Germany as in Danzig. The possibility remained, however, that in Danzig, as in the Reich, the chaotic state of affairs would clear up, and the true problems—economic, foreign and military— would make their importance felt.

In spite of my isolation, I endeavoured to continue my work. I was strengthened in this purpose above all by the foreign relations of Danzig, which continued to deteriorate. My colleagues and the party, however, persisted in their attacks on myself as the sole hindrance to the full *Gleichschaltung* (equitable settlement) of Danzig. They

complained about me to Hess and to Hitler himself. They
accused me of estrangement from the party, and of actions
hostile thereto, so that, they said, I no longer possessed the
confidence of the people. Hess made a few attempts at
reconciliation. I offered to hand in my resignation, an-
nouncing my willingness at the same time to accept any
other post, provided *Gauleiter* Forster would, as president,
accept full responsibility for the Government. I assured
Hess that under pressure of actual difficulties, full responsibility would soon force Herr Forster to follow my policy.
Hess explained that Hitler would under no circumstances
tolerate any voluntary resignation. It was my duty to come
to an understanding with the party. Forster, however,
with the ruthless frankness to which this type of crafty
politician frequently succumbs, told me that he had not
the faintest intention of allowing his career to be jeopardised.

At length the whole matter was referred to Hitler himself.
It seemed to him important enough to justify a personal
hearing of all the Danzig Senators, who could thus express
their views about me. The most serious accusation that
could be made against me, however, was—as my successor
to the presidency subsequently explained—that I " really "
believed in the possibility of a German-Polish settlement,
instead of merely using it as a temporary measure. I was
not present at this inquiry, nor was I ever given the opportunity of justifying my conduct with regard to particular
accusations. For this purpose Hitler invited me to a private
interview. This was in February, 1934. I justified my
position by outlining the existing political condition of
Danzig, the background for the line pursued by myself as
opposed to the desires of the party. Objectively there was
little to be said against it.

Hitler began, however, by declaring that I was practically
asking for absolute powers. If politics were as simple as
that—if all that was necessary was to act according to the

objective requirements of the situation, then indeed it would be an easy matter, and we could contentedly rely on the experts. Unfortunately, we had to deal with human imperfections, with malice and lack of understanding. Now certainly the party were not malicious. Or did I contend that they were? Men in responsible positions under National Socialism little knew, he told me, how lucky they were, compared with the politicians of the Weimar Republic, who had at every step to combat not only stupidity, but the malice of all against all. It was one of the great accomplishments of National Socialism to have eliminated this poison from the life of the nation, this evil rancour existing between the different parties, who were not interested in objective achievements, but merely jealous of their own prestige and profit.

" The party is well-intentioned," the Führer assured me. " *The party understands everything.* It is only a matter of explaining properly. If you do not succeed in making your intentions clear to the party, then either you do not yourself see things simply and clearly enough, or you are not the right man. If you become estranged from the party, so that it no longer understands your speech, it is always your own fault. That is why I constantly insist that you should talk, discuss, hold meetings, remain always in close touch with the mass of the party. If you lose that contact, you may have the best intentions in the world, but no one will understand you. We must not make the mistake of the *bourgeois* representatives, who are strangers to the people, and have perhaps one or two meetings, usually a fortnight before elections, and then never bother about their constituents again.

" It may be," he went on, " that our party comrades fail to understand certain matters because they have hitherto been unacquainted with them. But you cannot reproach them with being *unwilling* to understand. It is my mission, as it is that of each one of my assistants, repeatedly to explain my views to the party comrades, until they have understood them, and have voluntarily accepted them. Of course it is evident that in this continual striving, the sharp corners of your own views will be rounded off, and your judgment will often have to be re-adjusted. So much the better ! This is the fruitful outcome of such a constant interchange of ideas. The party is an incorruptible judge. However correct your own motives and ideas may be, if the party rejects them, you must seek the fault first and foremost in yourself."

Hitler spoke in a loud, firm tone, but without hostility. I cautiously ventured to say that I should certainly not fail to explain and make comprehensible the policy I considered the right one. But I had reason to believe that in some quarters there existed little interest in allowing the public to gain any understanding of this policy.

Hitler turned on me brusquely. Did I think he could always do as he thought right ? He had to make allowances, and adapt himself to the will and the understanding of others. He had obligations which he meant to fulfil to the letter. Above all he had to consider the " old gentleman," whose memory and receptivity were dimmed, who frequently, with the stubbornness of age, rejected things without investigating them. He would have to accept this state of affairs and adapt his policies to it. Or did I believe he was a dictator who might do as he pleased ?

He paused dramatically, and then uttered with solemn emphasis these memorable words :

" I am no dictator, and never will be a dictator."

Even if he succeeded in breaking the fetters that bound his actions at that time, he explained, he would never make a decision according to his own arbitrary views. No individual could carry the great responsibility involved in such a status. I was under a complete misapprehension as to the meaning of "leadership," and made the current mistake of confounding leadership with dictatorship.

"The fact that we do not vote and carry out our policy by majority decisions does not mean that we evade all control, whether it comes from the mass of the party or from factors outside the party. Do you propose to be more independent than I?"

Hitler moderated his tone. Any fool could play the dictator, he went on, while the possibility of doing so lasted. But it could not last long.

"You ask for full powers. You want to eliminate the party. And who will guarantee that you are the one who was right? How could I be sure I myself was right if I wanted to rule as absolutely as you want to do? I can only obtain such assurance by, again and again, consulting the will of the party. In your case, I have that assurance only when other men, when the incorruptible party, have tested each and every one of your measures. When you are in agreement with these men, I shall know you are on the right road. There is no such thing as unlimited power, and I should never dream of pretending to it myself. The word *dictatorship* is misleading; there is no such thing as dictatorship in the accepted sense. Even the most extreme autocrat is compelled to correct his absolute will by existing conditions. Considered soberly, there are only various means of giving shape to the public will. At times you may be more absolute and less dependent as a parliamentary officer than I am to-day or ever will be.

"'Being a dictator' is a catch-phrase with no reality behind it. My way of taking an average of the innumerable observations, judgments and desires in the party is an eminently difficult and continually fresh problem. It is my foremost problem—never to find myself in opposition to my party. If I am of a different opinion, then it is my duty to change either my own, or the party's view. But no one

can give you what you ask for. You want to operate in a
vacuum, instead of reaching some agreement between the
opposing forces—forces without which there can be no life."

Hitler went on talking past the actual problem, which
was an entirely concrete one, and lost himself in the maze
of a general dissertation on the nature of the party.

" What is, in fact, the meaning of our party ? Why have
we eliminated all the other parties, and fought against the
whole of the parliamentary, democratic system ? Did you
think it was because we wanted to destroy all contact with
the people ? On the contrary : we have destroyed outworn
institutions just because they no longer served to produce a
fruitful relationship with the body of the nation, but led
only to gossip and brazen deceit. We have eliminated
parasites who insinuated themselves between the people and
their leaders. Of course the part played by the masses is
thereby also cut out. There is no longer a voting herd
periodically intoxicated with words. In place of the mass,
there is now the people's community, developed from the
masses, the incorporated nation awakened to self-conscious-
ness : our party.

" The term ' party,' " he added in parenthesis, " is a
misnomer. I should prefer ' order ' myself. But perhaps
this is romantic. The Young German Order has destroyed
its significance ; one is reminded of monastic orders.

" Now," he concluded, " what is the meaning of our
party ? Only he who accepts duties has a right to a voice
in them. But he who does so, he who joins our ranks, who
is thought *worthy* of joining our ranks (and this without
regard to person)—that man has a right to be heard, and
is heard. We stand in close contact with this flower of the
nation. We submit all questions to it. We are doing a
work of political education such as no other party has ever
done before. I shall never take an important decision
without first being assured of the approval of the party.

I cannot give orders as I please. What I command is not
arbitrary, but the result of close understanding with the
party. We go far beyond any parliament on earth in our
constant reference to the will of the people. Only thus can
a real people's unity be attained. I am not dependent on
the man in the street. But I am responsible to my party
comrades. The parliamentary democracies can influence
public opinion as they like. I am subject to an incorruptible judge, my party."

Hitler talked on about the greatness of the National
Socialist movement. The shape our national destiny was
now taking, he said, was the essential thing.   It was
discipline that kept people together, not this or that aim,
this or that item of the programme. I must confess to having
been swayed by his impassioned speech, yet I could not
help thinking what a strange spectacle this was. Here was
a man enthusiastically idealising his actions, which in
reality sprang from quite different motives. Was this
conscious misleading of opinion ? Or did he believe his
own professions ? I think he did. In order to rise above
the daily squabbles in the party, he was compelled to create
for himself a fictitious world, and had to lash himself into
a frenzy to believe in it. In that state, I am convinced that
he no longer saw the reality, but only what he so passionately wanted to see. Hitler, the creator of a new form of
democracy—that was the true *motif* of his speech. The
democracy that had degenerated into parliamentarism
would be rescued by National Socialism.

I asked him whether it would not be in the interests of
clarity that this new form, which was to-day escaping from
the framework of the still legal Weimar Constitution, should
be embodied in a new set of laws. As things were, responsible politicians found themselves constantly in a state of
conflicting duties. The old status no longer had the force
of law, yet the new one appeared in the guise of a

revolutionary force, and as such, based on violence. The new rule seemed arbitrary, not because it signified something new, but solely because it was not subject to law.

Hitler curtly rejected my suggestion. The moment the new status could be formulated constitutionally, its revolutionary force, he declared, would be exhausted. The revolutionary status must be retained as long as possible, in order not to paralyse its creative power before its time. It was the fundamental error of the jurists and law-makers to think they could create life by means of a constitution and a code of laws. The true life of the nation would then go on outside the constitutional status, as the hair-splitting Weimar Constitution had proved.

" Constitutions can only conclude real developments ; they can never precede them. Artificial construction violates life. Disease in the body of the nation, and continual unrest and disturbance of growth, will be the inevitable results."

As long as possible, he would allow things to remain in their present condition. It was not yet possible to see the direction in which the new shape of the German destiny was going to develop. Everything must be allowed to grow and mature.

" I can wait," Hitler said with strong emphasis. " Let my successors after my death codify the great life of our nation. It is still too early now."

Hitler then began to speak of the reform of the Reich. Conditions here were similar. He was being urged to give the Reich its new district (*Gau*) constitution, dissolving the old, historical provinces, and making the new districts the permanent components of the Reich. But he was not going to be pushed. As an artist, he knew exactly when an idea had matured, but here everything was still in the early stage of ferment. Besides, before he could really model the permanent shape of the new Germany from the raw clay, he must have the countries of Austria and Bohemia, and the Polish and French areas. The new parts must grow, old and new traditions must be welded with the revolutionary forces into a new unity, before the final stroke, in the shape of a constitution, could be put to the completed picture. Over and over again he must exhort his party comrades to have patience.

The same thing was true of legal development. Everything here was still in a state of flux, but this very fact was his surety that new life was being breathed into the administration of justice. There was, of course, no such thing as objective justice.

" Justice is a means of ruling. Justice is the codified practice of ruling."

In this field, too, he deprecated the suggestion that he was a dictator who wished to force development ; he was rather a builder. But he was like those great builders of cathedrals who laboured generation after generation on some massive structure, and were more interested in the innate life of this structure than in any brilliant ideas of their own.

" So I, too, build the new Germany, not like a self-centred and in the profoundest sense unproductive artist of the present day, but like the pious cathedral builders of the Middle Ages."

Hitler had by this time talked himself into a state of exaltation. He had quite forgotten the occasion of our interview, namely my justification.

" I need ten years of law-making," he cried excitedly. " The time is short. I have not long enough to live, and first I must wage our war of liberation. I must lay the foundations on which others can build after me. I shall not see it fulfilled," he finished suddenly.

Hitler dismissed me in friendly fashion. I was confused. My own problem remained unsolved. As we exchanged farewells, he gave me a further piece of advice :

" I should like to warn you against two things. Don't associate with those *bourgeois* Nationalists. Don't take them more seriously than they deserve. The day of these gentry is past. The *bourgeois* age is ended. These men are ghosts. Don't allow yourself to be impressed by their so-called expert knowledge. They don't understand the new world that is arising, and they know nothing of its laws. These people will help neither me nor you. My other warning is against the League and its representative in your city. That world, too, is on its deathbed. See the self-importance of these people for what it is : the unreality of the theatre. Once the performance is over, you find yourself again in the street. You must shake off all scruples ; only then will you understand the party, and the party understand you."

TRUTH AND PHANTASY

The truth was very different. The party was neither well-intentioned nor anxious to understand. The party wanted power. Each individual party member wanted a place in the sun, cost what it might. Each one sought security for himself, and hoped by active work and a military bearing to attract the attention of the leaders and gain promotion. Those who blustered most, and had no scruples about technical knowledge, had the best chance of jobs and favours. Anyone who raised objections on the grounds of competence was regarded as inconvenient and pushed into the background. Thus the conflict between the rival elements of the party sharpened and grew heated. Motives of competence were looked on as outworn *bourgeois* scruples. It was impossible to make head or tail of this confusion, and to anyone standing as high as Hitler, the unvarnished truth rarely succeeded in breaking through. Everyone did his best to impress his immediate superiors. " A job well done must rattle," was an old proverb of the

Prussian soldiery. But the number of false pretences now indulged in by people who wished to appear in the most favourable light before *Gauleiter* or other, higher, officials surpassed anything previously seen.

These conditions prevailed in the highest circles, and the following is only one example of many. Todt, the Director-General for road-building, wanted, as early as 1934, to build a motor-road through the Polish Corridor, a plan warmly supported by Hitler. Over-estimating my relations with Polish governing circles, he asked me to obtain Polish agreement for the part passing through Polish territory. This was a political task of the first rank, and not, as this gentleman seemed naïvely to believe, a matter to be settled offhand. Nevertheless, I agreed to put out a feeler in the course of conversation. Imagine my amazement when, a month or two later, on a visit to Hitler, I was told by him that he had now bound East Prussia closer to the Reich. A new motor-road was being built—he informed me with the utmost unlimited complacency. I asked about the part passing through the Corridor, where, to my knowledge, there were difficulties. That was all arranged to the best advantage, he returned. Todt had already made a contract with a well-known Italian road expert, who in his turn had a fixed agreement with the Polish Government.

On returning from my interview with Hitler, I found an invitation from Todt at my hotel. I visited him that evening in his office, which at that time was in the Pariser Platz—I believe it was in the old, feudal club of the former infantry guards. He showed me his plans and maps, a vast network of planned, and in part already completed roads. Then he asked me about the progress of my talks with the Polish Government, and whether there was any chance of getting the road through the Corridor, as the Führer was most anxious for it. I let him talk, making sure there was no truth in what I had heard only a short while before from Hitler as a settled matter.

Todt came to a full stop at last, and then I told him of my conversation with Hitler that morning. I must confess that it gave me the greatest pleasure to watch the painful embarrassment of this gentleman who was so swollen with his own importance.

" That was a misunderstanding," he stammered, " there must be some misunderstanding." After this our conversation came to a rapid end. The truth, of course, was that, on the strength of my vague promise to sound the possibilities, Todt had given Hitler entirely inaccurate information in order to convince him that everything was settled, and the motor-road on the point of being constructed. As everyone knows, it is still awaiting construction.

By such methods, though not always as crude as this, these Ribbentrops made use of all their relations with Hitler to further their own ambitions. They threw sand in Hitler's eyes. They were assiduous in presenting themselves as peculiarly competent, in order to improve their own positions. Each one studied to tell Hitler what he wanted to hear, and sought to outshine his rivals and competitors in the matter of favourable and agreeable news calculated to show up his own ability and skill in bringing about desired results. The German people, once the most objective and scientific of peoples, now went to unbelievable extremes of lying servility.

Hitler was never told the uncomfortable truth. By favourably coloured reports he was pushed ever further along the road to ruin. It began with the minimising of difficulties and the magnifying of favourable prospects, with the slightest shifting of emphasis, and ended with out-and-out falsification. A policy grew up of keeping from him everything that might excite him. His excessive fits of rage tempted few people to provoke such a storm. This policy of concealment soon became general, and was practised by the other great ones of the party.

Danzig faced bankruptcy. We needed bills of exchange in order to maintain the backing of our currency on the prescribed level. The Reichsbank refused me the amount I asked for, and lamented that the whole of the rearmament plan was being jeopardised by Danzig. But Forster, the young man crowned with the halo of the Führer's special favour, went to the same bank—directed, incidentally, by a very honourable man—and obtained the required sum, and more, without difficulty. Was it not natural that Hitler and his lieutenants should come to believe that there were no difficulties, that everything could be done if only these " experts " were managed properly?

In reality, the problem was merely postponed. In the end it reappeared in such an urgent form that something had to be done. Usually it was by then a far more expensive business. The Danzig financial and currency problems were no exception. The party prevented me from taking the proper measures in time by behaving as though it possessed the lamp of Aladdin. Six months after my resignation, little could be saved from the wreckage. The Danzig *gulden* had to be devalued by about thirty per cent.

This currency trouble was one of the bones of contention which had increasingly worsened my relations with the party. Two months after I was to have justified my actions to Hitler, and had listened instead to a fervent lecture on the nature of the party, I laid the financial position of Danzig before a small Cabinet meeting. Hess presided, and Neurath, Schwerin-Krosigk, Schmidt, the then Minister of National Economy, and a number of other gentlemen took part. It was amazing how difficult these gentlemen found it to understand the special condition in Danzig, which was certainly not favourable, but only became hopeless after the mismanagement on the part of the National Socialists—a mismanagement I had been powerless to prevent. We were already faced with the results of financial experiments which in Germany had not yet borne their inevitable fruit. It was like throwing a pebble into a small pond. The waves, thrown back by the too-near shore, return, cross and rise. In a larger pond, the waves take a considerably longer time to return. We, in Danzig, had the results of certain measures of extending credit far sooner than Germany. This was something new to the gentlemen in Berlin. We never got beyond debates and suggested half-measures. The party drew the conclusion that they might continue their extravagance. " Money is no object " was still their guiding principle.

In my desperation I appealed, among others, to Keppler, later the Secretary of State, and at that time Hitler's special agent in economic matters. He had his offices in the Reich Chancellery in Berlin. Keppler was a civil engineer, and like all engineers, at any rate in Germany, childishly naïve and ignorant in regard to everything outside his technical knowledge, but full of self-assurance. He consoled me with stories of epoch-making inventions which were on the threshold of realisation. I had conceived a plan to improve Danzig's export industries, but he waved it away as a waste of time. Within the year, Danzig would be German, he claimed. The Reich had such inventions and means to attain power that no coalition in the world was strong enough to prevent Germany from taking Danzig back into the Reich. He regretted that he could give me no information as to what was being prepared, " but," he assured me, " if you only knew as much about it as I do you would simply let everything slide and wait."

Not contented with this vaguely splendid forecast, I obtained an interview over Keppler's head with Hitler. But here, too, the result was unsatisfactory. I repeated what I had told the Cabinet session, namely, that if Danzig did not succeed in re-establishing her balance of payment, she would in six months have to devaluate her currency.

Hitler raged and screamed. He would not permit it ! He would never allow an inflation !

" I have given my word. I shall not inflate. The people don't understand inflation. It can be done without inflation."

He became so incoherent that I failed to understand all he said. It was some time before he regained his calm. The interview was not an enjoyable one.

Incidentally, Schwerin-Krosigk had on one occasion, while we were both waiting in Hitler's ante-room, told me quite frankly his opinion that Germany would not escape another devaluation. Hitler had no objection to disguised or concealed devaluation, but he wanted at all costs to avoid the naked fact. On this point he was once more the shrewd demagogue who knew exactly how far to trespass on the gullibility of the man in the street, and at what point that patient person would begin to be refractory. Inflation and ration cards were to Hitler the essence of a mistaken mass psychology.

" Do anything you please," he repeated on this occasion, " except devaluation. I shall never give my consent to it, any more than I shall ever permit ration cards. There are plenty of other measures if you will only use your brain."

It was, he went on to declare, because of this unbelievable lack of understanding for the feeling of the masses, the small investors and the housewives, that the last war had been lost. He would not allow the same mistake to be made again, least of all before war had even started. He would sooner abolish money altogether, and instead of ration cards, introduce communal care of the whole nation. If the worst came to the worst, he could justify such measures to the masses. He could explain it as the new war Socialism, and proclaim it as a tremendous social advance. The people would believe that. But his government must never be associated with measures that had once already plunged the Reich into misery and defeat. This would only call to life feelings that would soon turn against everything National Socialism was trying to do. The confidence of the nation would be destroyed in very few months.

"Every state depends first and foremost on the craving for security and the confidence of the small investor and the housewife. Any government that has not these two classes as its friends cannot stand."

The Secret of Ruling the Masses

Hitler began in this connection to discuss leadership of the masses. He had an unerring instinct for what the masses felt, what could be expected of them, and what must, at all costs, be avoided, he told me. This was an inborn gift, and no one could teach him anything here. But this gift alone was not sufficient. It was necessary to be sure of one's means. The leadership of the masses was an art in the truest sense of the word, and mastery of this art presupposed a good deal of exacting labour.

"My enemies have turned up their noses at me. They have asked, full of envy : ' Why is this man so successful with the masses ? ' These Socialists and Communists thought they had a monopoly over the masses. They even had all the meeting-places and owned the streets. Yet suddenly a man appeared who created a really great mass movement. Was this just a lucky fluke, was it due to the uncritical mind of the masses ? No, it was thanks to us, to our assiduity, and to the technique we perfected.

"It is true that the masses are uncritical, but not in the way these idiots of Marxists and reactionaries imagine. The masses have their critical faculties, too, but they function differently from those of the private individual. The masses are like an animal that obeys its instincts. They do not reach conclusions by reasoning. My success in initiating the greatest people's movement of all time is due to my never having done anything in violation of the vital laws and the feelings of the mass. These feelings may be primitive, but they have the resistance and indestructibility of natural qualities. A once intensely felt experience in the life of the masses, like ration cards and inflation, will never again be driven out of their blood. The masses have a simple system of thinking and feeling, and anything that cannot be fitted into it disturbs them. It is only because I take their vital laws into consideration that I can rule them.

" I have been reproached for making the masses fanatic and ecstatic. In the opinion of these wiseacres the masses must be soothed and kept in apathy. No, gentlemen, the reverse is true. I can lead the masses only if I tear them out of their apathy. Only the fanatic mass can be swayed. A mass that is apathetic and dull is the greatest threat to unity. Apathy is to the masses a defensive form of rejection. They hide behind apathy, till suddenly they break out in entirely unexpected actions and reactions. The statesman who fails to take immediate measures against a growing apathy of the masses ought to be impeached."

He had made the masses fanatic, he explained, in order to fashion them into the instruments of his policy. He had awakened the masses. He had lifted them out of themselves, and given them meaning and a function. He had been reproached with appealing to their lowest instincts. Actually, he was doing something quite different. If he were to go to the masses with reasonable deliberations, they would not understand him. But if he awakened corresponding feelings in them, they followed the simple slogans he presented to them.

" At a mass meeting," he cried, " thought is eliminated. And because this is the state of mind I require, because it secures to me the best sounding-board for my speeches, I order everyone to attend the meetings, where they become

14

part of the mass whether they like it or not, ' intellectuals ' and *bourgeois* as well as workers. I mingle the people. I speak to them only as the mass."

He paused to reflect for a moment. Then he resumed with increased eagerness :

" I am conscious that I have no equal in the art of swaying the masses, not even Goebbels. Everything that can be learnt with the intelligence, everything that can be achieved by the aid of clever ideas, Goebbels can do, but real leadership of the masses cannot be learnt. And remember this : the bigger the crowd, the more easily is it swayed. Also, the more you mingle the classes—peasants, workers, black-coated workers—the more surely will you achieve the typical mass character. Don't waste time over ' intellectual ' meetings and groups drawn together by mutual interests. Anything you may achieve with such folk to-day by means of reasonable explanation may be erased to-morrow by an opposite explanation. But what you tell the people in the mass, in a receptive state of fanatic devotion, will remain like words received under an hypnotic influence, ineradicable, and impervious to every reasonable explanation. But just as the individual has neuroses which must not be disturbed, so the mass has its complexes that must not be awakened. Among them are all reminders of ration cards and inflation.

" I can safely demand much greater sacrifices from the masses, but I must get them to view those sacrifices in the proper light. How can I expect to wage war if I drive the masses into the same state of apathy that they were in during 1917-18 ? "

Up to this point I had had no chance of saying anything, but I interposed a question now. Was it not the function of the party, I asked, to make things clear to the individual, not as a mere component of the masses ?

" No," Hitler replied, " that may be possible for a short

time, but in critical times, the mass arises everywhere—in the street, in the factory, at the baker's shop, in the underground, in every place where ten to a dozen people congregate—and they will react in the mass, forgetting reason and persuasion. The entire weight of the masses rests on the party, and the party is itself a constituent part of the mass."

Hitler then began to discuss the use of propaganda to defeat opponents—a problem he strongly emphasised, that was quite distinct from the previous one. The two must on no account be confused. He had been discussing the mastery of the masses, but propaganda meant the defeat of opponents. The two had one thing in common : both must eschew all discussion of reasons, all refutation of opinions—in short, there must be no debating or doubting. But apart from this, the aim of a propaganda battle with one's opponents was quite a different one.

" Mastery always means the transmission of a stronger will to a weaker one. How shall I press my will upon my opponent ? By first splitting and paralysing his will, putting him at loggerheads with himself, throwing him into confusion."

He conceived the transmission of the will, he said, as something in the nature of a physical and biological process. Foreign bodies penetrated the circulation of the enemy, gained a foothold, and gave rise to disease and infirmity till he was ready to surrender. The instrument of terrorism was indispensable, less for its direct effects than for its undermining of the opposing will.

Once more Hitler began to speak of the coming war. The rules he had been laying down were also, he said, the fundamental rules of a war with psychological weapons. The world would be amazed at the methods he had in preparation for this purpose. The enemy propaganda of the last war would be child's play to his methods. War would not be waged by him solely as a military operation. If a bloody war did ever develop, he was confident of causing astounding breakdowns in the enemy ranks, on whom he would be in a position to force his will in the midst of battle.

Hitler's views on what is known to-day as the "war of nerves" were familiar to the initiated circles. They were the same as those to which he had adhered in the struggle for power. These tactics of political warfare were something quite peculiar to Hitler, and he could rightly claim that they were based on a wide range of psychological experience and study. Always he returned to these rules, and insisted that his *Gauleiter*, even in the smallest provincial districts, should acquaint themselves thoroughly with his ideas.

"Do anything you please," were the words with which he dismissed me. "But not another word about devaluation or inflation. Besides, the masses see no difference between the two."

Chapter XVI

MAGIC, BLACK AND WHITE

ONE day when Hitler seemed in an approachable mood, a far-sighted woman in his circle said to him warningly :

" My Leader, don't touch black magic. As yet both white and black are open to you. But once you have embarked upon black magic it will dominate your destiny. It will hold you captive. Don't choose the quick and easy successes. There lies before you the power over a realm of pure spirits. Do not allow yourself to be led away from your true path by earth-bound spirits, which will rob you of creative power."

Hitler was fond at times of this sort of mystical talk. Only in such guise could any serious warning be offered to him. This woman friend expressed in her way what everyone who came into touch with Hitler was bound to feel : Hitler was abandoning himself to forces which were carrying him away—forces of dark and destructive violence. He imagined that he still had freedom of choice, but he had long been in bondage to a magic which might well have been described, not only in metaphor but in literal fact, as that of evil spirits. And instead of a man emerging step by step from the obscurity of his youth, and freeing himself from its dross in his upward course, we witnessed the development of a man possessed, the helpless prey of the powers of darkness.

Had he been a free agent ? Could he have chosen any other course ? Many of us who knew him believed that he could. Many of us still hoped to see a change when it was already too late. But he was hampered, for one thing,

by the dead-weight of the obscure associates of the past
who had accompanied him in his rise. He had failed to
drive them back into the obscurity to which they properly
belonged, and this omission weighed on his whole career.
How much good-will there was in the party, what forces
would have been at his call, if these crooks and gangsters
had not thronged round him ! But the real reason why
he pursued the path to the abyss lay in an infirmity of
will. Hitler seems a man of tremendous will power, but
the appearance is deceptive. He is languid and apathetic
by nature, and needs the stimulus of nervous excitement to
rouse him out of chronic lethargy to a spasmodic activity.
He had chosen the easier path, and had abandoned himself
to the forces that led him to destruction.

There were talks that showed that he had a conception of
his true task. But these talks were no more than flights
into an unreal world, flights which strengthened his belief
in himself. The die had long been cast. It was an
illusion that this man had any freedom of choice left, even
if he possessed qualities which might have enabled him to
rise higher. He followed a course which brought him, in
externals, to the summit of power ; in essentials it
condemned him to more and more hopeless dependence.

Hitler was no dictator. Nor was he merely carried
like a cork to the surface. He always marched with the
big battalions. Over and over again in conversation he
declared that we must always choose the weaker for opponent
and the stronger for ally. It might sound a commonplace,
he would say, but it was the essential rule for all political
activity. One thing, especially, Hitler never did—he
never ran counter to the opinion of his *Gauleiter*, his district
commissioners. Each one of these men was in his power,
but together they held him in theirs ; and accordingly,
whenever differences arose, he so steered his course as to
carry the overwhelming majority of them with him. The

secret of his leadership lay in knowing in advance what
course the majority of his *Gauleiter* would decide on, and in
being the first to declare for that course. Thus he was
always in the right, and the opposition was put in the
wrong. These *Gauleiter* watched jealously over their pre-
rogatives. They admitted no new members into their
ranks. They resisted with robust unanimity every attempt
to set limits to their rights of sovereignty. Hitler was at
all times dependent on them—and not on them alone.

He was no dictator. He allowed himself to be guided
by the forces at his back, often against his better judgment.
It was the sum of these forces that at all times kept him to
the fore. But the result was that his policy continually
developed along wholly different lines to those which he had
envisaged. He maintained his position of supremacy, but
he had lost his freedom of decision.

My own relations with the party had become impossible.
After my return from Geneva the party demanded that the
Danzig Statute should be abrogated, that an agitation
should be started for liberation from the tutelage of the
League of Nations, and that a policy of ruthlessness should
be embarked on. To introduce this campaign I was to
have some of the Catholic priests arrested, the Socialist
party dissolved, and special measures taken against the
Jewish population.

I refused. My own proposals were an immediate
devaluation of the Danzig gulden and the widening of the
Government to a national basis, in order resolutely to face
the serious economic troubles. I appealed for Hitler's
decision.

Hitler was taking his ease at Obersalzberg and would
not give me an audience. I remained in Berlin, waiting.
I had drawn up a memorandum sketching the only possible
policy for Danzig as I saw it. As I had no access to the
party, I tried to get this memorandum to Hitler through the

intermediary of von Neurath, the Foreign Minister, request-
ing an opportunity to discuss it. Neurath was away,
hunting chamois. The question did not interest him. The
protection of " compromised " people was a delicate
business. I tried to interest von Bülow, the *Staatssekretär*
(Permanent Under Secretary). He promised to do his
best. But I knew that I stood no chance of carrying the
day for my policy unless I could reach Hitler before Forster,
the Danzig *Gauleiter*.

I do not know whether my memorandum ever came
into Hitler's hands. If it did, he certainly did not read it.
Hitler never read reports or memoranda. But Lammers
would have been able to make him acquainted with its
contents. Forster, however, forestalled me. He was
admitted to Obersalzberg, and to an audience.

Hitler capitulated to his *Gauleiter*. He refused to let me
defend my memorandum in person. This made my course
perfectly clear. I resigned.

Many times in our talks Hitler had expressed his particular
friendliness towards me. He had told me various things
that were certainly beyond the ken of his district commissioners. Now, however, he plainly could not escape from
the entanglement of his dependence on these old supporters.
He had placed himself at their mercy. And it was
impossible for him to render justice to anyone against them.
This was not realised at the time in Berlin. It was still
generally supposed, as I had done, and it long continued
to be supposed, that it would be possible to separate Hitler
from his entourage, and gradually to enable him to follow
a riper and more stable policy. Here in Berlin it was
still imagined that it would be possible to bring a patriotic
task to fulfilment by holding the fort and bearing up against
difficulties. It was all in vain. One after another, the
men who harboured these patriotic hopes sacrificed their
imagined influence and were reduced to capitulation before

the gangsters of Hitler's entourage. To-day they are despised experts whose opinions no longer carry weight.

At this time, in the autumn of 1934, I was staying, while awaiting a decision, in a Christian hostel, a sort of Y.M.C.A., in Berlin. My usual hotel was too full of spies for my comfort. I had learned that I was an invalid, and was to be sent to a notorious sanatorium near Berlin. I knew the fate in store for me there. I should never have reached home.

I had done all that it was possible to do. I had informed some of the most influential citizens of Danzig, particularly the men prominent in finance, commerce, and industry, of the impending dangers, and had asked their support in a joint complaint about the Nazi mismanagement, of which they had long been complaining to me. This step had been necessary in order to absolve me from the odium of merely carrying on one of the current personal rivalries in my campaign for a reasonable policy.

But in this Free City of Danzig there was no longer a vestige left of the old independent Hanseatic spirit. Every man I approached showed himself to be concerned for nothing beyond his own precious self, and to be in terror of " backing the wrong horse." This spinelessness of the German business men could not but be fatal to their country. It may be that Hitler was merely the instrument of an inexorable verdict of history—the dissolution of the German middle class, which never had manifested any serious ambition for political independence.

I found support elsewhere. Every potential opponent of my ultimate successor, Forster, approached me with the desire to assist me. These men were ready to come into the open. They advised me not to attack Hitler's hench-man but to strike at other opponents, and so to get back into the saddle. Typically Nazi tactics ! These persons saw everything under one aspect only, that of a struggle for positions and against rivals.

In another quarter—the army—the sweeping away of party control of Danzig would have been witnessed with satisfaction. One very well-known General urged me to quell the monster and set an example to Germany. Why not, he said, expel Forster as an undesirable alien, put the loudest shouters for the party under lock and key, form a new provisional Government on the broadest possible basis, and arm the trade-unionists, as the backbone of the workers, using them as a militia ?

There was something in that. But it needed different forces. I could not in the same breath call in the Opposition for the maintenance of the Statute and carry out a *coup d'état*. Apart from that, we should have been financially on the rocks in a few weeks, as we could not maintain our currency without the support of the Reich. At that time it was impossible to get rid of National Socialism in Danzig by extra-legal means. Six months later legal means almost succeeded. At the elections, in spite of extreme terrorism, the party only just obtained a majority of votes for National Socialism. The League of Nations might have set aside the result, on account of illegal practices, and ordered a new election. The result would have been an overwhelming victory for the Opposition. The opportunity was allowed to slip by.

But these were mere fancies. Germany's destiny had to be fulfilled. It was not difficult to forecast it, given knowledge of the factors, especially the personal one. Hitler avoided a decision ; von Neurath explained to me that the Leader could not intervene in the affairs of Danzig. It was an independent State, and he had no competence to interfere.

There I was in Berlin, sick with apprehension, completely isolated, and expecting every moment to be carried off by Himmler's minions, the secret police. The burden of Germany's gloomy future, for which we were all responsible through our mistakes and omissions, was beyond bearing. In despair I turned to the New Testament, which is placed at every bedside in the German hospices, and turned over its pages. The first passage on which my eyes fell contained these comforting words from the Second Epistle to Timothy :

" But they shall proceed no further : for their folly shall be manifest unto all men."

I read the passages preceding and following the verse quoted, read of the men who are lovers of their own selves, boasters, proud ; read of those who shall be turned unto fables, who after their own lusts shall heap to themselves teachers.

MAGIC, KNOWLEDGE, AND CONSCIENCE

Black magic, white magic—Hitler is the typical person with no firm foundation, with all the shortcomings of the superficial, of the man without reverence, quick to judge and quick to condemn. He is one of those with no spiritual tradition, who, being caught by the first substitute for it that they meet, hold tenaciously to that, lest they fall back into nothingness. He belongs also to the type of German who is " starving for the unattainable." For all those who have been unsuccessful in the battle of life National Socialism is the great worker of magic. And Hitler himself is the first of these ; thus he has become the master-enchanter and the high priest of the religious mysteries of Nazidom.

Hitler's henchmen make more and more play with this quality of his of supreme magician, a quality supposed to outdistance those of a great statesman. And amid the ecstasy of his speeches, or in his solitary walks in the mountains, he feels that he does possess this quality. But in the many vacant hours of lethargy he feels humiliated and weak. At such times he is irritated and unable to do or

decide anything.   He tries then to acquire the semblance
of creativeness by endless talk.   This requires an audience.

It was in this mood that Hitler once conferred on me
the privilege of learning his views on morality and the
things of the spirit.   They were a mixture of misunderstood
Nietzsche and popularised ideas of a certain tendency in
current philosophy.   All this stuff he poured forth with
the air of a prophet and a creative genius.   He seemed to
take it for granted that the ideas were his own.   He had
no notion of their actual origin, and considered that he had
worked them out himself, and that they were inspirations,
the product of his solitude in the mountains.   I give here
some of these dicta, noted down at the time, but not all of
them now in their original context.   They are fragments
from various talks.

" We are now at the end of the Age of Reason.   The
intellect has grown autocratic, and has become a disease
of life."

" Our revolution is not merely a political and social
revolution ; we are at the outset of a tremendous revolution
in moral ideas and in men's spiritual orientation."

" Our movement has at last brought the Middle Ages,
medieval times, to a close."

" We are bringing to a close a straying of humanity."

Of truth and conscience :

" The Ten Commandments have lost their validity."

" Conscience is a Jewish invention.   It is a blemish,
like circumcision."

" A new age of magic interpretation of the world is
coming, of interpretation in terms of the will and not of
the intelligence."

" There is no such thing as truth, either in the moral or
in the scientific sense."

Of science :

" The idea of free and unfettered science, unfettered by

hypotheses, could only occur in the age of Liberalism. It is absurd."

" Science is a social phenomenon, and like every other social phenomenon is limited by the benefit or injury it confers on the community."

" The slogan of objective science has been coined by the professorate simply in order to escape from the very necessary supervision by the power of the State."

" What is called the crisis of science is nothing more than that the gentlemen are beginning to see of their own accord how they have gone off the line with their objectivity and independence. The simple question that precedes every scientific activity is : who is it who wants to know something, who is it who wants to find how he stands in the world around him ? It follows necessarily that there can only be the science of a particular type of humanity and of a particular age. It is reasonable to say that there is a Nordic science, and a National Socialist science, which are bound to be opposed to the Liberal-Jewish science, which, indeed, is no longer fulfilling its function anywhere, but is in process of stultifying itself."

Of action :

" We approach the realities of the world only in strong emotion and in action. I have no love for Goethe. But I am ready to overlook much in him for the sake of one phrase—' In the beginning was action.' Only the man who acts becomes conscious of the real world. Men misuse their intelligence. It is not the seat of a special dignity of mankind, but merely an instrument in the struggle for life. Man is here to act. Only as a being in action does he fulfil his natural vocation. Contemplative natures, retrospective like all intellectuals, are dead persons who miss the meaning of life."

" We Germans above all, with our long-established habit of brooding and dreaming to excess, needed to be brought back to the great truth that only deeds and perpetual activity give meaning to life."

" Every deed has its place, even crime."

" All passivity, all inertia, on the other hand, is senseless, inimical to life. From this proceeds the divine right of destroying all who are inert."

" The world ' crime ' comes from a world of the past. There are positive and negative activities. Every crime in the old sense towers above respectable inactivity. Action may be negative from the viewpoint of the community, and must then be prevented. But it is at least action."

Of the intelligence :

" We must distrust the intelligence and the conscience, and must place our trust in our instincts. We have to regain a new simplicity."

" People set us down as enemies of the intelligence. We are. But in a much deeper sense than these conceited dolts of *bourgeois* scientists ever dream of."

" I thank my destiny for saving me from the State-granted privilege of acquiring blinkers in the form of a so-called scientific education. I have been able to steer clear of many naïve assumptions. Now I am reaping the benefit. I approach everything with a vast, ice-cold freedom from prejudice."

" Providence has ordained that I should be the greatest liberator of humanity. I am freeing men from the restraints of an intelligence that has taken charge ; from the dirty and degrading self-mortifications of a chimera called conscience and morality, and from the demands of a freedom and personal independence which only a very few can bear."

" To the Christian doctrine of the infinite significance of the individual human soul and of personal responsibility, I oppose with icy clarity the saving doctrine of the nothingness and insignificance of the individual human being, and of his continued existence in the visible immortality of the nation. The dogma of vicarious suffering and death through a divine saviour gives place to that of the representative living and acting of the new Leader-legislator, which liberates the mass of the faithful from the burden of freewill."

Pronounced with the authority of the recognised leader in the presence of his entourage, such *dicta*, studding a conversation, gave the impression of deep revelations. Hitler, moreover, was offended if anyone gave expression to his feeling that they had been said before or were being said by others who shared his opinions. He wanted to feel that he had thought out all of them, alone and unaided. He regarded it as a belittling of his stature if we mentioned similar opinions. Like other self-taught men, he was unaware that the ideas that seemed to him to be mysterious inspirations were the product of the general intellectual outlook of to-day, of which he was constantly absorbing the germs.

But this was not mere jealousy. He hated the suggestion of predecessors and contemporary thinkers on his lines because, however similar their ideas, they had given expression to them in an entirely different connection. It is true that no one else drew the same revolutionary conclusions from them, combining cultural and social, political and moral elements in a single general conception of a vast world change. This was his original contribution. What this world change amounted to in his idea was a point that he left unexplained. He spoke of it only in pictures, of doubtful originality. But we had the feeling that in his exaggeration of his own importance he came dangerously near to the limit beyond which Nietzsche passed when he announced that he was the Dionysus-God, the Anti-Christ become flesh.

The outcome of this contempt for intellect and science a few places lower in Hitler's entourage was shown in a short

talk I had with Himmler, head of the Gestapo and the
S.S.—the secret police and Hitler's vastly inflated bodyguard.
Himmler had had a public school education. He was
able to express himself with more brutal pregnancy than
Hitler. Himmler was my guest one evening at Danzig.
He had burst in with a horde of S.S. men, and there was
plenty of noise. Among them was the young Prince
Dohna-Schlobitten, who had the honour to be serving as
Himmler's chauffeur on a tour of inspection in East Prussia.
It was not a pretty spectacle to see the old East Prussian
nobility thus degraded to the service of these gangsters.

Himmler called me to account about a professor who
lectured on prehistoric times both at Danzig and at Königsberg. This man, he said, had been criticising current ideas
about the origin of the Teutons and the age of their civilisation, and had condemned these ideas from alleged
scientific points of view. At that time a sensation had been
created by an exceedingly silly book, a manifest forgery, the
" Uralinda Chronicle." The book traced back the history
of the Teutons to an infinitely remote period ; and it
proved once more that the original German-Teuton race
was the true creator of European civilisation. The professor had treated this book with proper severity, and
Himmler wanted me to dispose once for all of scientific
mischief-making of this sort. He himself would put the
fear of God into the professors in Königsberg and Breslau ;
I was to do the same in Danzig.

What ideas, he said, these gentlemen got into their heads !
Their scientific views were of no interest to anybody, they
were just their private opinions. But if the State or the
party had declared that a certain view was regarded as the
desired starting-point for scientific research, that view must
be accepted simply as a scientific axiom, and there must be
no shilly-shallying about it, still less malevolent criticism.

" We don't care a hoot whether this or something else

was the real truth about the prehistory of the German tribes. Science proceeds from hypotheses that change every year or two. So there's no earthly reason why the party should not lay down a particular hypothesis as the starting-point, even if it runs counter to current scientific opinion. The one and only thing that matters to us, and the thing these people are paid for by the State, is to have ideas of history that strengthen our people in their necessary national pride.

" In all this troublesome business we are only interested in one thing—to project into the dim and distant past the picture of our nation as we envisage it for the future. Every bit of Tacitus, in his *Germania*, is tendencious stuff. Our teaching of German origins has depended for centuries on a falsification. We are entitled to impose one of our own at any time. Prehistory is the doctrine of the eminence of the Germans at the dawn of civilisation."

In another *milieu*, that of the dreamers and credulous cranks, these ideas of the end of rational science reappeared, in the guise of a great retrogression of civilisation from the age of reason to that of " sleepwalker's assurance," that of a super-rational magic. I heard a lecture by the professor who had edited the peculiar " Chronicle," Professor Wirth ; he had written some queer books on the " Origin of Humanity," and had engaged in research into the primitive symbolism of prehistoric ages in signs and designs. Hitler was interested in the subject. Wirth spoke at meetings in which the fundamentals of a new conception of God and the basis of the coming civilisation were discussed ; the chair was taken by an ex-diplomat, von Leers. Humanity, we learned, stood on the threshold of a new day. Every principle accepted at the present day was far gone in obsolescence. Nothing could be of any service to us in the new era now dawning but recollections and resuscitations of the earliest ideas and customs of the dawn of humanity.

15

HITLER, WAGNER, GOBINEAU

Hitler recognised no predecessors—with one exception :
Richard Wagner.

He asked me whether I had ever been to Bayreuth.   I
replied that in my youth I had been an enthusiastic student
of music, and had often been at Bayreuth.   I had also
studied music fairly seriously in Munich.   I had been a
pupil of Thuille.

"I won't discuss music," said Hitler.   "I know Thuille
and these neo-romantics.   It's decent music, but that's all.
But none of these lesser lights know the real Wagner.   I
don't mean simply the music, but the whole revolutionary
doctrine of civilisation, down to the details that may seem
trifling and immaterial."

Did I know, he continued, that Wagner had attributed
much of the decay of our civilisation to meat-eating ?
"I don't touch meat," said Hitler, "largely because of
what Wagner says on the subject, and says, I think,
absolutely rightly."   So much of the decay of our civilisation
had its origin in the abdomen—chronic constipation,
poisoning of the juices, and the results of drinking to excess.
He did not touch meat or alcohol, or indulge in the dirty
habit of smoking ; but his reason had nothing to do
with considerations of health, but was a matter of
absolute conviction.   But the world was not ripe for this
advance.

Wagner, said Hitler, had really proclaimed the eternal
tragedy of human destiny.   He was not merely a musician
and a poet ; he was the supreme prophetic figure among
the Germans.   He, Hitler, had come early to Wagner, by
chance or by the disposition of Providence.   He had
discovered, with almost hysterical excitement, that everything written by that great man that he read was in agreement with his own innermost. subconscious, dormant
conviction.

" The problem," he cried, " is this : How can we arrest racial decay ? Must what Count Gobineau says come true ? We have acted politically on it—no equality, no democracy ! But are we to allow the masses to go their way, or should we stop them ? Shall we form simply a select company of the really initiated ? An Order, the brother-hood of Templars round the holy grail of pure blood ? "

Hitler pondered a moment and then went on :

" We must interpret ' Parsifal ' in a totally different way to the general conception, the interpretation, for instance, of the shallow Wolzogen. Behind the absurd externals of the story, with its Christian embroidery and its Good Friday mystification, something altogether different is revealed as the true content of this most profound drama. It is not the Christian-Schopenhauerist religion of compassion that is acclaimed, but pure, noble blood, in the protection and glorification of whose purity the brotherhood of the initiated have come together. The king is suffering from the incurable ailment of corrupted blood. The uninitiated but pure man is tempted to abandon himself in Klingsor's magic garden to the lusts and excesses of corrupt civilisation, instead of joining the *élite* of knights who guard the secret of life, pure blood.

" All of us are suffering from the ailment of mixed, corrupted blood. How can we purify ourselves and make atonement ? Note that compassion, through which man gains comprehension, is only for the corrupted man at issue with himself. And that this compassion knows only one treatment—the leaving of the sick person to die. The eternal life granted by the grail is only for the truly pure and noble ! "

Hitler continued with vivacity :

" For myself, I have the most intimate familiarity with Wagner's mental processes. At every stage in my life I come back to him. Only a new nobility can introduce the

new civilisation for us. If we strip "Parsifal" of every
poetic element, we learn from it that selection and renewal
are possible only amid the continuous tension of a lasting
struggle. A world-wide process of segregation is going on
before our eyes. Those who see in struggle the meaning of
life, gradually mount the steps of a new nobility. Those
who are in search of peace and order through dependence,
sink, whatever their origin, to the inert masses. The
masses, however, are doomed to decay and self-destruction.
In our world-revolutionary turning-point the masses are the
sum total of the sinking civilisation and of its dying representatives. We must allow them to die with their kings, like
Amfortas."

Hitler hummed the *motif* "comprehending through
compassion . . ." (*durch Mitleid wissend. . . .*)

" In a natural order," he continued, " the classes are
peoples superimposed on one another in strata, instead of
living as neighbours. To this order we shall return as soon
as the *sequelæ* of Liberalism have been removed. The
Middle Ages were not yet ended when the liberal dissolution
began of the firm bonds which alone guaranteed the rule of a
nobility of pure blood—until finally in our glorious day we
find all values subverted—the meaner components of the
European nations on top, and the valuable ones dependent
on them."

" But this," I interposed, " means the setting up of a new
feudal order."

" No, no ! " said Hitler, and he told me to disregard all
these ridiculous comparisons. " Don't let us waste time on
these naïve criteria. Such conceptions of an age of which
not a vestige is left have no bearing on what we are called to
create. Imagination is needed in order to divine the vast
scale of the coming order. But," he continued, " when a
situation is created that favours noble blood, the man of the
great race always comes to the top, as, for instance, our own

movement shows. The creation and maintenance of this situation is the great preparatory political action of the Leader-legislator."

" Once," I mentioned, " I heard you say, I think, that the days of conventional nationalism are over. Did I rightly understand you ? "

" The conception of the nation has become meaningless. The conditions of the time compelled me to begin on the basis of that conception. But I realised from the first that it could only have transient validity. The ' nation ' is a political expedient of democracy and Liberalism. We have to get rid of this false conception and set in its place the conception of race, which has not yet been politically used up. The new order cannot be conceived in terms of the national boundaries of the peoples with an historic past, but in terms of race that transcend those boundaries. All the adjustments and corrections of frontiers, and of regions of colonisation, are a ploughing of the sands."

I tried to object that there were very great difficulties in the way of this for Germany, but Hitler cut me short with a wave of his hand.

" I know perfectly well," he said, " just as well as all these tremendously clever intellectuals, that in the scientific sense there is no such thing as race. But you, as a farmer and cattle-breeder, cannot get your breeding successfully achieved without the conception of race. And I as a politician need a conception which enables the order which has hitherto existed on historic bases to be abolished and an entirely new and anti-historic order enforced and given an intellectual basis. Understand what I mean," he said, breaking off. " I have to liberate the world from dependence on its historic past. Nations are the outward and visible forms of our history. So I have to fuse these nations into a higher order if I want to get rid of the chaos of an historic past that has become an absurdity. And for this purpose the conception of race serves me well. It disposes of the old order and makes possible new associations. France carried her great Revolution beyond her borders with the conception of the nation. With the conception of race, National Socialism will carry its revolution abroad and recast the world."

Hitler concluded, with growing fervour :

" Just as the conception of the nation was a revolutionary change from the purely dynastic feudal states, and just as it introduced a biological conception, that of the people, so our own revolution is a further step, or, rather, the final step, in the rejection of the historic order and the recognition of purely biological values. And I shall bring into operation throughout all Europe and the whole world this process of selection which we have carried out through National Socialism in Germany. The process of dissolution and reordering will run its course in every nation, no matter how old and firmly knit its social system may be. The active section in the nations, the militant, Nordic section, will rise again and become the ruling element over these shopkeepers and pacifists, these puritans and speculators and busybodies.

" This revolution of ours is the exact counterpart of the great French Revolution. And no Jewish God will save the democracies from it. There is a stern time coming. I shall see to that. Only the tough and manly element will endure. And the world will assume a new aspect.

" But the day will come when we shall make a pact with these new men in England, France, America. We shall make it when they fall into line with the vast process of the reordering of the world, and voluntarily play their part in it. There will not be much left then of the clichés of nationalism, and precious little among us Germans. Instead there will be an understanding between the various language elements of the one good ruling race."

The Jews

Hitler's anti-Semitism is an essential element in his general policy, but it is also part of his mental make-up. To him the Jew represents the very principle of evil. His feeling about the Jews has much in common with that of the pornographer Julius Streicher and with that of the ordinary storm-trooper or SS man, but there are also elements of difference. To the great majority of the Nazi clique of leaders the whole racial doctrine is " Adolf's bunkum." They regard the ousting of the Jews as an exercise in revolutionary activity. They are able to do with the Jews as they would have been glad to do with the whole middle class, which is not so defenceless. To Streicher and his following anti-Semitism is a splendid stroke of business and, at the same time, a satisfaction of their vile instincts. Among the mass of the Germans there is no deep-rooted anti-Semitism ; they have their grudges against the Jews, but these are no great matter.

I had in my own experience a practical demonstration of the fact that the majority of the party members did not take the anti-Semitic shouting of the Nazis seriously, and certainly had no expectation that anything drastic was really intended. On April 1st, 1933, when the first systematic persecution of the Jews began in Germany, I was rung up on my estate by a number of old party members in Danzig, where, of course, nothing of the sort was attempted. If, they said, these disgusting outrages continued, or were introduced in Danzig, they would not dream of remaining in the party. This was not their idea of the struggle for the New Germany.

In the pogrom of the autumn of 1938 the general attitude showed the extent of the degradation into which Hitler has plunged the German people. " What does it matter to us ? Look away if it makes you sick. It is not our trouble." That was the general reaction to the chasing of thinly-

clothed men and women, and old and sick people, through
the streets. Natural feelings of indignation had been
overcome by the growth of callousness and of fear of the
all-powerful tyranny. Still, the scenes did not increase
the popularity of anti-Semitism.

Hitler, however, believes in the natural wickedness of
the Jew. For him the Jew is evil incarnate. He has made
a myth out of the Jew, and has made capital out of it ;
but behind this is a manifestly genuine personal feeling of
primitive hatred and vengefulness.

Explanations of this may be sought in his personal
experience, and, incidentally, it may be that under the
Nuremberg racial legislation Hitler himself is not entitled
to be classed as " Aryan " ; but the intensity of his anti-
Semitism can only be explained by his inflation of the
Jew into a mythical prototype of humanity. It cannot be
said, indeed, that he is illogical in this. His own esoteric
doctrine implies an almost metaphysical antagonism to the
Jew. Israel, the historic people of the spiritual God, cannot
but be the irreconcilable enemy of the new, the German,
Chosen People. One god excludes the other. At the back
of Hitler's anti-Semitism there is revealed an actual war
of the gods. This was so, of course, only for Hitler himself.
His party comrades had no notion of the fantastic
perspectives in which their master saw their concrete
struggle.

Was not this degenerate race the protagonist of the
independence of the spirit, and thus the mortal enemy of
the coming age ? Were not its members among the most
eminent in science, that insubordinate outsider which,
in Hitler's view, destroys life instead of promoting it ?
And was not the whole hated doctrine of Christianity,
with its faith in redemption, its moral code, its conscience,
its conception of original sin, the outcome of Judaism ?
Was not the Jew in political life always on the side of

analysis and criticism ? Hitler had plenty of arguments to bring forward in justification of his loathing.

The extent to which he was obsessed by his hatred of the Jews was shown by the way he could scarcely speak without bringing in sooner or later at least one scathing reference to them. On one occasion he gave me a fairly full account of his ideas on this subject. It was perfectly true, he said, that anti-Semitism is a useful revolutionary expedient. He had often made effective use of it, and would do in the future. It was valuable both as an implicit threat to the whole middle class in Germany, a class with a greatly exaggerated faith in itself, and as a warning to the short-sighted democracies.

" My Jews are a valuable hostage given to me by the democracies. Anti-Semitic propaganda in all countries is an almost indispensable medium for the extension of our political campaign. You will see how little time we shall need in order to upset the ideas and the criteria of the whole world, simply and purely by attacking Judaism.

" The Jews themselves are our best helpers in this. In spite of their dangerous situation, the poor Jews continually associate with the enemies of the established order, and the rich Jews are envied because they are much in view as possessors of great fortunes. Thus it is easy to justify ourselves by quoting concrete instances from close around. And, once the principle of race has been established by the exposure of the particular case of the Jews, the rest is easy. It logically follows step by step that the existing political and economic order has to be ended and attention paid to the new ideas of biological politics."

Anti-Semitism, continued Hitler, was beyond question the most important weapon in his propagandist arsenal, and almost everywhere it was of deadly efficiency. That was why he had allowed Streicher, for instance, a free hand. The man's stuff, too, was amusing, and very cleverly

done. Wherever, he wondered, did Streicher get his
constant supply of new material ! He, Hitler, was simply
on thorns to see each new issue of the *Stürmer*. It was the
one periodical that he always read with pleasure, from the
first page to the last.

But, he said, we cannot rest content with that : it is
only the beginning of a merciless struggle for world
domination.

" The struggle for world domination will be fought
entirely between us, between Germans and Jews. All else
is façade and illusion. Behind England stands Israel, and
behind France, and behind the United States. Even when
we have driven the Jew out of Germany, he remains our
world enemy."

I asked whether that amounted to saying that the Jew
must be destroyed.

" No," he replied. " We should have then to invent
him. It is essential to have a tangible enemy, not merely
an abstract one."

Hitler instanced the Catholic Church : it did not content
itself, he said, with the Devil ; it had to have visible enemies
in order not to relax in the struggle.

" The Jew," he said, " is always with us. But it is easier
to combat him in the flesh than an invisible dæmon.
The Jew was the enemy of the Roman Empire, even of
Egypt and Babylon ; but I have been the first to go all
out against him.

" Jews have been ready to help me in my political
struggle. At the outset of our movement some Jews actually
gave me financial assistance. If I had but held out my
little finger I should have had the whole lot of them
crowding round me. They knew well enough where there
was a new thing on, with life in it. It was the Jews, of
course, who invented the economic system of constant
fluctuation and expansion that we call Capitalism—that

invention of genius, with its subtle and yet simple self-acting mechanism. Let us make no mistake about it—it is an invention of genius, of the Devil's own ingenuity.

" The economic system of our day is the creation of the Jews. It is under their exclusive control. It is their super-state, planted by them above all the states of the world in all their glory. But now we have challenged them, with the system of unending revolution. Has it not struck you how the Jew is the exact opposite of the German in every single respect, and yet is as closely akin to him as a blood brother?

" I have read ' The Protocols of the Elders of Zion '—it simply appalled me. The stealthiness of the enemy, and his ubiquity! I saw at once that we must copy it—in our own way, of course. Think of it—these people constantly on the move, and we with our new faith in unceasing activity, two groups so closely allied and yet so utterly dissimilar. It is in truth the critical battle for the fate of the world!"

" Don't you think," I objected, " that you are attributing rather too much importance to the Jews?"

" No, no, no!" exclaimed Hitler. " It is impossible to exaggerate the formidable quality of the Jew as an enemy."

" But," I said, " the ' Protocols ' are a manifest forgery. I saw the book in 1920, through a certain Müller von Hausen. It was evident to me that it can't possibly be genuine."

" Why not?" grunted Hitler. He did not care two straws, he said, whether the story was historically true. If it was not, its intrinsic truth was all the more convincing to him. " We must beat the Jew with his own weapon," he continued. " I saw that the moment I had read the book."

" So you derived inspiration for your struggle from the ' Protocols '?" I asked.

" Yes, certainly, down to the veriest detail," he replied.

" I found these Protocols enormously instructive. I have always learnt a great deal from my opponents. I studied revolutionary technique in the works of Lenin and Trotsky and other Marxists. And I got illumination and ideas from the Catholic Church, and from the Freemasons, that I could never have obtained from other sources. The man who is not ready to learn from his enemies, and from them above all, is a fool. Only a weakling will be afraid of losing his own inspiration by studying the enemy."

" Even the Freemasons and the Catholic Church? Is not that going rather far? "

" Not a bit of it," retorted Hitler. " Nothing could be more natural. I learned above all from the Jesuits. So did Lenin, for that matter, if I remember rightly. There has been nothing more impressive in the world than the hierarchical organisation of the Catholic Church. I have taken over many elements of it in the organisation of my party. To have lasted almost two thousand years, under changing fortunes, is an achievement."

" I remember hearing you say something of the sort once," I ventured. Hitler ignored the remark, and pursued his theme :

" The Catholic Church is a model above all in its uncommonly clever tactics and its knowledge of human nature, and in its wise policy of taking account of human weaknesses in its guidance of the faithful. I have followed it in giving our party programme the character of unalterable finality, like the Creed. The Church has never allowed the Creed to be interfered with. It is fifteen hundred years since it was formulated, but every suggestion for its amendment, every logical criticism or attack on it, has been rejected. The Church has realised that anything and everything can be built up on a document of that sort, no matter how contradictory or irreconcilable with it. The faithful will swallow it whole, so long as logical reasoning is never allowed to be brought to bear on it. But if there is one thing that will perplex and demoralise the flock of believers it is an alteration of a solemn confession of faith, no matter how remote it may have become from practical realities, no matter if it has become simply a venerable ancient monument."

" I can't help wondering," I said, " what you could possibly have taken from the Freemasons."

" That's simple. Needless to say, I don't seriously believe in the abysmal evilness and noxiousness of these people. In Germany they are just a harmless union for the mutual protection of interests. I have had a careful report made on them. I placed the investigation and the framing of the report in Major Buch's hands. All the supposed abominations, the skeletons and death's-heads, the coffins and the mysteries, are mere bogeys for children. But there is one dangerous element, and that is the element I have copied from them. They form a sort of priestly nobility. They have developed an esoteric doctrine, not merely formulated, but imparted through the medium of symbols and mysterious rites in degrees of initiation. The hierarchical organisation and the initiation through symbolic rites, that is to say without bothering the brains but by working on the imagination through magic and the symbols of a cult—all this is the dangerous element and the element that I have taken over. Don't you see that our party must be of this character ? "

He banged the table.

" An Order, that is what it has to be—an Order, the hierarchical Order of a secular priesthood. But, mind you, the only one. Ourselves or the Freemasons or the Church—there is room for one of the three and no more. The Catholics entirely agree with us as regards the Freemasons. There you are—and we are the strongest of the three and shall get rid of the other two."

I recapitulated—" The Church's hierarchical organisation, the Freemasons' principle of an Order, with its inviolable oath of obedience and secrecy and its esoteric doctrine revealed in stages through symbols. And what," I asked, " have you taken over from the ' Protocols of the Elders of Zion ' ? "

" Political intrigue, the technique of conspiracy, revolutionary subversion ; prevarication, deception, organisation. Is that not enough ? "

A regular collection, I admitted.

" But we have been speaking," said Hitler, " of the Jew only as the ruler of the economic world empire. We have been speaking of him as our political opponent. Where does he stand in the deeper struggle for the new world era ? "

I confessed that I had no notion.

" There cannot be two Chosen People. We are God's People. Does not that fully answer the question ? "

" That is to be understood symbolically ? "

Again he banged the table.

" Symbolically ? No ! It's the sheer simple undiluted truth. Two worlds face one another—the men of God and the men of Satan ! The Jew is the anti-man, the creature of another god. He must have come from another root of the human race. I set the Aryan and the Jew over against each other ; and if I call one of them a human being I must call the other something else. The two are as widely separated as man and beast. Not that I would call the Jew a beast. He is much further from the beasts than we Aryans. He is a creature outside nature and alien to nature."

Hitler seemed to have more to say. But words failed him amid the onrush of his surging thoughts. His face was distorted and working. He snapped his fingers in his excitement. " It's an endless subject," he spluttered.

CHAPTER XVII

THE HUMAN SOLSTICE

A CATHOLIC priest and a Jewish rabbi were clearing
the latrine in a concentration camp. Working up to
their hips in filth, they were mockingly asked by the S:S. man
who was standing guard over them,

" Where's your God now ? "

" We don't know," replied the priest ; " but he who
seeks Him shall find Him."

But the rabbi said :

" God is here. God is even here."

But where is the god whom Hitler sometimes addresses
in his speeches, the god he calls Providence or the Almighty ?
That god is the handsome, the god-like man whose statue
stands in the *Ordensburgen*, the vast training institutions for
future Nazi leaders. Hitler's god is Hitler himself.

On one occasion, before he had immersed himself in
foreign policy and his military plans, Hitler passionately
exclaimed that he wanted to build up, to do constructive
work as statesman and legislator. He was full, he said, of
gigantic plans. The world would see in him the greatest
creative genius of all ages.

" I have so little time . . . too little time ! "

And he went on to say that we had, as yet, only the
faintest idea of what manner of man he really was. Even
his most intimate colleagues, he insisted, did not know
what was in his mind, what it was that he wanted
to build, or at least to start building.

Now and then he was obsessed by frightful nervous
apprehension that he was going to fail to attain his goal.
Or he would bury himself in technical puzzles, pottering

239

about with motors and new inventions. At such times he
was an intolerable nuisance to his entourage.

We had come to a turning-point in world history—that
was his constant theme. We uninstructed persons, it was
clear, had no conception of the scale of the revolution that
was to take place in all life. At these times Hitler spoke
as a seer, as one of the initiated. His inspired pronounce-
ments were based on a biological mysticism—or shall we
call it a mystical biology ? The pursuit of the " random path
of the intelligence," we learned, was the real defection of
man from his divine mission. To have " magic insight " was
apparently Hitler's idea of the goal of human progress. He
himself felt that he already had the rudiments of this gift.
He attributed to it his successes and his future eminence.

A savant of Munich, author of some scientific works, had
also written some curious stuff about the prehistoric world,
about myths and visions of early man, about forms of
perception and supernatural powers. There was the eye of
Cyclops or median eye, the organ of magic perception of
the Infinite, now reduced to a rudimentary pineal gland.
Speculations of this sort fascinated Hitler, and he would
sometimes be entirely wrapped up in them. He saw his
own remarkable career as a confirmation of hidden powers.
He saw himself as chosen for superhuman tasks, as the
prophet of the rebirth of man in a new form.

Humanity, he proclaimed, was in the throes of a vast
metamorphosis. A process of change that had lasted
literally for thousands of years was approaching its completion. Man's solar period was coming to its end. The
coming age was revealing itself in the first great human
figures of a new type. Just as, according to the imperishable
prophecies of the old Nordic peoples, the world has continually to renew itself, the old order perishing with its gods,
just as the Nordic peoples took the sun's passing of the
solstices as a figure of the rhythm of life, which proceeds

not in a straight line of eternal progress but in a spiral, so must man now, apparently, turn back in order to attain a higher stage.

Did Hitler believe all this? Was it anything more than a sort of propaganda, with which to gain prestige and support in certain quarters? There were only a few people, mostly women, among whom he used to talk in this style. Perhaps that was simply because his rough political comrades would have had nothing but laughter for such portentous stuff. But how did this revolutionary and propagandist get hold of these notions? Perhaps they were his " white magic." Yet he may have believed in it all. He is capable of entertaining the most incompatible ideas in association with one another. One thing is certain—Hitler has the spirit of the prophet. He is not content to be a mere politician.

In our talks he put these ideas before me in a rather more materialistic form.

" Creation is not yet at an end," he said. " At all events, not so far as the creature Man is concerned. Biologically regarded, man has clearly arrived at a turning-point. A new variety of man is beginning to separate out. A mutation, precisely in the scientific sense. The existing type of man is passing, in consequence, inescapably into the biological stage of atrophy. The old type of man will have but a stunted existence. All creative energy will be concentrated in the new one. The two types will rapidly diverge from one another. One will sink to a sub-human race and the other rise far above the man of to-day. I might call the two varieties the god-man and the mass-animal."

That, I commented, was very reminiscent of Nietzsche and his superman. But I had always taken all this as metaphorical.

" Yes," Hitler continued, " man has to be passed and
16

surpassed. Nietzsche did, it is true, realise something of this, in his way. He went so far as to recognise the superman as a new biological variety. But he was not too sure of it. Man is becoming God—that is the simple fact. Man is God in the making. Man has eternally to strain at his limitations. The moment he relaxes and contents himself with them, he decays and falls below the human level. He becomes a quasi-beast. Gods and beasts, that is what our world is made of.

" And how simple, how elementary it all becomes ! It is constantly the same decision that has to be made, whether I am faced with new political decisions to be made or with problems of the reordering of our social system. All those who cut themselves off from our movement, who cling to the old order, die away and are doomed. But those who listen to the immemorial message of man, who devote themselves to our eternal movement, are called to a new humanity. Do you now appreciate the depth of our National Socialist movement ? Can there be anything greater and more all-comprehending ? Those who see in National Socialism nothing more than a political movement know scarcely anything of it. It is more even than a religion : it is the will to create mankind anew."

Now, I said, I began to realise the deeper significance of his Socialism. It was the preparation for a division of humanity into the new *Herrenmensch*, the man of the *élite*, of the dominant few, and the *Herdenmensch*, the man of the herd. The new masses were, in the political field, the first indication of what Hitler called the atrophying type of humanity.

Hitler agreed. " Politics to-day is, literally, the frame of destiny. Don't you agree that the process of selection can be accelerated by political means ? "

" We certainly can't breed the superman," I replied. " But, strictly speaking, what do we mean by breeding ?

Simply selecting." That, after all, was all that we farmers did, I told him. If a variety turned up, we kept it alive, deliberately selected it for propagation, and so hurried on the natural process. In scientific language, we sought for the homozygous plus-variation and cultivated it. "This, after all, is all that breeding amounts to, and I can conceive that a particular political system might make possible a process of human selection."

"Exactly so," said Hitler brightly. "You have put it well. Politics to-day is completely blind without a biological foundation and biological objectives. Only National Socialism has recognised this. My policy is not a national policy in the conventional sense. It draws its criteria and its objectives from a complete and comprehensive recognition of the essential nature of life."

"But you can only assist nature. You can only shorten her path when she chooses to grant you the new variety. All the breeder can do is to foster and propagate mutations when they appear."

"The new man is among us ! He is here ! " exclaimed Hitler triumphantly. " Now are you satisfied ? I will tell you a secret. I have seen the vision of the new man—fearless and formidable. I shrank from him ! "

ESOTERIC DOCTRINE

" I will tell you a secret. I am founding an Order."

The idea was not new to me. It had probably come from Rosenberg. At all events, I first heard it put forward by him. In the rooms of the Marienburg, the old castle of the Teutonic Order of Knights, he had been lecturing to a small group of members of the higher Nazi hierarchy. His subject was nominally an historic retrospect, describing the Teutonic Order and its work in Prussia, but the underlying message was the need for turning National Socialism into a similar Order. He described

that ancient Order of armed knights who had to be
capable administrators, but also formed a priesthood with its
mysteries, a hierarchical organisation, with a special type of
leadership : but it all seemed to imply a moral for the
moment.

After the lecture we sat in the *Ratskeller*, the basement
restaurant in the medieval town hall.   Rosenberg continued
to expound his ideas. With him was *Gauleiter* Koch,
commissioner for East Prussia, and close colleagues of the
two were also in the party.

" It's time," said Rosenberg, " that we changed the
character of the party." Its mass organisation, he
explained, should be wound up. Once its purpose, the
acquisition by constitutional means of Parliamentary power,
had been achieved, its dependence on Parliament must be
ended.   The party now had another function and needed
a different basis.

Hitler, said Rosenberg, wanted to leave things as they
were ; the internal organisation of the party, in Hitler's
view, should not be changed until the new generation had
come to maturity. Rosenberg himself felt, however, that
it would hamper the future of the party to retain its mass
character. The mass of the members and officials would
not be affected by the changes he wanted.   But already an
inner circle of the really initiated was forming everywhere
and drawing away from the mass. This tendency should
be deliberately furthered. The old political ideas of
National Socialism could perfectly well be kept alive—for
the masses. But a circle of the initiated should be formed
within the party. This would not only clarify the organisation, but give the party the character of an Order, with
degrees of initiation and responsibility.

He did not mean, continued Rosenberg, the creation of
a party within the party. But the membership wanted
sorting out and rearranging on the basis of intelligence and

devotion, in order to take in hand the great problems that faced them, over and beyond the day-to-day issues.

" It is quite possible," he concluded, " that we may suffer serious set-backs in foreign policy or in economic matters ; at such times it is essential that the well-informed members shall be on the spot, as a secret priesthood existing independently of any organisation in the public view, in order to conserve the great cultural ideas of National Socialism, and to be ready to bring them forth again at a more favourable moment."

Koch thought we might do well to consider the question without reference to set-backs. But something had got to be done. Hitler had given his assent to the idea of an Order being carried into effect, at all events in the training of future leaders. " But I agree," he added, " that the sooner we make it clear that we are not just a political party of the old type, the better."

Nothing tangible resulted from all this at the moment. Hitler knew what his most active *Gauleiter* and storm-troopers thought of all bookish ideas and schemes. He himself was obviously interested in the idea of an Order. But he went forward cautiously, beginning with the introduction of National Socialist " Junker schools," under Ley, the head of the Labour Front. These schools were not merely for the training of future leaders ; as their name suggested, they were intended for the creation of a new Order of nobles, to be bound together as a sworn body.

Hitler was perfectly well aware of the weaknesses of his *Gauleiter* and the men in high command in the S.A. and S.S. Once, when I complained of the stupidity of some of the Danzig leaders, he remarked that he had not been able to pick and choose ; he had had to make use of any who came forward in readiness to help. Why did not the educated people come along at the time when membership of the party meant a sacrifice ? He could not now sack men who had served him loyally. Sometimes it was the devil of a job to keep the team together, but he made a point of it, in order to preserve the unity of the party. He might be able to find more intelligent colleagues, but never more faithful ones. " Unfortunately, intelligence and loyalty are never very closely associated with each other," he remarked.

He knew, he said, that these men were inaccessible to lofty ideas. They were political veterans who had grown to greatness amid the fury of the battle. They had never had more than a smattering of the " philosophy " of National Socialism, most of them had forgotten even that in the heat of the struggle, and their ideas went no further than a few practical rules. But they had learnt how to keep the masses in order and themselves in power. The present generation would have to be used up before the party could grow into the new and unfamiliar shape of a secular priesthood in control of the State. The present leaders were entirely out of reach of the deeper speculations which were more and more engaging Hitler's thoughts, the new world-religion, the creation of a new humanity.

Hitler resisted the temptation to make any premature mention in public of his deeper purposes. National Socialism was only at the outset of its career. He had first to carry the political struggle to completion and to prepare himself for the decisive war that must inevitably come. Only when, like old Frederick, King of Prussia, his venerated hero and model, he had his wars behind him, could he proceed to the actual building up of Germany. Many times he touched on these ideas in conversation. And we could see behind his outward resignation the consuming impatience to get at last to his real work, the work of the creative statesman and legislator, the pioneer artist and city builder, the prophet and founder of a religion.

" In my great educative work," said Hitler, " I am beginning with the young. We older ones are used up. Yes, we are old already. We are rotten to the marrow. We have no unrestrained instincts left. We are cowardly and sentimental. We are bearing the burden of a humiliating past, and have in our blood the dull recollection of serfdom and servility. But my magnificent youngsters ! Are there finer ones anywhere in the world ? Look at these young men and boys ! What material ! With them I can make a new world.

" My teaching is hard. Weakness has to be knocked out of them. In my *Ordensburgen* a youth will grow up before which the world will shrink back. A violently active, dominating, intrepid, brutal youth—that is what I am after. Youth must be all those things. It must be indifferent to pain. There must be no weakness or tenderness in it. I want to see once more in its eyes the gleam of pride and independence of the beast of prey. Strong and handsome must my young men be. I will have them fully trained in all physical exercises. I intend to have an athletic youth— that is the first and the chief thing. In this way I shall eradicate the thousands of years of human domestication. Then I shall have in front of me the pure and noble natural material. With that I can create the new order.

" I will have no intellectual training. Knowledge is ruin to my young men. I would have them learn only what takes their fancy. But one thing they must learn—self-command ! They shall learn to overcome the fear of death, under the severest tests. That is the intrepid and heroic stage of youth. Out of it comes the stage of the free man, the man who is the substance and essence of the world, the creative man, the god-man. In my *Ordensburgen* there will stand as a statue for worship the figure of the magnificent, self-ordaining god-man ; it will prepare the young men for their coming period of ripe manhood."

More than that, concluded Hitler, he could not say. There were stages of which he must not allow even himself to speak. Even this, he said, he only intended to make public when he was no longer living. Then there would be something really great, an overwhelming revelation. In order completely to fulfil his mission, he must die a martyr's death.

" Yes," he repeated, " in the hour of supreme peril I must sacrifice myself for the people."

REVOLUTION WITHOUT END

I must add a few words on the subject of this doctrine of Hitler's. Few know about it. Yet his political purpose can only be understood with this background of his ideas. Hitler is not superstitious in the ordinary sense. His interest in the horoscope and the cryptic elements in nature is connected with his conviction that man exists in some kind of magic association with the universe. The political element is for him only the foreground of a revolution which he pictures on the most stupendous scale.

The study of apocryphal literature gives him the material for his doctrine. But what is of more importance than the doctrine is the will behind it. Hitler never tires of proclaiming, with endless variations on his theme, that the movement into which he has led the German people and the world is an unending movement, an unending revolution. This revolution embraces the whole existence of mankind. It is the liberation of mankind, which, according to Hitler's doctrine, advances a step every seven hundred years. This liberation is at the same time, for the great majority of mankind, a subjection to a new form of bondage. For the liberation is that of the sons of God. It is the revolution of the new nobility against the masses.

He has gone far, if we recall where he began. Hitler the conspirator and paid propagandist has become the prophet of a new religion. Is this merely the megalomania of a sick man, or is it not, after all, the outcome of a logical process ? A red thread may be plainly seen running through all the

inconsistent, contradictory activities of this most extraordinary man. "Activity is everything. Keep always on
the move." His natural restlessness finds expression in
everything. But at the back of it there is not only his own
"haunting hysteria," as he himself so significantly calls it.
A world in full process of dissolution, and a people no less
hysterical than himself could not but come under the
leadership of a man of this sort.

"Time," he says, "is working for us. I need but give
them a kick, and we shall be free of the chains of a world
that has outlived its day. All these things that seem so solid
are rotten and ready to collapse."

All things do, indeed, seem to be inwardly rotting and in
dissolution. In its dismay humanity seems to be abandoning
itself to restless movement, perpetual change. And self-
surrender to the uncontrollable impulse to wreak destruction
seems to be the essence of the spirit that guides this insane
adventurer. "We do not know yet," said Hitler on one
occasion, "the full scope of our objective. But we have it
in our blood, and we are living it." That is literature—bad
literature. It dates from the outset of the present century.
At that time there existed a sort of hysterical romanticism
in Germany and Austria. It flourished especially in Vienna
and Munich.

It is not the first time that the sick fancies of a whole
fevered nation have found concrete shape in figures that have
worked havoc for centuries thereafter. Whole peoples have
broken suddenly into an inexplicable restlessness. They
undertake pilgrimages of penance, they are seized with an
hysterical dancing mania. The present is one of these
cases. A nation has become sick in mind; the
circumstances may be investigated, but the root cause
remains undiscoverable.

National Socialism is the Saint Vitus's dance of the
twentieth century.

CHAPTER XVIII

HITLER HIMSELF

IS Hitler mad?

I think everyone who has met the Führer two or three times must have asked himself this question. Anyone who has seen this man face to face, has met his uncertain glance, without depth or warmth, from eyes that seem hard and remote, and has then seen that gaze grow rigid, will certainly have experienced the uncanny feeling: " That man is not normal."

Then again he may be seen to sit in apathy for a quarter of an hour, without speaking a word, without even looking up, picking his teeth abominably. Has he heard anything that was going on? Has he been dreaming? Never was a real conversation with Hitler possible. Either he would listen in silence, or he would " speechify " and not allow one to speak. Or he would walk restlessly up and down, interrupt constantly, and jump from one subject to another as if unable to concentrate.

I cannot judge whether Hitler is near madness in the clinical sense. My own experience of him and what I have learned from others indicate a lack of control amounting to total demoralisation. His shrieking and frenzied shouting, his stamping, his tempests of rage—all this was grotesque and unpleasant, but it was not madness. When a grown-up man lashes out against the walls like a horse in its stall, or throws himself on the ground his conduct may be morbid, but it is more certainly rude and undisciplined.

Hitler, however, has states that approach persecution mania and dual personality. His sleeplessness is more than

250

the mere result of excessive nervous strain. He often wakes up in the middle of the night and wanders restlessly to and fro. Then he must have light everywhere. Lately he has sent at these times for young men who have to keep him company during his hours of manifest anguish. At times these conditions must have become dreadful. A man in the closest daily association with him gave me this account : Hitler wakes at nights with convulsive shrieks. He shouts for help. He sits on the edge of his bed, as if unable to stir. He shakes with fear, making the whole bed vibrate. He shouts confused, totally unintelligible phrases. He gasps, as if imagining himself to be suffocating.

My informant described to me in full detail a remarkable scene—I should not have credited the story if it had not come from such a source. Hitler stood swaying in his room, looking wildly about him. " He ! He ! He's been here ! " he gasped. His lips were blue. Sweat streamed down his face. Suddenly he began to reel off figures, and odd words and broken phrases, entirely devoid of sense. It sounded horrible. He used strangely composed and entirely un-German word-formations. Then he stood quite still, only his lips moving. He was massaged and offered something to drink. Then he suddenly broke out—

" There, there ! In the corner ! Who's that ? "

He stamped and shrieked in the familiar way. He was shown that there was nothing out of the ordinary in the room, and then he gradually grew calm. After that he lay asleep for many hours, and then for some time things were endurable.

It is terrible to think that a madman may be ruling Germany and driving the world to war. And hysteria is infectious. Anyone who has seen splendid youngsters, entirely normal, slowly but steadily become demoralised through association with hysterical women, will not wonder that hysteria should be extending to high dignitaries of the Reich, *Gauleiter*, officials, officers, and a whole nation.

But how comes it that so many visitors are charmed to
the point of ecstasy over this man, and consider him an
outstanding genius ? Not only very young people, but men
of knowledge and experience and critical judgment, are
unable to speak of their experience without emotion.
What is the magic that has captured them ? Max Halbe,
the poet, a close friend of Gerhart Hauptmann, told me of
the meeting between Hitler and the veteran German
dramatist. Hauptmann had the feeling that this might
prove to be a counterpart of Goethe's meeting with
Napoleon, and was eagerly looking forward to hearing some
striking remark from Hitler. Hitler, himself an artist—
which of Hauptmann's works would he penetrate to the
heart, with the eye of genius ? Not the " Weavers " ;
perhaps " Florian Geyer."

Hauptmann was introduced. The Führer shook hands
with him and looked into his eyes. It was the famous
gaze that makes everyone tremble, the glance which once
made a distinguished old lawyer declare that after meeting
it he had but one desire, to be back at home in order to
master the experience in solitude.

Hitler shook hands again with Hauptmann.

Now, thought the witnesses of the meeting, now the
great phrase will be uttered and go down in history.

Now ! thought Hauptmann.

And the Führer of the German Reich shook hands a
third time, warmly, with the great writer, and passed on
to his neighbour.

Later Gerhart Hauptmann said to his friends :

" It was the greatest moment of my life ! "

This man, awkward and ill at ease, and always at a loss
for words when he cannot be rhetorical, has not even the
irritating attractiveness of the wayward. What, then, is
it in him that so powerfully affects his visitors ?

There is an instructive parallel—mediums. Most of

these are ordinary, undistinguished persons ; yet suddenly
they acquire gifts that carry them far above the common
crowd. These qualities have nothing to do with the
medium's own personality. They are conveyed to him
from without. The medium is possessed by them. He,
himself, however, is uninfluenced by them. In the same
way undeniable powers enter into Hitler, genuinely
dæmonic powers, which make men his instruments. The
common united with the uncommon—that is what makes
Hitler's personality so desperate a puzzle to those who come
into contact with him. Dostoevsky might well have
invented him, with the morbid derangement and the pseudo-
creativeness of his hysteria.

I have frequently heard men confess that they are afraid
of him, that they, grown men though they are, cannot
visit him without a beating heart. They have the feeling
that the man will suddenly spring at them and strangle
them, or throw the inkpot at them, or do something senseless. There is a great deal of insincere enthusiasm, with
eyes hypocritically cast up, and a great deal of self-deception,
behind this talk of an unforgettable experience. Most
visitors want their interviews to be of this kind, because so
many others have said that such were their own. One is
reminded of that invisible picture of Till Eulenspiegel's,
which no one was ready to admit that he could not see.
But these visitors who were fain to hide their disappointment gradually came out with it when they were pressed.
Yes, it is true he did not quite say that. No, he does not
look impressive, it is impossible to pretend that he does.
Why, then, imagine things about him ? Yes, if you look
critically at him he is, after all, rather ordinary. The
nimbus—it is all the nimbus.

But is that really all it amounts to, that the visitor was
simply under the influence of auto-suggestion during his
" great experience " ? The case is not quite so simple as

that. I have often had the opportunity of examining my
own experience, and I must admit that in Hitler's company
I have again and again come under a spell which I was
only later able to shake off, a sort of hypnosis. He is,
indeed, a remarkable man. It leads nowhere to depreciate
him and speak mockingly of him. He is simply a sort of
great medicine-man. He is literally that, in the full sense
of the term. We have gone back so far toward the
savage state that the medicine-man has become king
among us.

" I, Emperor and God "—that is not the formula of his
existence. There is nothing Cæsarian about him, no
deification of the State in the person of the Emperor. The
parallel with the Roman Emperors is entirely misleading.
It is the Shaman's drum that beats round Hitler. Asiatic,
African cults and bewitchments are the true element of
his spell, and furious dances to the point of exhaustion.
The primitive world has invaded the West.

It is supremely important to avoid raising this man
to undue significance, giving him immortality, making a
myth out of him. He will dominate the imagination of his
fellow-countrymen long enough without that, and not
theirs only. He himself believes that his influence will be
greatest after his death. And in spite of every caution his
spell might revive, like that of the imprisoned jinn in the
Arabian tale who when set free suddenly grew into a
giant. It is useful and salutary, therefore, to realise fully
this man's ordinariness, to see Hitler as he is and not as he
orates or as he interprets himself. It is not a pleasant study.

Hitler is exacting, spoilt, avaricious, greedy. He does not
know how to work steadily. Indeed, he is incapable of
working. He gets ideas, impulses, the realisation of which
must be feverishly achieved and immediately got rid of.
He does not know what it is to work continuously and
unremittingly. Everything about him is " spasm," to use

a favourite word of his. Nothing about him is natural. His professed love of children and animals is a mere pose.

He has been a Bohemian all his life. He gets up late. He can spend whole days lazing and dozing. He hates to have to read with concentration. He rarely reads a book through ; usually he only begins it. Yet he has a large library. He loves books ; loves fine editions and fine bindings. In his Munich residence there were walls covered with bookcases. Hess's sister, a craftswoman, bound his books by hand. He is characteristically fond of thrillers. But in the drawer of his bedside table there is also literature of less reputable character.

He loves solitary walks. The mountain forests intoxicate him. These walks are his divine service, his prayers. He watches the passing clouds, listens to the moisture dripping from the pines. He hears voices. I have met him when in this mood. He recognises nobody then : he wants to be alone. There are times when he flees from human society.

He has acquired the most curious habits. He can only get to sleep if his bed has been made in a particular way. The quilt must lie folded exactly as prescribed. Men whom he trusts must make the bed. Is he afraid of poisoning, of some secret contrivance, poison on the pillow, an infernal machine in the mattress ? Himmler busied himself in the early days with a poisonous white powder. Strewn on the pillow, it would be inhaled in sleep and injure the lungs, bringing a painful death.

Göring is naturally brave ; Hitler is not. He is excessively nervous, and insanely self-important. He has nothing of the brave man's readiness to challenge and defy fate. He sees to it that he is guarded like a precious antique. If he exposes himself to any risk, the protective arrangements are perfection. The onlooker may imagine that Hitler is taking a risk ; he is not.

He is timid and sensitive. He has to force himself by

much preparation to put on a bold front ; he then becomes aggressive. He is without natural coolness.

For everything he needs to be worked up. He must prepare beforehand for the smallest decision, the simplest action : he must screw himself up to it. In the past he used to complain for weeks at a time, blaming the ingratitude of his followers or the unkindnesses of fate for his own inactivity. He was fond of posing as a martyr and dwelling on the idea of premature death. At such times he would seem to be giving up. He was then full of compassion, but only for himself.

All the more astonishing are the explosions of his " determined will," his sudden activity. Then he neither tires nor hungers ; he lives with a morbid energy that enables him to do almost miraculous things. Everything is done then, in his own words, " with determination," " without tolerating " (whatever obstacle may be in question), " fanatically ". But everything about him is jerky and abrupt. He is entirely without balance. And in this respect he shows not the slightest improvement as he grows older. He has no natural greatness, even in the vastest of his new and vast rooms.

Hitler used to like to be seen with a riding whip in his hand ; he has given up this habit. But the qualities it revealed remain—contemptuousness, arrogance, brutality, vanity. Hitler has never mounted a horse ; but the tall riding boots and the riding whip bore witness to his resentment at past years of submission to his officers. What a vain and touchy creature the man must have been in his obscure youth ! He is full of resentments. A chance word, an association of ideas, may arouse them at any time. Visitors have been completely dumbfounded at a sudden transition in the Führer from obvious goodwill to violent scolding, for some imagined slight, and defensive self-praise. In some harmless remark the visitor will have unwittingly touched one of the leader's sore points, reopened some wound left by past injuries to his self-confidence and vanity.

But Germany's Führer is not only vain and as sensitive as a mimosa : he is brutal and vindictive. He is entirely without generosity. He lives in a world of insincerity, deceiving and self-deceiving. But hatred is like wine to him, it intoxicates him. One must have heard his tirades of denunciation to realise how he can revel in hate.

Brutal and vindictive, he is also sentimental—a familiar mixture. He loved his canaries, and could cry when one of them sickened and died. But he would have men against whom he had a grudge tortured to death in the most horrible way. He eats incredible quantities of sweetmeats and whipped cream ; and he has the instinct of the sadist, finding sexual excitement in inflicting torture on others. In Roman history he gloats over such a figure as Sulla, with his proscriptions and mass executions. Once he recommended to me as instructive reading a banal novel of which Sulla was the hero.

Most loathsome of all is the reeking miasma of furtive, unnatural sexuality that fills and fouls the whole atmosphere round him, like an evil emanation. Nothing in this environment is straightforward. Surreptitious relationships, substitutes and symbols, false sentiments and secret lusts— nothing in this man's surroundings is natural and genuine, nothing has the openness of a natural instinct.

" Oh ! " said Forster once to me—" Forster Boy," one of Hitler's closest intimates, the *enfant terrible* among the *Gauleiter*—" Oh, if Hitler only knew how it does one good to have a fresh, natural girl ! " Forster had just begun " courting." " Poor Hitler ! " he said. I did not pursue the subject.

Hitler has a room with obscene nudes on the wall, concealing nothing. Such pictures have no artistic intention or appeal. He revels in this style of painting. Is he merely

17

aping Frederick " the Great " and his cynicism ? Was
that his intention, too, when he was paying court to dancers
—was he trying to dupe the world by pretending to be
involved in amorous adventures while his troops were
preparing to march on Prague, in imitation of Frederick's
invasion of Saxony ?

Frederick II of Prussia is his great exemplar. He feels
akin to him. He accords to Frederick II the posthumous
honour of recognition as Hitler's forerunner.

But in Hitler even this bit of hero-worship is debased
to a means of satisfying his vanity and of political deception.
Even in the praise of others he is so self-centred that it is
only his own self that he thus honours. Yet this man, so
convinced of his own godlike stature, is grateful for every
bit of praise and for the crudest flattery. He lives on praise
and recognition. He needs constant reassurance by expressions of enthusiastic approval. He depends at all times on
the agreement of those round him. It is to women's
encouragement that he owes his self-assurance. It is absurd
that he of all men should always be surrounded by a crowd
of women, most of them rather over-blown—that women,
indeed, launched him on his career.

HITLER AND WOMEN

Hitler was discovered by women, society ladies who
pushed him forward, when still a young man, after the
Great War. It was the wives of some great industrialists,
before their husbands, who gave him financial support,
surreptitiously supplying him with money, and in the
inflation period with valuables. It was in the company
of a clique of educated women that the paid propagandist
developed into a political prophet. How much they con-
tributed to his stock of ideas may be doubtful. But it was
they who pampered him and ministered to his conceit
with extravagant advance laurels. Women's gushing

adulation, carried to the pitch of pseudo-religious ecstasy, provided the indispensable stimulus that could rouse him from his lethargy. It is curiously reminiscent of the feminine adoration lavished on the arid and unattractive Robespierre.

Hitler knew very well what he was about. He " cultivated " these connexions as carefully and calculatingly as any adventurer in pursuit of a rich wife. He gave his *Gauleiter* cynically concrete instructions, urging them to devote particular attention to propaganda among women. In the struggle for power it was the women's vote that brought Hitler to triumph. In the mass meetings in every town the front rows were always filled with elderly women of a certain type, married and single. Anyone looking down from the platform on those front seat women and watching their expression of rapturous self-surrender, their moist and glistening eyes, could not doubt the character of their enthusiasm. The S.S. men who guarded the hall at these meetings soon had a coarse phrase for these women enthusiasts : they were the " varicose vein squad."

Eroticism is an important political factor in modern mass propaganda, the erotic effect of a speaker's voice, of tonality and speaking melody. These are much more important elements of a speech than its content. Hitler has taken factors of this sort into account, and owes not a little of his political success to their cynical exploitation. How much of his relations with women has been a genuine sublimation of erotic intensity and how much cold calculation, I do not know. Hitler, as I see him, is a personality so exclusively wrapped up in himself that he is incapable of genuine devotion. And thus the more or less morbid women who swarm round him and pay him homage, women with more than a touch of hysteria, are a deliberately selected company.

Later I frequently found with him strikingly pretty young blondes. They sat beside him at meals. He stroked their hands. He permitted himself little intimacies. The whole thing was play-acting. The whole conceit and unnaturalness of this man shows itself even in the most elementary relations in human life. He has shaken off nothing of his past. He still carries it with him, and with its insincerity and uncleanness and monstrousness it burdens the whole German people.

It is true that Hitler is no longer the young man of 1923. In 1933, when he came into power, he was already more realistic, more calculating, more cynical. Since then he has further changed. The Byzantines of the new German court speak of a process of ripening to greatness. They praise Hitler's rise to be the most eminent of statesmen and predict that some day he will also prove himself the greatest of army commanders. But the essential Hitler is unchanged. He has remained the same hopelessly immature man, with the same morbid lusts. His technique, his routine, may have ripened. Otherwise he is tragically identical with the Hitler of twenty years ago. He may well claim that he laid the foundations of his philosophy of life in his Vienna days, and since then has added nothing to his mental and spiritual stature.

Hitler cannot shake off his past. In everything that he does he remains true to type. But can anyone shake off his past? Only by spiritual development; and of this Hitler is incapable. This man of the unending revolution, of unending movement and change, is confined in his own tragic nature that shuts out every creative influence that ripens a man. He remains unchanged.

To this day he is the hireling of whoever offers the best terms. To this day he is the vain and touchy person of his boyhood. To this day he is the excitable, theatrical revolutionary of the years of inflation, his hand on his heart as he swears tremendous oaths; and then, when he breaks them, tearfully entreating forgiveness and comprehension of his claim that he had to obey the higher call of the Fatherland.

Chapter XIX

THE EAGLE'S EYRIE

VAST architectural schemes have been carried out at Hitler's orders—Government departments, private buildings, party offices. His mania for building is the expression of his constant itch to assert himself. People have admired this architecture ; others have been aghast at its dimensions and at the indifference it reveals to extravagant expenditure. It was all this building that first set everybody, and particularly thinking people, wondering what would be the end of it all. There were new party offices far exceeding all reasonable proportions, and correspondingly costly. Their architect entirely ignored the conditions demanded by the site. Great difficulties arose, one learned, over the foundations alone for the party offices at Nuremberg. Hitler was completely unconcerned.

He not only built a new Chancellery ; he put up a branch of it in his mountains. He had Berlin rebuilt, and busied himself with plans for the reconstruction of Vienna. Vast plans, and all merely incidental, casual additions to armament expenditure ran almost into hundreds of thousands of millions. And by and by there were to be workmen's dwellings and garden cities. The suburban housing system was to be completely reconstructed, and spread far over the countryside ; not merely in view of future air raids, but in order to remove the cleavage between town and country, and to create a new feeling of attachment to the soil and of love of home.

When he had completed the work of rearmament, Germany should put on a new face, he often said. The scale of it all might be gauged from the new party buildings.

There were plenty of admirers, at home and abroad.   They
would come away from a national party congress deeply
impressed with the immense scale of everything ;   they
would see in the cupola of light thrown by searchlights on
the night sky the beginning of a new era of civilisation of
unprecedented magnificence.   What mattered the unintelligible speeches and the queer proclamations ?   Here was
visible evidence of the creative will of a whole people.

At the time of my conflict with the party I represented to
Hitler my concern at Forster's ambitious building schemes
for Danzig.   When we were in opposition we had criticised
the modest buildings put up by past Governments, usually
buildings that served practical purposes, health insurance
offices, industrial housing estates, and so on :   now we
ourselves were building theatres and party palaces.

Hitler was inclined to take offence at my criticism.   Did
I suppose that these buildings were a luxury ?   Could I get
no further than the idea of workmen's housing and the like
—was that all my imagination would run to ?

" In my buildings I am giving the people visible symbols
of my plans for the new order," he told me.   " We are all
influenced by the places in which we work and rest.   Only
by the dimensions and the purity of our buildings can the
people measure the scale of our ideas.   I should have made
the greatest possible mistake if I had begun with housing
estates and workers' tenements.   All that will come—
obviously.   Any Government could do that, any Marxist
or *bourgeois* Government.   But only we, as a party, can work
freely and on a generous scale at this noblest of all arts.   We
are the first, since the time of the medieval cathedrals, to
provide the artist with important and imposing tasks.   Not
homes and little private buildings, but the most tremendous
architecture that has been seen since the gigantic buildings
of Egypt and Babylon.   We are erecting the shrines and
symbols of a new and noble culture.   I had to begin with

these. Through them I am impressing on my people and my age their ineffaceable spiritual stamp."

But building plans had to give place to the great problems posed for Hitler by foreign policy and the military situation. He could only devote leisure moments to building plans and models. He sat now poring over maps and strategic plans, playing the never-ending game, the never-ending gamble, of his foreign policy. More and more clearly he was developing into the army commander of the new world war.

Strategic and political moves, and deliberate working on opponents' nerves in " psychological warfare," were but the elements now of a vast building plan of another sort, that of a new world empire. Things at which in the past Hitler had merely hinted, perhaps as objectives for the remote future, were now being worked for with uncanny deliberation. Chance came to his aid in furthering their attainment. Everything and everyone seemed to be playing amazingly into his hands, and carrying him on from success to success. Visitors came and went ; they came by command, summoned with threats. A new and remarkable political method made its appearance. Germany and the world looked on passively while this man threw to the winds all the rules of diplomacy. The ruler of the country stayed at his mountain seat in remote southern Bavaria ; and the administrative machine and the foreign diplomats had to make the best of this hindrance to their labours.

The mountain seat grew into a remarkable building, in which boys' dreams or the fantastic ideas of detective story writers found concrete realisation. Bavarians were reminded of their romantic King Ludwig II, with his fairyland castles, his isolation, and his final madness. In a rocky ravine, concealed and shut off from the world, a lift rises several hundred yards. It leads to a glass-walled building, hidden away in the rocky wilderness of the Bavarian mountains, looking across to the Watzmann. Here, high

above the world, far beyond reach, the German Führer sits
enthroned.   It is his eagle's eyrie.   Here he looks out to
eternity.   Here he challenges his æon.

He has converted his dreams into reality.   But with him
also are troubled dreams of the past and torturing doubts
as to the future.   Again and again he is convulsed by
paroxysms that bring him near to insanity.   But now, if he
cannot sleep for agitation, he is no longer alone.   He
presses a button, and aides-de-camp come hurrying in.
He wants to speak at once to someone : aircraft and motor
cars set out to bring him.   Often he only wants young men
to come at night from their beds ; they must help their
master to forget the fear and anxiety and solitude that are
torturing him.   They sit or stand round the fire in the huge
room, ignorant, uncomprehending, unfeeling ; they bandy
jokes and stories, banal or indecent.   Their task is to divert
Hitler's thoughts, to help him to stop thinking and worrying.
Hitler himself walks restlessly up and down, like John
Gabriel Borkman.

This Master Builder, this Solness, is himself not immune
from dizziness.   A whole nation watches anxiously as he
climbs to the top of his building to crown it with a wreath.
It expects to see him suddenly stagger and fall, and lie
mangled and lifeless on the ground.

But as yet every wish of his can be fulfilled.   Every whim
is given effect.   Only in invention he has not the success
he ardently desires.   Here it is not sufficient to command ;
everything has to be achieved, point by point, by steady
labour.

Hitler has also joined the company of inventors.   He
invents in the same way as other powerful lords, with the
brains of other people.   And we almost seem to be back in
the days of the Philosopher's Stone, when princes thirsting
for gold locked up their adepts in solitary towers until the
formula had been discovered and the gold produced.   But

the search now is for secret military inventions, aerial torpedoes, death-rays. Hitler has always toyed with technical problems. His *Gauleiter* are astonished at his knowledge of the merits and shortcomings of every motor car. He particularly enjoys giving technical advice to his colleagues. The *grands seigneurs* of the past talked endlessly of their horses and studs ; these new peers spend hours discussing their cars and private planes. Hitler excels them all. He sketches, improves, designs. He was, at one time, a draughtsman. He has unquestionably a certain skill. And in the eyes of his admirers he can achieve anything. He is a universal genius, the new Leonardo ! He puts ideas into the heads of everybody—architects and Generals, savants and authors, statesmen and captains of industry : each of them receives from Hitler the brilliant idea that crowns his efforts with success. Nobody leaves the Leader's presence without confessing, like Schacht, that he goes back to his work refreshed and with new courage.

So, in his own Sanssouci, Hitler feels like Frederick of Prussia, who in the intervals between his wars, and before the last and hardest of them, united with the life of the statesman and soldier that of a thinker and poet and musician, while laying the foundations of victory and of constructive work. Hitler's thoughts, like Frederick's, revolve round the inevitable war to come. He looks forward to it though he fears it. For his horoscope has warned him against war. In war, it has predicted, he would lose all he has gained. Yet his ambition constantly draws him back to occupation with military problems. He has long been an impassioned student of the noble art of strategy. He is interested only in one side of it, the fascinating part that is concerned with devices and bright ideas. The laborious work of calculating and checking every possible detail is not to his taste. He loses patience with it, gets tired of it. In throwing out a sketch with a few strokes of genius—that is where he finds supreme satisfaction.

But he does work, day and night, seriously and with determined tenacity, on plans of foreign policy. One idea after another is considered and dropped. It is a complicated game. He holds all the threads in his hands. He has his own sources of information. He controls a vast organisation. Material is within immediate reach on every question. He watches the whole surface of the earth. He has long grown out of the simple East European, continental policy of the past. There are no isolated problems in foreign policy. The remotest of them affects his situation. And his own moves affect the whole world.

To gain influence over the people who matter, to get information about them, about their passions, their tastes, their friends, their way of life—that is politics. Women are his spies, strikingly beautiful women play a critical part in his political calculations. What type of woman is this man's fancy, and that man's ? These are problems no less important than the number of submarines or aeroplanes. With extraordinary subtlety each man's type of womanhood is found for him, delicately and with great caution. This is done not only for heads of states and dictators, but for powerful bankers, foreign politicians, perhaps Generals. So secrets of state are learnt, and influence is won. All this is no fevered fancy, no plagiarism from spy fiction, but historic reality. One man gives their orders to these women, and they carry them out for his sake, for the sake of his great and noble aims.

These are indeed no ordinary times. They combine the methods of the Renaissance with the usages of Imperial Rome in decay, the customs and conventions of Byzantium or the Merovingian court. And at the centre of it all is— Hitler—Hitler, who calls himself Machiavelli's greatest disciple, and who, whatever truth there may be in that, will never be able to overcome his lower-middle class awkwardness and quarrelsomeness. It is absurd, ridiculous. Yet it is the reality which we have to face.

THE NEW MACHIAVELLI

Hitler once told me that he had not only read but studied " The Prince." The book, he said, is simply indispensable for every politician. For some time he had it always at his bedside. He had found unexampled purification and emancipation in reading it. It had liberated him from mistaken, sentimental ideas. It had revealed to him for the first time how many inhibitions fetter us at every step. It was not until he had read this Florentine's book that he realised that we have to learn what the science of politics really is.

He mentioned the book in the talk I had with him on my return from Geneva. " I have just been busy," he said, " with what amounts to the study of human weaknesses. We do well to speculate on human vices rather than on human virtues. The French Revolution may have appealed to virtue ; we shall do better to do the opposite. And it is not enough to work on the weaknesses of the masses ; those of the men at the head of affairs are of more importance. I cannot embark on a policy without knowing them. A thorough knowledge of the weaknesses and vices of each one of my opponents is the first condition of success in any policy."

Hitler complained of the spinsterly methods of German foreign policy and diplomacy. These people were continually groping in the dark. They had no intelligence service worth the name, and so nothing to work on. Nothing reached them but now and then a tedious embassy report. You might regard this stuff either as light literature or as scientific disquisitions, but in either case he was not

interested in it. It was just consequential, portentous
tripe. What he, Hitler, wanted to know was where Lord
So-and-so liked to throw his line and who was the mistress
of X, the managing director of Messrs. Y, Limited. " The
whole Foreign Ministry is choked with bureaucracy and
formalism."

I remarked that it was just the same with the military
espionage and counter-espionage during the War. When
I became unfit for military duty I was employed for a time
on counter-espionage. The whole system at that time was
ridiculous.

" It's better now," said Hitler. Military espionage was
working exceedingly well. Even more wretched had been
the political secret service—it simply did not exist. " I am
doing my utmost to make up for lost time. What we need
is something like the British secret service, an Order, doing
its work with passion."

" Passion will not make up for everything," I objected.
" A great deal of accumulated experience is needed, and
that is not acquired all at once."

" Anyhow," said Hitler, " we shall get nothing achieved
without a staff who have their hearts in the work. The
officials don't like this job ; it's too dirty for them. So they
say, but in reality it is they who are too cowardly and too
stupid. But consider the women, the society ladies thirsting
for adventure, sick of their empty lives, no longer getting
a ' kick ' out of love affairs. And I shall not shrink
from using abnormal men, adventurers from love of the
trade. There are countless men of this sort, useless in
respectable life, but invaluable for this work.

" I told those Father Christmases at the Foreign Ministry
that what they were up to was good enough for quiet times,
when they can all go their sleepy way ; but not good enough
for creating a new Reich. They must take the trouble to
learn more modern methods. Neurath is unimaginative.

Shrewd as a peasant, but with no ideas. At the moment it's his benevolent appearance that is of most use to me. You can't imagine a man like that going in for a revolutionary policy, they will say in England."

Neurath, I suggested, was amiable, but inclined to patronise. He seemed to be saying, " Let us give the young men a sniff of the mysteries."

" Yes, the lordliness and conceit of these people is huge. They think wonders of the mysteries of their craft. An efficient Ambassador must be a master of ceremonies ; at all events, he must be able to work as procurer and forger. The least of all his duties is to be a correct official !

" Besides," Hitler continued, " I am not going to wait until these gentlemen wake up to the fact that they have got to start learning over again. I am building up a great organisation of my own. It costs a lot of money, but it gets things moving for me. I have drawn up a *questionnaire* covering details of the persons I am interested in. I am having a comprehensive card index compiled of every influential person in the world. The cards contain every detail of importance. Will he take money ? Can he be bought in any other way ? Is he vain ? Is he sexual ? In what way ? Is he homosexual ? That is of the utmost value, because it provides close associations that can never be escaped from. Has he anything in his past to conceal ? Can he be subjected to pressure ? What is his business ? His hobby, his favourite sport, his likes and dislikes ? Does he like travel ? And so on. It is on the strength of these reports that I choose my men. That really is politics. I get hold of men who will work for me. I create a force of my own in every country."

" A huge and expensive job, is it not ? "

" Have we ever shirked a job ? There's no sense in attempting propaganda without adequate resources—on the contrary, it merely arouses opposition and achieves nothing.

People have an entirely mistaken notion of what propaganda is. Open influencing of the masses is only one side of it, and a perfectly innocent side. The masses have got to be worked on, in order to prepare the ground. But the real problem is to get hold of prominent people, and whole sets.

" I should have thought," continued Hitler, " that that was obvious enough. I have to provide myself with a sphere of influence. That is all ; but it is also ample. The results at which I have to aim are only to be attained by systematic corruption of the possessing and governing classes. Business advantages, erotic satisfactions, and am- bition, that is to say, the will to power, are the three main stops in our propaganda organ.

" We shall only see the fruits of my activity in the coming war. For none of my opponents will have anything of the sort to use against me. In the past the French produced a Talleyrand and a Fouché ; to-day they have become humdrum and circumspect, a nation of dried-up clerks. They will venture to play for halfpence, but no longer for a great stake."

At the time I did not take all this seriously. I said something to the effect that the possibilities of underground political influence of this sort must not be over-estimated.

Hitler replied tartly that they could not possibly be over-estimated.

" If these gentlemen," he said, " with their outworn ideas, imagine that they can go on pursuing policy like the honest merchant with his business, in accordance with precedent and convention, let them go on. But I am concerned with power politics—that is to say, I make use of all means that seem to me to be of service, without the slightest concern for the proprieties or for codes of honour. And if people come blubbering to me, like that man Hugenberg and his tribe, complaining that I am breaking my word, that I am paying no regard to treaties, that I am making a practice of trickery and deception and mis-representation, I reply :

" ' Well, what of it ? You are free to do the same. Nobody is preventing you.' "

He laughed sourly.

" All these gentry have got to realise that I can no longer carry on politics in the style of the *bourgeois* democracies and monarchies of the nineteenth century, with their totally obsolete rules and conventions. When has a revolutionary regime ever confined itself to conventional limitations ? I am carrying on power politics, with the aid, if I choose, of naked, ruthless force, and what earthly difference can there be between using every means of trickery and misrepresentation and ordering my armies to march ? One method is regarded as respectable, and, now and then, unhappily unavoidable between well-bred people ; at the other, people throw up their hands in horror. Why ? Such distinctions are moral fancies for old women. I certainly have an advantage over these *bourgeois* democrats in my freedom from pedantic and sentimental inhibitions. Am I to be so generous as to throw away this advantage, simply because my opponents have not progressed so far ? If anyone is prepared to be deceived, he must not be surprised that he is."

I tried to suggest that these might be two-edged weapons : trickery invites counter-trickery.

" Maybe," replied Hitler, " but anyhow I get there first. My great political opportunity lies in my deliberate use of power at a time when there are still illusions abroad as to the forces that mould history."

A renascence, said I, of Machiavellianism.

" If you like," assented Hitler. " I have no objection to describing myself as a disciple of Machiavelli. But I consider that only we who realise the biological foundations of policy are in a position to act accordingly."

Trickery, deception, treachery, misrepresentation, flattery, murder—all these political instruments soon lost their efficacy, I objected. The history of the Italian city states seemed to me to offer direct evidence that a policy of that sort could not long continue to serve.

Nor need it, said Hitler. He would be content if it worked long enough to enable him to break through the political walls that surrounded Germany.

"After all," said Hitler, "my opponents ought to be grateful to me for falling in with their pacifism, and preferring political weapons for attaining what others before me attained only by armed struggle.

"Let us not deceive ourselves," he continued. "Those people no longer have any desire to resist us. Their anxiety to come to terms with us cries aloud from every word that comes from that camp. All these democracies and abdicating classes want nothing better than to disburden themselves of their tiresome responsibility, and to have the peace I guarantee to them. These men are not of the sort that want power and enjoy having it. All their talk is of duty and responsibility, and they would be only too delighted to be able to tend their gardens in peace, and go fishing when the time comes round, and, for the rest, to spend their life in pious meditation."

Quite so, I agreed—so far as concerned our German Liberals and Conservatives. But I was not so sure about England and France.

Hitler ignored my remark.

"But we, sir, are feverishly in pursuit of power," he almost shouted, "and we are not a bit afraid to say so. We are madly keen on it. We are fanatically pursuing it. For us the pursuit of power is not an anæmic theory : the will to power is for us literally the whole meaning of this life. We are alive," he shouted triumphantly, "alive ! Let the others sleep ! Fafnir, the wild worm : ' I lie still on my possessions; let me sleep!'" He roared with scornful laughter.

"To-day," he resumed, "the old wives of the literary world are everywhere croaking at me, charging me with 'betrayal of the spirit!' And they themselves have been betraying the spirit to this day in their fine phrases. So long as it was just a literary pastime, they prided themselves on it. Now that we are in earnest with it, they are opening wide their innocent eyes."

"But is not all life made possible only by conventions?" I asked.

"That is beside the point. At critical periods in history all the tinsel falls away and the great rhythm of life alone rules the hour. I am restoring to force its original dignity, that of the source of all greatness and the creatrix of order."

So Hitler ran on, carried away by phrases of this sort about the greatness of his new type of politics. Finally he returned to our theme :

"It is characteristic of the narrowness of these outlived classes that they should be indignant with me, indignant at our contempt for past customs and assumptions in political life. I recognise no moral law in politics. Politics is a game, in which every sort of trick is permissible, and in which the rules are constantly being changed by the players to suit themselves."

He came then to the disappointment of the German Nationalists, who had expected quite different things from him.

"It is not my fault," he said, "if these men took me for a simpleton and found afterwards that it was they who had been fooled."

He rejected as idiotic the charge that he was a dictator. "People want to brand me as a bloodthirsty tyrant. All rule is at bottom tyranny. It can come into existence in no other way. If this does not fit in with what the

18

Hugenberg people want, or with the ideas of my well-meaning English friends, they must wait until they have grown accustomed to the new order of things. Every new regime seems to be a tyranny, simply because it applies compulsion in an unfamiliar style. Rule and the maintenance of order are inconceivable without compulsion."

He came once more to the reproaches constantly made against him on account of the men who are his best colleagues. " I am charged with surrounding myself with ambitious and pushing elements. What rubbish ! Am I to build my Reich with saintly sisters ? If a man is not ambitious, I don't want him. Only on those whose own personal advancement is so bound up with the general movement that there is no longer any separating the two things—only on those men can I depend. Men who not only spout patriotism but make it the sole motive of their actions, are suspect. In any case, my task is not to make men better, but to make use of their weaknesses.

" The men I want round me are those who, like myself, see in force the motive element in history, and who act accordingly. Not that I have any desire to appear as more contemptuous of the moral code than the generality of men. Why make it easy for people to attack me ? I myself can quite easily give my policy a colouring of morality and show up my opponents' motives as hypocritical. Moral commonplaces are indispensable for the masses. Nothing is more mistaken than for a politician to pose as a non-moral superman. That is a fool's game. Those who try to play it are usually sons of respectable families who have been carefully brought up and gone to the bad, and who want to pass their off degeneracy as strength. I shall certainly not make it a matter of principle to act immorally in the conventional sense. I am ready to stick at nothing—that is all."

Hitler spoke of the necessity of terrorism and brutality. He had not the slightest liking for concentration camps and secret police and the like, but these things were simply necessities from which there was no getting away. " Unless you are prepared to be pitiless, you will get nowhere. Our opponents are not prepared for it, not because they are humane or anything of that sort, but because they are too weak. Dominion is never founded on humanity, but, regarded from the narrow civilian angle, on crime. Terrorism is absolutely indispensable in every case of the founding of a new power. The Bolsheviks applied it in the old style : they killed off the whole of the former ruling class. That is the ancient, classic method. To the best of my memory, it is recommended by Machiavelli ; or, at least, he recommends extending goodwill only to the second stratum, those who were immediately below the ruling class. I go further. I make use of members of the old ruling class itself. I keep them in fear and dependence. I am confident that I shall have no more willing helpers. And if they become refractory, I can always return to the ancient, classic method.

" Too much frightfulness does harm. It produces apathy. Even more important than terrorism is the systematic modification of the ideas and feelings of the masses. We have to control those. It is incomparably easier nowadays with the radio."

That, I said, involved a tremendous responsibility. With the modern technique the masses could be made to believe or disbelieve anything at will.

" Yes," replied Hitler, " those who are responsible to history grow more and more visibly to worldwide omnipotence. Consequently they must be as free as gods from the outlook of the masses. Their supreme, their only purpose in all they do must be to maintain their power. Our path," he continued, " is not unsullied. I know of no case in which a man has trodden the path to power without wading through mud. We are content to leave it to our successors to set store by morality."

The sources of Hitler's extremist views were evident enough. I asked him whether he had read Sorel's essay on violence, and whether he had heard of Pareto's cycle of the *élite*. But Hitler disliked questions of that sort. He evaded mine by saying that he had devoted a great deal of time to the literature of the subject, and having thoroughly absorbed it all did not know, and did not care which of his ideas were suggested from without and which were his own. In any case, whatever ideas had been put forward and whoever had put them forward, he was the first to carry them out on a grand scale and with consistency. That was the only thing that mattered. " The Bolsheviks are only now, by devious routes and after having sent packing the whole body of Marxist doctrine, coming round to the clarity of my own policy." As for Mussolini, he lacked breadth and boldness of outlook. He could never get beyond the completely misleading prototype of the *Imperium Romanum*.

Premonition of Martyrdom

At the time of the conversation just recorded, it was still possible to hope that our nation would withstand the temptation of this grotesque doctrine of violence. But that would be possible only if Hitler could be forced to abdicate, and his place taken by a statesman who would bring reconciliation and a new constitutionalism. But could Hitler be overthrown ?

His horoscope spoke of a sensational progress, of victory after victory. Then it became confused and ambiguous. A prophecy spoke of an unparalleled downfall.

The Middle Ages had been resuscitated. Comets and dark prophecies were expected to bring the truth to light, where other sources were banned or restricted to the political struggle. The whole nation was affected. The

sect of Bible Searchers searched the Scripture, and came
in the Book of Daniel to the vision of the tyrant. " He,"
they whispered to one another, is he of whom it is written
(Dan. xi. 37) : " Neither shall he regard the God of his
fathers, nor the desire of women, nor regard any god : for
he shall magnify himself above all. But in his estate shall
he honour the god of forces." For their prophecy they
were condemned to concentration camps and death. But
the masses ask, " How long ? "

That question, the question how this nightmare can be
shaken off and this man removed, without plunging the
German nation into the destruction and ferocity of civil
war, has occupied the minds of all thinking people in
Germany since 1934. Those who ask themselves this
question have not grown fewer : they are to be found even
within the party.

Hitler has always threatened to let loose infinite bloodshed if there is any attempt at overthrowing him by force.
Is there any remedy save through force ? Could the party
be split in two ? It might have been in 1932, and it might
still have been in 1934. But not after that for a long time.
The masses had become apathetic, and blindly credulous.
The party members were utterly dependent for their
livelihood on the continuance of the regime. Hitler could
only be overthrown if the masses rose against him and
if the many small men in the party saw their position
threatened by an imminent collapse of the party and
became anxious to escape from their compromising association with it. Hitler's downfall would only be possible if
he made manifest mistakes and suffered manifest defeats
that produced doubts of his superlative quality. Only if
he was obviously leading Germany to destruction could a
coup d'état be carried out without producing sanguinary
civil wars. A coup implied a nucleus of power which could
challenge the party. Without such a nucleus, the armed

forces of the party could crush any rising. The time of
mass risings and barricades was gone for ever. This nucleus
of power could be found only in the army.

A second consideration was whether the process of
destruction of the regime from within, of its self-destruction,
could be hastened. The economic situation was not
sufficient for this : the regime might yet vegetate for years.
But suppose Hitler were brought into a completely hopeless situation in foreign affairs—would he not then make
mistake after mistake, and, once he had lost his self-assurance, end by completely losing his head ? The man's whole
temperament made him only able to carry on with his
policy so long as he continued to have unshaken faith in
himself. His fall must be prepared by destroying his self-
confidence. If his nimbus were dissolved, he would lose all
prestige and authority with the party and the masses.
The whole regime would then very soon collapse like a
card castle.

There were some honourable open opponents of the
regime in Germany. The party very quickly made an end
of them. It was a vain sacrifice to come out into the open.
All that remained possible was underground opposition.
Hitler's own methods compelled his opponents to adopt
secret and, to be frank, underhand methods. There were
opponents who affected to be ardent supporters of the
extremest Hitlerist ideas. Among them are two Nazis who
are particularly closely associated with Hitler. They, and
with them many of the best of the junior office-holders of the
party, are as thoroughly convinced as the firmest among
the *bourgeois* opponents of the regime, that Hitler must
be sacrificed for the sake of Germany's future.

There have been subtle plans to induce Hitler to com-
promise himself beyond recovery. But these have failed
for two reasons. His riskiest enterprises have succeeded,
and in doing so have turned into his greatest triumphs.

In the second place, for Hitler to get into difficulties involves Germany's doing the same.

The only thing left to do is to leave Hitler to bear full and exclusive personal responsibility for the war, defeat, and destruction that must inevitably come. He will try to evade this responsibility, to shift it on to the shoulders of the party, to share it out among his advisers. He will try above all to make the army leaders answerable for the course of the war. And then he will find that, with the exception of a few of those grown-up cadets who have not learnt to think things out, not one of the army leaders or high officials has any other answer than : " It's up to you, Herr Hitler ! You led us into this. Now get us out."

But will this happen ? Will not such men as Hjalmar Schacht see behind Hitler's fall the irreparable downfall of Germany ? Will they not then, after all, identify Hitler's cause with the nation's ?

The party's thinking is less involved. The old guard always had its own opinion about " Ahi " (Adolf Hitler) ; the very nickname was a contemptuous dig at him. When his *tremolo* came into his speech, or he appealed with convulsive sobs to the hardened criminals of the S.A., there was scornful laughter over the " fidget." Even the " intense " believers did not agree with Hitler's policy. A prominent politician of one of the provinces around Danzig said to me once that the Führer would have to give his life for the party, like Christ. Only then would the whole world realise his quality. The time might soon come when he must disappear into the wilderness ; no one must know where ; he must be surrounded with mystery and become a legend. A whisper of something portentous to come must run through the masses. The tension must become intolerable. Finally Hitler must reappear, metamorphosed, a gigantic figure. He must no longer conduct day-to-day policy ; he will be too great for that. As a great law-giver

and prophet he must bring from the sacred mountain the
new tables of commandments. Then, after this last act,
he must disappear for ever. But his corpse must not be discovered. For the mass of the faithful he must end in mystery.

So this man let his fancy run on. He was not alone.
Others expressed the same idea in more primitive fashion,
but their meaning was the same : sooner or later, Hitler
must go. He must sacrifice himself. The greatest service
he could do to the movement was to suffer a martyr's death.

Some of the leaders make use of this feeling and do their
best to promote it. The faithful Rudolf Hess himself said
some time ago that the new State must not be coupled with
the vast proportions of the Leader, or at his death it would
all be shaken like the State of Frederick II and that of
Bismarck. " New and independent personages, who will
be able in the future to guide the steed of the reseated
Germania, do not thrive under the dictator. Consequently,
he will carry out the last great act—instead of tasting his
power to the dregs he will lay it down and, as a respected
elder statesmen, stand aside."

A suspicious prophecy ; it has recently been repeated.
But who is to decide that Hitler shall stand aside like an elder
statesman ? Hitler himself is aware that he is no dictator.
But, say the *Gauleiter* and the national leaders, there were
general councils in the Teutonic Order who deposed their
Grand Masters ; and destiny may have the same end in
view for the new Grand Master of the German Order-State.
Was not one of the greatest of the Grand Masters deposed
because he wanted to renew a war with Poland out of due
season ? That happened many hundreds of years ago, but
similar situations might arise again.

It is quite conceivable, too, that Hitler might become
impossible for Germany. She might find herself with a
weak-willed Führer at her head, inert and apathetic. It
would not be for the first time. *Gauleiter* and national

leaders note with anxiety his exaltation, at least bordering on insanity. So far it has been tolerable, but suppose the borderline is crossed ?

Hitler has long since sensed the growing discussions around him. He is surrounded by premonitions. Could he retire of his own will, and return with increased prestige ? Would it not soon prove that the regime cannot exist without him ? And would not his return be the greatest triumph of his life ? Or will he die, shot by one of his most trusted comrades ; and will not his sudden end, so long feared, come at the very moment when he alone knows the way out of Germany's severest trial ? It was old Hugenberg who said to Hitler to his face : " You will only fall through shots fired by your own men ! "

Thus, some want the living Hitler to bear responsibility to the bitter end, as the only way to destroy this man with his devilish ideas ; others want to save the Hitler myth and to make him disappear at the summit of his success, so that the responsibility for the inevitable setbacks may fall on others. In either case, Germany marches to destruction, to the inevitable end—war.

Hitler has never left his supporters in any doubt that war must come, however much he may try to prevent it. " We shall not be spared the great testing-time," he said in my presence at a leaders' conference. " We must be prepared for the hardest struggle that a nation has ever had to face. Only through this test of endurance can we become ripe for the dominion to which we are called. It will be my duty to carry on this war regardless of losses. The sacrifice of lives will be immense. We all of us know what world war means. As a people we shall be forged to the hardness of steel. All that is weakly will fall away from us. But the forged central block will last for ever. I have no fear of annihilation. We shall have to abandon much that is dear to us and to-day seems irreplaceable. Cities will become heaps of ruins ; noble monuments of architecture will disappear for ever. This time our sacred soil will not be spared. But I am not afraid of this. We shall clench our teeth and go on fighting. Germany will emerge from those ruins lovelier and greater than any country in the world has ever been."

So, in winged words, he gave play to his imagination, in the effort to talk his close colleagues out of their anxiety. He went on to speak of the ruthless way in which he would have to wage war. All means would be justified. For everyone would know that the issue would be one of life and death for Germany. If Germany did not win, there would be no Germany thereafter. It would be well that his troops should be aware of this, so that the knowledge should steel them to the utmost courage and daring. And with the same daring he must use every expedient, however desperate and criminal it might appear to the outer world. He would not shirk making the sacrifice of lives needed to pierce the Maginot Line. He would respect no neutrality. Poison gases and bacteria he would not reject as weapons if they promised success. With an unprecedented application of all means at his command, with the most ruthless dispatch to the front of all reserves, he would nail victory to his mast in one gigantic knock-out blow.

THE RECKONING

There are times of exaltation when, dreaming at his mountain seat, Hitler feels that he is his country's greatest genius, and the greatest of law-givers for future mankind. Has there ever been in all history, he says to himself, a man who in so short a space, seven years, has achieved so much ? He has really fulfilled his mission already, at least so far as laying the foundation-stone is concerned. He counts his successes, with the " untamable " pride that he

has felt even amid his greatest humiliation. He is the
creator of a new type of power, of a new vast dominion
such as never before existed in Germany's history. He has
created the new army ; the new social legislation. Is it
not he who is in process of solving the social problem ; is
not his new economic order the economic foundation of a
new epoch ? And the novel constitution of his Order ; and
the organisation of the Reich ; the new strategy, the
population policy, the new art ! Is there a single field of
human activity into which he has not introduced the most
subversive ideas ? He, Hitler—a man greater than
Frederick II, greater than Napoleon, greater than Cæsar !

For seven years more he wants to struggle for the external
greatness and the permanent moulding of the Greater
Germanic Reich ; and then for another seven years to
devote himself to the last and greatest tasks, prophecy, the
proclamation of the new faith, with which his work will
really be completed. For if the Christian era is now to
give place to the thousands of years of the coming Hitlerian
era, it will not be because of an external political order,
but because of the revelation of the new doctrine of salva-
tion for which mankind has been waiting.

But then he begins to think of the coming struggles, the
inescapable labour of detailed execution ; and his hands
begin to tremble. The very idea of the daily burden makes
him feel physically ill. He can no longer endure these men
of his entourage, these unvarying, stupid faces. He has
been growing more and more irritable. His nerves are
upset by the smallest trifle.

These dull colleagues, with their pedantry, their pettiness, their persistence ! They do not keep their distance
as they should. They presume with confidences to which
he objects. He should never have to leave this place. He
ought to give his commands from this solitude, like a god
in the clouds. From here, where nobody disturbs him, his

glass-walled house in the mountains, his eagle's eyrie. The reports he needs should be sent to him here. He would rule from here.

But need he go on plaguing himself with all this detail ? Is it his business to carry on an administration ? Let the others see to all that. He must keep himself free for the great decisions. Why must he wage war ? He is overcome with weariness. He thinks now fairly frequently of death.

He remembers his " Testament." It provides for every-thing. He will live on in that, even if he is now to die. The thought of the testament is a relief to him. The things still to be done are contained in it. His young comrades will carry them out. For them the testament will be sacred.

This testament provides for the building up of the Order, the definitive framing of his National Socialist Party Order. It names his successors. He thinks with hatred of Göring. To yield his place to that man ! But there is no way out of it. It will not be for long. Göring will not live long.

This testament contains the plan of the Reich, the structure of the new Greater Reich, its Constitution, and the new " Declaration of Rights." This Constitution was to be proclaimed in Versailles, after the victories. It was to be proclaimed with the new perpetual peace, at the end of the war. This testament contains the internal organisation of his Reich, the social statute, and the new economic system. And this testament contains, last and highest of all, the religious revelation, the first tentative sentences of the new Holy Book which he will confer on the world, if he lives.

But he will not live. He feels that he will not. He has been marked down by death. Others will have to complete his work.

He is filled with anguish. The feelings of happiness that were uplifting him only a moment before have gone. Traps are being set for him, ambushes. He hears whispering that stops as he approaches. People look more and more curiously at him. They are discussing him. What can these people want to say about him? They are not joking; they all have a sinister look. These people are up to something.

What will they do with his testament? Will it not have the same fate as Hindenburg's? They will substitute another one for it. Everything will be changed. These creatures will mangle his work. They will rob him of his immortality. That Göring will reintroduce the monarchy. The Hohenzollern will step into his vacant place. The hour of the monarchy has struck, says Göring. Has he (Hitler) laboured in order to restore the Hohenzollern? That is what old Hindenburg wanted. He had to promise the old man that he would see to it. He did not keep his promise.

Everyone is suddenly turning against him. There is no one he can trust any longer, not even Hess. Horribly ugly chap, to tell the truth, that Hess, with those deep-set little eyes, those unlovely prominent cheekbones. Hess, too, is disloyal. They are all lying in wait for him. They have borrowed his technique, his cunning and trickiness. There is no sincerity and honour among the party members. Each one of them watches the next like a mortal enemy. That was a good plan at the outset, when he was making his way and approaching power with this insubordinate crew. He was able to play off one against another. But now he has no one he can rely on, no one who is not thinking first of himself and his own future.

And his old opponents? Are not these more numerous than ever? Are they not raising their heads again, with impudent daring? Those officers and junkers, in whose presence he always felt a little uncomfortable, those conceited officials, those unimaginative industrialists!

And the masses? They are beginning to elude him. He notices it. His unfailing sense is not to be deceived. The people have no determination now ; they are weakening. And how is he to wage war now—with this sort of human material ?

Suddenly his problems begin to press on him ; they are beginning to be independent of him. He used himself to be the one to push on ; now everything has begun to take charge. He is being carried away. He is only able with difficulty to keep on his feet. And suddenly all the problems are pressing at once ! He no longer has any freedom of decision. These deadly problems have acquired a will of their own. They are dragging him the way he does not want to go. Must he now carry out the things he has passionately fought against ? Is he not being carried along, step by step, in the opposite direction to the one he meant to take ?

Really, has he achieved anything ? Will not everything collapse when he is no longer at the head ? If only he had introduced his Constitution, if only he had carried his statute into law ! Now nothing will go down to posterity. His successors will mutilate and falsify everything, they will trample on his memory and befoul it, just as he did with his predecessors and his opponents. Nothing of his will remain, except a few buildings as curiosities. The buildings ! Perhaps after all he was no more than an architect, and all the rest was just a roundabout way of enabling him to build—him, the stumped candidate for entry into the school of architecture !

Grotesquely devious life's path !

He has really done nothing that has permanence. Everything will be transitory like a confused morning dream. He knows the masses well enough. He has lived among them. He has been too close to them not to despise them for all time. And they will hate and despise him. With all the breathless, panting greed of the stunted, they will take their revenge for having once believed in him and acclaimed him—a man no better than themselves. Just a guttersnipe like themselves. A guttersnipe who pushed himself up by fraud where he had no place. They yelled the loudest in his praise ; now they will be the first to stone him. Their women will spit at him. They will shriek for his execution—or would, if he were not already long dead.

Is he not dead already ? Is he not just dreaming all this ? He grows faint. His life was a feverish dream. He will be called the great culprit. He has achieved nothing, except destruction. The foundation on which he meant to build has suddenly disappeared. It is all a phantasm. Where now is his new Reich ? Are not Austria and Czechoslovakia falling away already ? Can he stop them ? Has he not dug a cleft for all time between the Reich and Austria ? Where is the Constitution, the new *Gau* (regional) structure, by means of which he intended to extirpate the memory of the historic past, of the princes ? Where is the Greater German Union, that federalisation under Germany of all Europe ? What is becoming of his social system, his army ?

Doubts and apprehensions clutch at his throat. He is hoarse again. He feels his pulse. He is afraid. The threads are closing round him. " I do not want to die ! " Sweat breaks out on him. He shivers. The prophecy, the last horoscope ! He threw that warning to the winds.

The solitude oppresses him. He is in terror of it. Something frightful is closing in on him. He must get into company. He must do something, anything. Anything but think ! Find something to do—at once.

He goes to the lift.

THE END